Raswell
The Guide
N
W
E
S
FUEL
Sun cream
Factor
50+
UPF
Protection

WANTED:

MYSTERY INVESTIGATORS

Are you looking for adventure? Are you curious? Do you like solving challenges – and, most of all, do you want to uncover some of the Great Mysteries of the World?

YOU		RICHARD
Adventurous?	☐	Adventurous? (Adventure is fine as long as there are no big spiders . . . eek!)
Like a challenge?	☐	Like a challenge? (There's nothing I like better than really challenging challenges!)
Curious?	☐	Curious? (Oh yes! Some might say 'nosy'.)

If you can tick all the boxes, join me on a global journey to investigate the unexplained, the bizarre and the downright weird. From cursed 'ghost' ships and visiting alien spacecraft to menacing monsters and disappearing planes, you'll be stunned at some of the strange and spooky goings-on around the world . . .

All these mysteries have baffled the experts and left investigators clueless. My mission is to find out the truth. And I need your help.

Together, we'll weigh up the evidence, look at all the explanations – then you decide which is the best solution. You can even keep track of your solved mysteries by turning to page 426 and recording your verdict!

A word of warning: If you're the nervous type, put this book down now. Some of the mysteries we'll be investigating are pretty scary. The kind of things that might make a person a bit, well, jumpy . . .

What was that?

Did you hear something?

OK, I'd better calm down . . . and breathe . . .

Let's go. Time to explore the world's greatest mysteries!

Richard Hammond

RICHARD HAMMOND'S

GREAT MYSTERIES OF THE WORLD

THE BODLEY HEAD

RICHARD HAMMOND'S GREAT MYSTERIES OF THE WORLD
A BODLEY HEAD BOOK 978 0 370 33237 6

Published in Great Britain by The Bodley Head,
an imprint of Random House Children's Publishers UK
A Random House Group Company

This edition published 2013

1 3 5 7 9 10 8 6 4 2

RANDOM HOUSE CHILDREN'S PUBLISHERS UK
61–63 Uxbridge Road, London W5 5SA

www.**randomhousechildrens**.co.uk
www.**totallyrandombooks**.co.uk
www.**randomhouse**.co.uk

Addresses for companies within The Random House Group Limited can be found at:
www.randomhouse.co.uk/offices.htm

THE RANDOM HOUSE GROUP Limited Reg. No. 954009

A CIP catalogue record for this book is available from the British Library.

Printed and bound by Clays Ltd, St Ives plc

Every effort has been made by the publishers to contact the copyright holders of the material published in this book; any omissions will be rectified at the earliest opportunity.

With special thanks to Amanda Li

CONTENTS

WEIRD WATERS

DEEP-SEA DIVING-KIT LIST

All water investigators know one thing. They're going to get wet. So I'm going to need some serious training – and some serious equipment – to help me on my mission to explore these weird watery mysteries. Here are a few of the basics:

DIVING WET SUIT – keeps you from freezing in a cold sea

DIVE SKIN – only for warmer waters, it protects you from jellyfish stings and sunburn

FLIPPERS – help you move faster and more efficiently through the water

DIVING MASK, OXYGEN TANKS AND REGULATOR – you need to be able to breathe!

DIVING WEIGHTS – to get down really deep. Weights attach to the body and help you descend

DIVING KNIFE – if you get caught up in weed or fishing line, this could be a lifesaver

WHISTLE, LIGHT OR SIGNALLING DEVICE – in case you're lost or swept out in a current

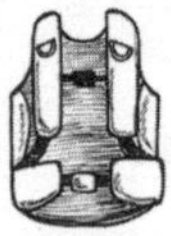

BCD (BUOYANCY CONTROL DEVICE) – wear it like a vest. You control the flow of air to move up or down once underwater

UNDERWATER FLASHLIGHT – it's really dark down there! Best to have a headlight too

BOAT – to take you to the diving location. The boat should have a red and white 'diver down' flag to alert others that divers are underwater in the area

BUDDY – no one should dive without a buddy to help them out

UNDERWATER CAMERA – to get the best shots possible. My model has a 100m depth rating and a macro lens for crystal-clear close-up shots. It also has a power flash for those dark, murky waters

Know your diving signals

Hand gestures are the best way of communicating when you're underwater. It's really important to know some basic signals – your life could depend on it!

1. *Are you OK?*

2. *Yes, I'm OK.*

3. *Not OK, something's wrong.*

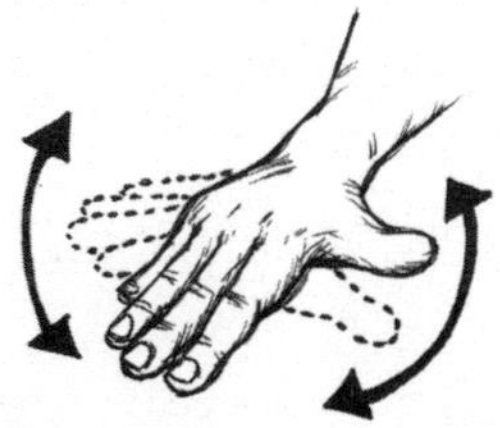

Hand moves from side to side

Right, so now I'm fully kitted up, join me on my first mystery hunt . . .

MYSTERY 1

The Lost City of Atlantis

THE MISSION . . .

. . . to search for the legendary lost city of Atlantis.

BURNING QUESTIONS

- Was Atlantis swallowed up by the sea more than 9,000 years ago?
- Can an entire city disappear without trace?
- Did Atlantis ever exist?

MISSION DETAILS

I'm looking for Atlantis – an ancient city built by an advanced civilization on a mysterious island. According to legend, Atlantis disappeared under the sea long, long ago. No trace has ever been found of its buildings or its people.

One of the reasons people find Atlantis fascinating is because it was supposed to have existed more than *10,000 years ago* (probably around 9600 BC). This, if you need reminding, was the time of the Stone Age. The humans we know about were still chipping away with sharpened bits of flint and trying to make fire!

But the Atlanteans – which is what you're called if you live in a city called Atlantis – were busy being brilliant architects, talented engineers and having intelligent discussions about politics and art. So if we ever found Atlantis, we would literally have to rewrite the history of human civilization . . .

THE EVIDENCE

There have been hundreds, maybe thousands, of investigations into Atlantis. Books have been written about it, divers have searched for it, films and TV programmes have been made about it.

But no one's ever found any trace of Atlantis. So how do we even know about it?

It's because Atlantis and its history were described in detail by none other than the famous Greek philosopher, Plato. In about 360 BC he wrote a long essay about an incredible island nation. His description has fascinated people ever since. Here are some of the things he said:

- Atlantis was ruled by ten kings
- The island of Atlantis was located close to the Pillars of Hercules
- The Atlanteans were clever, wealthy and powerful – an ancient superpower with a fleet of warships and more than a million soldiers
- They fought against Europe and Asia. They also tried, but failed, to invade Athens
- They were incredible engineers, architects and artists

Here is one of Plato's descriptions:

> Of the combatants on the one side the city of Athens was reported to have been the ruler, and to have directed the contest; the combatants on the other side were led by the kings of the islands of Atlantis, which, as I was saying, once had an extent greater than that of Libya and Asia; and, when afterward sunk by an earthquake, became an impassable barrier of mud to voyagers sailing from hence to the ocean.

Ever since Plato's time, people have wondered where this amazing place could have been – and if we can find it.

Was Plato making it all up? Or was Atlantis just an impressive work of fiction, Plato's own *Harry Potter*?

Potted Plato

Philosophers are people who think a lot about the big questions in life – a bit like me, really. Questions like 'Why are we here?' and 'What is wisdom?' – or, in my case, 'Why does my hair always stick up in the morning?'

Plato thought a lot about questions like these (except the last one, of course). He was born in Athens, Greece, in about 429 BC, to a rich, educated family. Later in his life, Plato wrote a famous book called *The Republic*, in which he discussed all his ideas about how to lead and govern people. He was thoughtful, wise – and extremely clever (again, the similarity!).

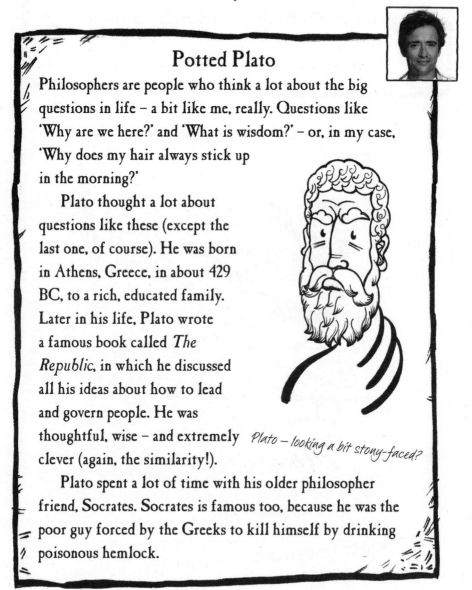

Plato – looking a bit stony-faced?

Plato spent a lot of time with his older philosopher friend, Socrates. Socrates is famous too, because he was the poor guy forced by the Greeks to kill himself by drinking poisonous hemlock.

We know all this because Plato wrote it down. And we believe him.

Plato is thought to have been one of the greatest philosophers of our time, admired and respected for centuries. So why shouldn't we believe his account of Atlantis?

As we can't ask him, we'll never know!

Atlantis – the Place

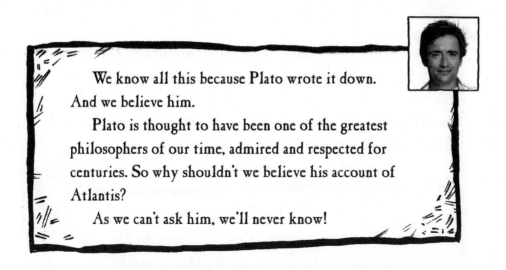

Amazing Atlantis!

COME TO THE DREAM CITY OF ATLANTIS! ENJOY SCENIC VIEWS FROM THE HARBOURS, RELAXING IN BEAUTIFUL SURROUNDINGS, WORSHIPPING IN THE FINEST TEMPLES AND WATCHING THE INCREDIBLE WILDLIFE ON THIS STUNNING ISLAND.

Atlantis sounds like a brilliant place to live. Plato says that it was made up of a large central island surrounded by three huge harbours. The harbours were in the shape of concentric circles – a series of circles that radiate outwards from one centre. There was a canal and tunnels for ships to pass through. On the island, there was a huge city of beautiful buildings, a large palace, temples, fountains, bridges, gardens, ports and docks.

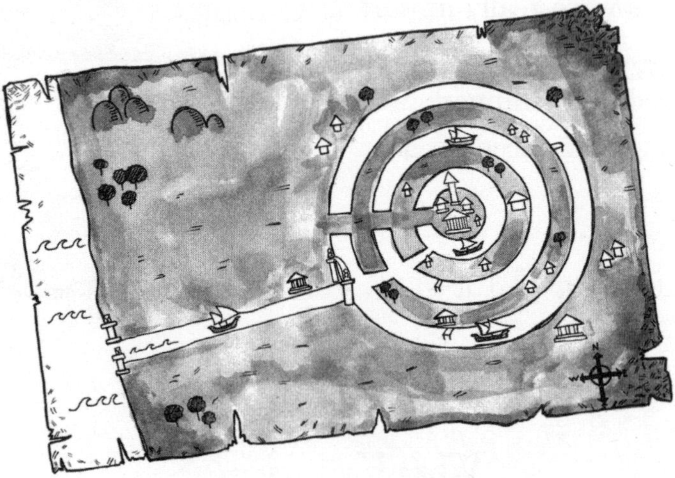

The Atlanteans had everything they could possibly need. The islands were full of exotic plants, fruits and animals, even elephants. There were precious metals too. The people made stunning gold and silver statues and displayed them around the city. There were large resources of a metal called *orichalcum*, which 'glowed like fire' – now thought to be copper. This lost treasure is another reason why adventurers seek Atlantis – whoever finds it could get *seriously* rich!

On top of the most central hill – called the Acropolis Hill – the Atlanteans built two huge temples. The most important was in honour of Poseidon. Inside this temple was a golden statue of the sea god on a chariot being pulled by winged horses. The Atlantean rulers came here to discuss important issues and to worship the powerful Poseidon.

All around the temples, bulls ran free. Bulls were really important to the Atlanteans – they regarded them as sacred, worshipped them and sometimes sacrificed them to the gods.

The Atlanteans had it all. But one day it fell apart . . .

What Happened?

Atlantis disappeared – literally overnight. What could have wiped out these beautiful islands and the people that lived on them?

Plato said that a 'terrible night of fire and earthquakes' was sent by the gods as a punishment to the badly behaved islanders, who had become too powerful and corrupt for their own good. Modern-day investigators think a natural disaster, most likely a tsunami, could have hit the island, destroying Atlantis and its people. If so, the island could now lie deep under the sea, undiscovered for thousands of years.

Tsunami Terror

'Tsunami' means 'harbour wave' in Japanese.

A tsunami is a gigantic wave caused by a massive underwater disturbance, usually an undersea earthquake or a volcanic eruption. Deep in the ocean, movement on the sea floor pushes the water above it, causing fast-moving waves. Once these waves reach shallower waters near the shore, they slow down but get bigger. This is when they can get to terrifying heights – as much as 40 metres.

A tsunami can wipe out everything in its path once it hits land, destroying entire cities, towns and villages. The speed and power of the water is unbelievable.

© AFP/GETTY IMAGES

The town of Otsuchi in Japan, following the devastating earthquake and tsunami of 2011

Certain parts of the world are prone to earthquake activity and tsunamis. One of these areas is called the 'Ring of Fire' and includes much of Asia and the Americas' Pacific coast.

THE LOCATION

We're not short of potential locations for Atlantis. It's a hot topic and there are lots of ideas out there: Egypt, Cuba, the Canary Islands, England, even chilly Antarctica, among many others.

Plato said that Atlantis was located *just beyond* or *in front of* the Pillars of Hercules, depending on your translation of ancient Greek. (I don't know about you, but my ancient Greek's just a little bit rusty . . .)

Most people believe that the Pillars of Hercules is the ancient name for the two huge rocks that lie on each side of what we now call the Strait of Gibraltar (one is called Gibraltar, the other Jebel Musa). They mark the entry point to the Mediterranean Sea from the Atlantic Ocean.

So all we have to do is dive down around the Strait of Gibraltar and we'll find Atlantis there? Well, if things were that straightforward, they would have found Atlantis years ago. Not everyone agrees about the location – and as you'll discover, trying to find Atlantis is anything but straightforward. There are countless 'experts' out there with different ideas and theories – and everyone makes mistakes.

Whoops!

It's easy to get carried away when you're mystery hunting. When excited researchers found an image with what looked like a grid of ancient roads under the Atlantic Ocean, they thought they had struck Atlantis gold. But the sunken 'city' was just an illusion. The 'roads' were actually lines reflecting the path of a boat as it was collecting data for maps!

Not everyone gets it right!

MY MISSION

Judging by what Plato said, the Mediterranean Sea and the Atlantic Ocean seem to be the obvious places to begin my investigation – but where exactly?

- ***A wetlands area in Southern Spain***

  Satellite photographs from space show images of large circles buried underneath the mud at Donaña, Europe's largest wetlands. I'm going to find out more about these circles and what they might mean. Some serious techie gadgets will be required!

- ***The Greek island of Crete***

  There are lots of similarities between an ancient civilization called the Minoans (who once lived on Crete) and the Atlanteans. I'm going to check out the Minoan history to see what it's all about. Digging and mapping involved.

An area of sea close to the island of Cyprus

There are rumours that man-made structures have been detected on the ocean floor southeast of Cyprus. I'll be diving down to take a look.

Note: There has been a suggestion that Atlantis is buried deep under a notorious area of ocean in the western part of the north Atlantic. Find out more on this in 'The Bermuda Triangle' (pages 63–90).

See you when I get back!

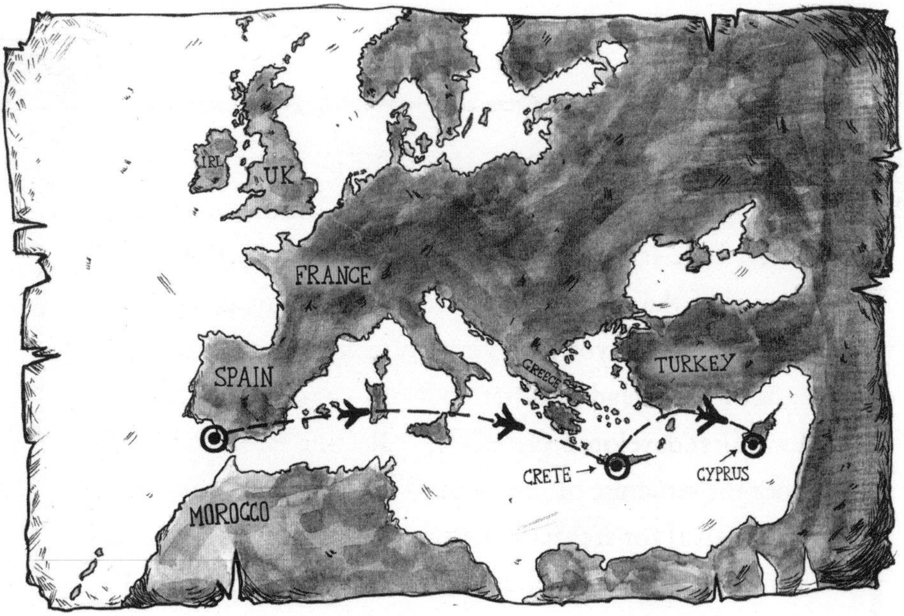

EXTRA KIT

Deep-sea diving kit is perfect for exploring water, but what if you're trying to find something buried underground? Guess what? – I'm going to need a gadget.

- ***The GPR*** – a machine that transmits high-frequency radio waves through the earth. OK, it may look a bit like a lawnmower, but in fact this is a high-tech piece of kit that can scan areas deep underground to detect what lies below. This is also called 'sonar imaging'.

A 'wheely' fun way to find out what lies underground . . .

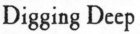

Digging Deep

Deeply buried sites have always been hard for archaeologists to deal with. It's pointless trying to dig up the earth with a shovel, if the site you're looking for is a kilometre underground and you're not even sure of its exact location.

GPR – Ground Penetrating Radar – has changed all that. It was first developed as a way of collecting information about the structure of the moon. The technology has proved really useful for archaeologists as well as astronauts, as it can be used to help find ancient remains deep below ground. The data it collects is then processed by a computer and turned into maps.

MISSION COMPLETED

Well – I've dived into the deepest oceans . . .

Spent hours surveying the land with my GPR machine . . .

Talked to lots of experts . . .

I haven't discovered the city of Atlantis yet – but I do have some very interesting information for you.

WHAT DO YOU THINK?

1. The Minoans and the Atlanteans Were One and the Same

When Plato wrote about the 'Atlanteans', was he describing a real group of people called the Minoans? They were a Bronze Age civilization who lived on the Greek islands of Crete and Santorini (and in other regions). We think the Minoans died out around 1500 BC, but they were around for hundreds of years before that.

The coincidences I have found are pretty amazing:

- Like the Atlanteans, the Minoans were very advanced for their time. They were the first Europeans known to have used a written language. They had hot and cold running water and were highly skilled plumbers –

archaeologists believe that Minoan Crete was home to the world's first flushing toilet!

- Their king, Minos, lived in a huge 150-room palace in Knossos. Plato described a great palace on Atlantis – could they be the same?
- Bulls were important animals in Atlantis. They were in Crete too. Archaeologists have unearthed paintings of Minoan bullfighters wrestling and jumping over bulls

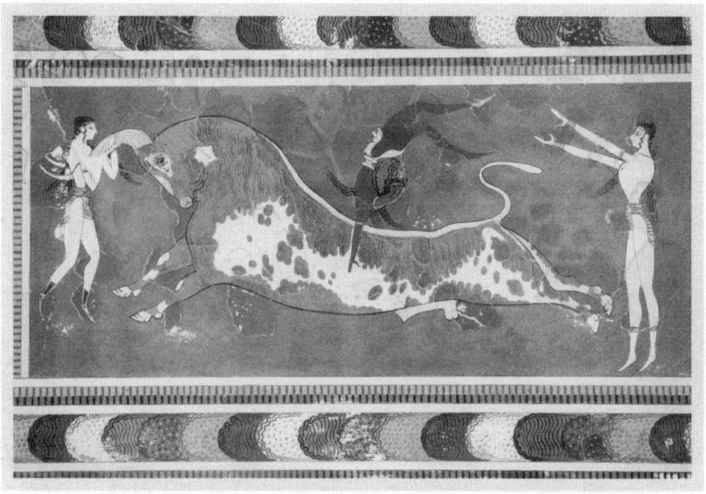

A Minoan wall painting showing the incredible things you can do with bulls!

- Both civilizations were excellent shipbuilders and had powerful naval fleets
- The Minoans disappeared, just like the Atlanteans. Around 1500 BC, a volcano erupted on the island of Santorini (then called Thera), not far from the island of Crete. It was a massive eruption, blasting out red-hot ash, gas and rocks, and it could have caused a later tsunami

- To back this up, archaeologists have found micro-organisms in the local soil that could only have come from the ocean floor. How did they get there? They're most likely what's left of a massive tsunami from long ago. So, did a tsunami wipe out the Minoans (who were really the Atlanteans)?

Not everything fits. Crete, though in the Mediterranean, is not very close to the Strait of Gibraltar. Also, the Minoans lived thousands of years *later* than Plato's Atlanteans. Some people think that the translations of his writings might not be exact, which could possibly explain the differences in date and location. For example, Plato said that Atlantis existed about 9,000 years before his time – but if that translation was wrong and it was actually *900* years before, then that would tie in with the Minoans nicely. Hmmm . . .

2. Atlantis Is Buried under Mud Flats in Spain

This is a really interesting one – and also the most recent of our theories. The images from satellite photos certainly indicate that there is *something* buried deep in the wetland area of Donaña, on the Atlantic coast of Spain. What it is exactly, no one can be sure, as the images can only show a vague outline.

What we do know is this:

- The wetlands were once a huge bay, but the ocean has receded over many years, leaving behind marshland
- The shapes discovered do look similar to the famed

circular harbours of Atlantis. There are also some rectangular shapes which the investigators think might be the remains of the Atlantean temples. Why not dig it all up and find out for sure? Well, the area is part of a National Park and one of Europe's most important wetland reserves – so that's not an option

- Plato said there was a plain and a range of high mountains behind the island Atlantis. In this area, there is a plain that runs from Spain's southern coast up to the city of Seville. The high mountains could be those of the Sierra Morena and Sierra Nevada
- Copper, another feature of Atlantis, is found in the mines of the Sierra Morena
- A research team, headed by Professor Richard Freund, found a large piece of stone with a carved symbol on it. It shows three concentric rings with a line in the centre, like a channel, and what looks like a simple human figure next to it. Could this carving represent the harbours and people of Atlantis?

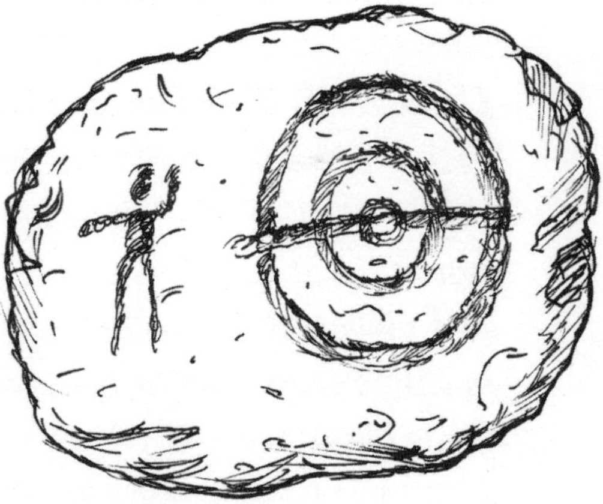

Even though the stone is not old enough to have come from Atlantis itself, the research team think it may have come from a 'memorial city' nearby – a city built years later by a group of Atlanteans who managed to escape the disaster that befell their island. Professor Freund thinks these survivors could have moved inland and built more cities. Perhaps they made the stone symbols in tribute to Atlantis, their true home. More than a hundred of these stone symbols have been found in central Spain – do they prove that the real Atlantis is here?

3. Atlantis Was Once Part of Cyprus

Everyone got very excited in 2004, when an archaeologist called Robert Sarmast found what appeared to be two large man-made structures beneath the ocean, close to the island of Cyprus in the Mediterranean. Sonar data images taken 1,500 metres below sea level showed what were possibly two straight, two-kilometre-long walls, sitting on a flat-topped hill. Sarmast studied Plato's measurements of the walled city and said they matched up. He is convinced that he has found the legendary Acropolis Hill that was at the centre of Atlantis.

Could Cyprus once have been part of Atlantis? Here are some reasons why:

- Sarmast thinks that part of the landmass sank under the sea thousands of years ago
- Plato said there were elephants on Atlantis. Well, surprisingly, there used to be a species of dwarf elephant on Cyprus (now sadly extinct)
- According to Plato, copper was abundant on Atlantis And what is the island of Cyprus named for? – you've got it – copper! Cyprus was once very famous for its copper reserves

- Every year in Cyprus, the people celebrate a Festival of the Flood – but no one knows why. Does the tradition go back thousands of years, marking the sinking of Atlantis under the sea?
- The highest mountain on the island is named Olympos. Could this be the original Mount Olympus, the sacred mountain of the Greek gods?

4. It's Just a Story

As everything we know about Atlantis comes from Plato, we only have his word for it. He may have been making it all up. Perhaps he was describing his fantasy, his ideal world. But if it *was* made up, why would Plato have brought his perfect world to an end? Seems a bit of a shame, doesn't it?

Well, Plato may have been trying to help people learn that actions have consequences. The people of Atlantis had everything, but they lost their way, became greedy and behaved badly. As a result, they were punished by the gods. This could have been an allegory – an important lesson told through a story. Was Plato's story made up for this reason?

5. Aliens on Atlantis

Some people believe that the Atlanteans weren't human. They think that Atlantis was populated by 'extraterrestrials'

– aliens from outer space! Could a group of advanced, intelligent aliens have landed on Earth and formed their own colony, thousands of years ago? If so, what happened to them? Maybe a natural disaster killed them or perhaps they destroyed themselves accidentally – with a nuclear bomb or with a weapon so weird and technologically advanced we can't even begin to imagine it!

THE HAMMOND-ATOR®
I've invented a highly dangerous death-ray gun. Now all I need is someone to invent the manual to go with it.

The alien believers think that this idea could solve some big unanswered questions – like, for example, how (and why) did the ancient Egyptians build the pyramids? And why are similar pyramids found in Central America and other far-away parts of the world? Some think that the knowledge needed to build them came from intelligent pyramid-loving aliens who passed it on to the ancient cultures of our world.

There is no scientific evidence for this idea that I know of – but it's certainly 'out of this world'!

YOU DECIDE

So, now we've come to the end of our Atlantis adventure, do you think it was a real place – or a just myth?

Why not turn to page 426 and vote for your favourite theory, or write your thoughts about the Atlantis mystery in the notes section.

The great Atlantis debate will continue – and the watery hunt will go on . . .

MYSTERY 2

The Mary Celeste

THE MISSION . . .

. . . to find out why the passengers and crew disappeared from a ship called the *Mary Celeste.*

© HULTON ARCHIVE/GETTY IMAGES

The ghostly, abandoned Mary Celeste

BURNING QUESTIONS

- How can ten people just vanish into thin air?
- Did the crew abandon their ship – and why?

MISSION DETAILS

I'm trying to get to the bottom of one of the biggest ever maritime mysteries, one that has had people scratching their heads for more than a hundred years.

On 5 December 1872 a ship was discovered drifting in the Atlantic Ocean – in good condition, with no signs of any major problems. Just one odd thing: the crew had completely disappeared.

What could have happened? Did the passengers panic and leave the ship for some reason – or was there a more sinister explanation?

THE EVIDENCE

The mystery of the *Mary Celeste* has fascinated people ever since the infamous 'ghost ship' was found silently floating alone, all those years ago. People have come up with all sorts of ideas about what could have happened, from attacks by bloodthirsty pirates to the entire crew being abducted by aliens.

The famous mystery writer Sir Arthur Conan Doyle even made up his own 'explanation' – more on that later.

But even though there was a full investigation at the time, we really don't have that much to go on. Just a spooky, empty ship and the eyewitness accounts of the sailors who found it.

The facts we know for sure are:

- There were ten people on board the *Mary Celeste*: Captain Benjamin Briggs, his wife, Sarah, their two-year-old daughter, Sophia, and a crew of seven men
- A small rowing boat, called a yawl, was missing. The railings on one side of the ship had been lowered so the yawl had probably been launched
- All the cargo (hundreds of barrels of alcohol) was intact, apart from just nine barrels, which were found to be empty
- The ship's clock wasn't working and the compass was destroyed
- The stove had been moved
- The sextant and chronometer were missing. (In the days before sat nav, these instruments would have been essential for navigating the ship)
- The ship's navigation book was missing – but the log book was still there
- The halyard (the rope used to hoist the sail) was broken and part of it was missing
- There was some water slopping around between the decks, and one of the pumps was broken. Two of the ship's hatches had been removed

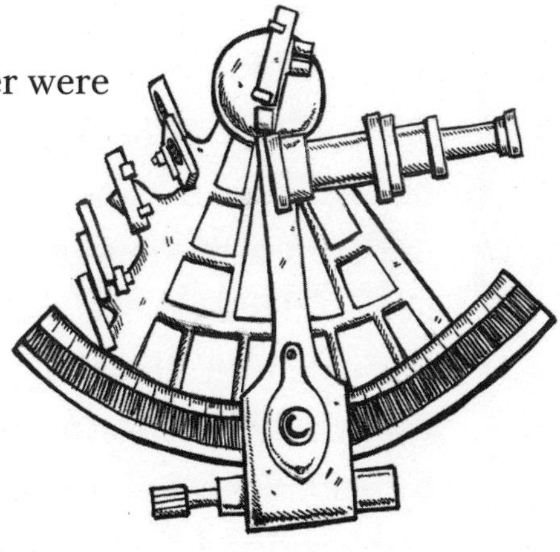

This is a sextant – even trickier to use than a sat nav . . .

Fact or Fiction?

Sir Arthur Conan Doyle – who later went on to create the brilliant violin-playing detective Sherlock Holmes – loved a good mystery (me too!).

Take a look at his photograph. Here's another mystery for you – how did Sir Arthur get his moustache to twirl upwards in that gravity-defying way? (I admit I don't have the answer to this – yet another great unsolved mystery of our time.)

© HULTON ARCHIVE/GETTY IMAGES

Conan Doyle was fascinated by the *Mary Celeste* case and decided to write his own story about the ghost ship. His gruesome version was published in 1884.

In his story:

- The ship is named the *Marie Celeste*
- Among the crew and passengers is a strange-looking character named Septimius Goring. Septimius has lost all the fingers on his right hand, leaving just a thumb, but no one knows why. (Sounds like he could do with a trip to a second-hand shop . . . ?)
- Turns out we were right to be suspicious about Goring – he's a bad guy. He shoots the captain, takes control of the *Marie Celeste* and sails her to Africa
- He then murders most of the crew and is last seen disappearing into the Sahara desert . . .

The story caused a lot of confusion as people weren't sure if it was the truth. And many still think the real ship was called the *Marie Celeste*. Even more confusingly, over time, other details about the real-life case have been exaggerated, or made up. For example, lots of people believe that the ship was found with half-eaten meals at the table and half-drunk cups of coffee. If this were true, it would have meant that the passengers had left the ship incredibly fast, without even having time to finish their food. But, just like the Conan Doyle story, it's pure fiction!

THE LOCATION

The *Mary Celeste* set sail from New York, USA, on 7 November 1872, bound for Genoa in Italy. She was a brigantine – a ship with two masts. (By the way, ships are always referred to as 'she' – an old sailor's tradition.)

On board was a cargo of 1,701 barrels of pure alcohol, used to fortify wine and destined for the vineyards of Italy.

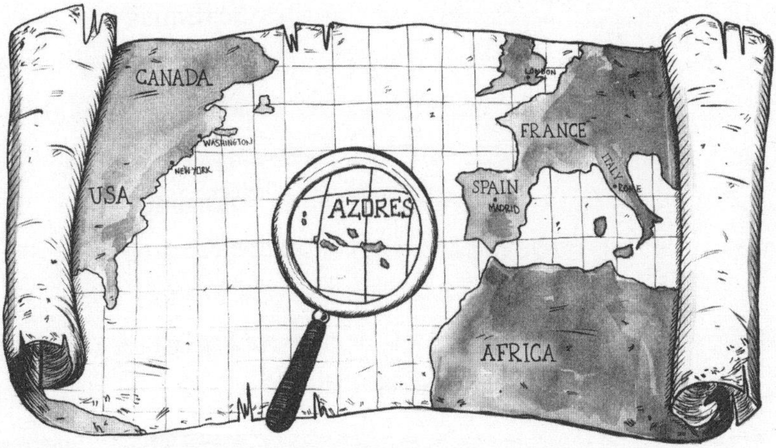

The log book's last entry was recorded on 25 November and described nothing unusual. At this point, the ship was just six miles away from the island of Santa Maria. Santa Maria is one of nine Portuguese islands called the Azores, in the North Atlantic Ocean.

When she was discovered, the *Mary Celeste* had drifted 400 miles east of Santa Maria and was heading towards the Strait of Gibraltar.

What Happened?

A Canadian ship called *Dei Gratia* had left New York harbour a few days after the *Mary Celeste.* On 5 December the *Dei Gratia* crew were puzzled to see a ship in the distance, apparently unmanned (that means no one was on board). They could tell this because of the way the *Mary Celeste* was moving. She was doing something sailors call 'yawing', which is swinging around to the right and left – clearly not under a captain's control.

Captain Morehouse of the *Dei Gratia* looked carefully through his telescope and recognized the ship. He knew the *Mary Celeste*'s captain – he'd even had dinner with Captain Briggs the night before she had sailed. After a couple of hours of observation there were still no signs of life on board and absolutely no response to their signals. So Morehouse decided to send out a boarding party in a small boat.

The men boarded a completely deserted ship. It must have been a really spooky sight – the ship's wheel spinning round with no hand to guide it, the deck and rigging creaking, but not a soul on board to reply to the men's shouts and calls. From the look of things – the sailors had left behind their boots and pipes and the captain's wife hadn't taken any of her jewellery – the crew had left the ship in a bit of a hurry.

Rather appropriately for a ghost ship, Captain Morehouse put a 'skeleton crew' on the *Mary Celeste*, and both ships were sailed back to Gibraltar.

Spooky Ships

Would you have volunteered to be the first to step aboard the scarily silent and empty *Mary Celeste*, not knowing what had happened? It's enough to literally 'shiver your timbers'! But it seems there might be even spookier ships out there, according to sailors' tales. Take the legend of the ghostly *Flying Dutchman*, for example.

Sailors are petrified of spotting this ghostly glowing ship. Why? Because anyone who sees it is supposed to die an awful death. This is what is known as a 'bad omen'. And, as omens go, seeing the *Flying Dutchman* is a really, really bad one.

The story goes that in 1641 a Dutch ship was caught up in a terrible storm near the Cape of Good Hope (on the Atlantic coast of South Africa). As the ship crashed into rocks and began to sink, the captain screamed out that he would *never* give up – that he would keep sailing round the Cape until Doomsday! (Quite a long time, then.) Unfortunately, the captain then drowned, along with the rest

of his crew. But, according to legend, his phantom ship carries on, doomed to sail the seven seas for eternity . . .

Years later, in 1881, the Royal Navy ship *Bacchante* was sailing round the Cape, when – yikes! A terrifying sight came into view. Yes, you've guessed it: it was the *Flying Dutchman*, glowing with a ghostly red light, as if she had sailed from the depths of hell itself. The crew were understandably terrified and panic broke out amongst the men. Soon afterwards the ship vanished from sight. Everyone breathed a sigh of relief. But worse was to come . . . the sailor who had first spotted the *Dutchman* later fell from a mast to his death. Eek!

MY MISSION

After hearing that story, I'm a teeny bit nervous about spotting any kind of ghost ship. Fortunately, the *Flying Dutchman* is supposed to haunt oceans in South Africa – a very long way away from where I'll be sailing to search out the wreck

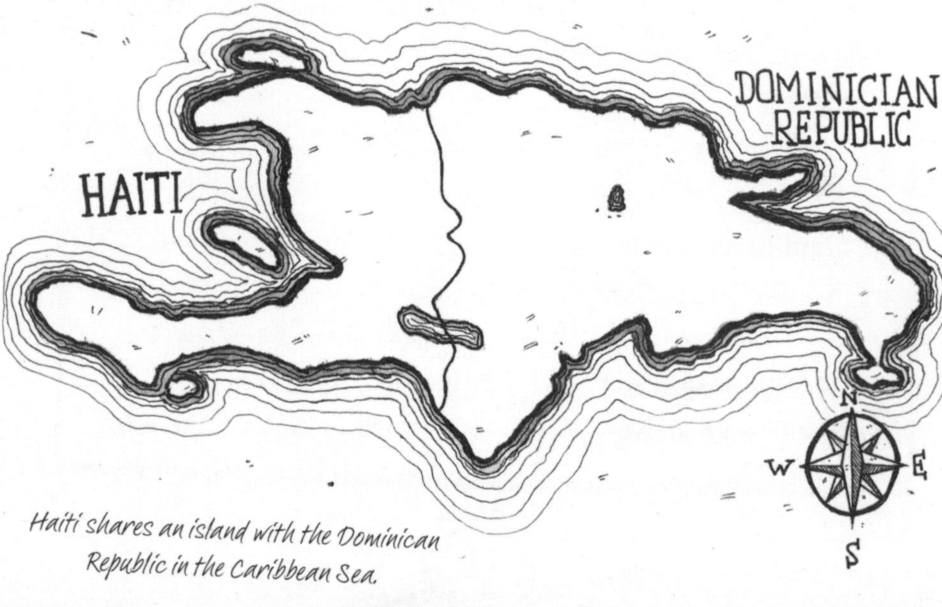

Haiti shares an island with the Dominican Republic in the Caribbean Sea.

of the *Mary Celeste.* I'm off to the Caribbean! But what is the *Mary Celeste* doing there?

In 2001 a team of divers found the remains of the legendary ship lying on a coral reef, just off the coast of Haiti. The poor old *Mary Celeste* had been abandoned by her last owner and left to rot.

I'll be diving down to the *Mary Celeste*'s final resting place to inspect the wreck. I'll need my full deep-sea diving kit to have a good old look around. Luckily, the Caribbean is one of the warmer seas of the world, and the coral reef should be full of amazing sea creatures. I'm just off to get a book and check out exactly which ones . . .

. . . OK, so there's good news and there's bad news. The bad news is that I now know what lives in coral reefs in the Caribbean Sea – the Caribbean reef shark!

The good news is that, apparently, shark attacks are extremely rare. In fact, most sharks only attack humans by mistake, thinking they are big fish. So – just in case a wandering reef shark mistakes me for a fish, I've invested in a whopping bit of kit to take along:

EXTRA KIT

- A shark cage. This super-strong submersible cage is constructed from marine-grade aluminium. It's not big – with a height of 3 metres and a width of just 2 metres, it's going to be cosy, but, most importantly, it should – hopefully – protect me from the fiercest reef shark!

MISSION COMPLETED

Back from my diving adventure – and you'll be pleased to hear (I hope!) that I wasn't eaten by a Caribbean reef shark. Even better – I found the *Mary Celeste*! She's not looking her best, though. Having been underwater for so many years, much of her wood has rotted and her sails have completely disintegrated. She is pretty much unrecognizable as a ship and is almost completely covered in coral. It's a sad sight . . .

I couldn't get right inside the wreck because the shark cage was, well, a bit limiting. And there was no way I was getting out of that cage to take a closer look!

It was fascinating to see the old wreck of this mysterious ship . . . but it couldn't really tell me anything new about the mystery. So, like the legendary detective Sherlock Holmes, we will have to use our incredible powers of deduction . . .

WHAT DO YOU THINK?

There are lots of theories, ranging from the ridiculous to the realistic. There was once even an episode of TV's *Doctor Who* (from 1965 – the Doctor really is ancient!) that blamed the *Mary Celeste* crew's disappearance on a rogue group of Daleks! Well, wouldn't *you* jump overboard if a bunch of one-armed metallic monsters suddenly appeared on board your ship?

Hmm – maybe best to 'exterminate' that idea and move on to some others . . .

1. Sea Monster Attack

Were the passengers devoured by a giant octopus? Perhaps 'squidnapped'?

Many people at the time believed that some kind of huge sea monster attacked the ship. This theory depends on a few other things. Firstly, believing that sea monsters actually exist. Throughout history, sailors have told tales of horrible monsters such as the Kraken, a gigantic squid-like creature with writhing tentacles that attacks ships at sea.

This artist painted a picture of the Kraken in 1801, based on real sailors' descriptions at the time. Not something you'd want to encounter on a relaxing boating trip . . .

'Mmm – fish and ships for dinner tonight!'

But if a hungry Kraken was responsible for the disappearance, surely the passengers would have had to be on deck for the monster to attack them? (I don't know about you, but I'd get *below* deck very fast if a massive monster with waving tentacles suddenly rose out of the waves.)

Also, why – and how – would a sea monster take the yawl, sextant, chronometer and ship's papers? Those great big tentacles aren't exactly made for picking up delicate objects, are they? Surely there would have been some bite marks in the deck, or at least some signs of a struggle?

2. Plundering Pirates

Yo ho ho! In days of old, posses of plundering pirates sailed the oceans on the lookout for ships to raid. Given their liking for a bottle of rum, the *Mary Celeste* – which was carrying barrels of alcohol – should have been an ideal target for a group of thirsty pirates. They might have got rid of the passengers and crew by throwing them overboard – or perhaps making them walk the plank!

But if pirates *had* attacked the ship, why would they have left all those valuable barrels behind? Plus, again, there were no visible signs of an attack or a struggle. Could pirates really be to blame for the crew's disappearance?

3. Foul Play

Was there a cunning plot to make a fortune out of the *Mary Celeste*? In those days, you could claim a very nice amount of cash – 'salvage money' – if you rescued a ship that had valuable cargo on board. Some believed that the captains of the two ships involved planned to do exactly this.

In Gibraltar, where the *Mary Celeste* was eventually taken by the *Dei Gratia*, the Attorney General, Mr Solly Flood, made some serious accusations against Captains Briggs and Morehouse. He suggested that a plot had been hatched between the two captains to get rid of the crew and claim the salvage money for themselves.

Mr Flood later accused Captain Morehouse and the crew of the *Dei Gratia* of murdering everyone on board the *Mary Celeste.* None of these accusations of 'foul play!' were ever proved, but they did have a big impact. People everywhere heard about the rumours and everyone got talking about the mysterious case. That's been going on ever since.

4. Mutiny!

If you were a captain of a ship, the one thing you would dread (apart from pirates, sea monsters and terrible storms, obviously) was mutiny. A mutiny happens when the crew takes over the ship and gets rid of the captain because they don't like him very much. Any group of sailors would have had to be really desperate to do this – because the punishment for mutiny was dire. If a mutineer was captured, it would be a case of 'Hang him by the yardarm!' – a particularly nasty way to die (the yardarm being a horizontal timber mounted on the mast of a ship).

Did a mutiny take place aboard the *Mary Celeste*? Were the crew so upset about something that they murdered the captain and his family, threw their bodies overboard, then escaped in the yawl, never to be seen again?

Mutinies always happen for a good reason – perhaps the sailors are badly treated, or suffering horribly on a very long voyage. As far as we know, Captain Briggs was a well-respected leader and there were no known troublemakers among the crew. Also the voyage was just a few weeks long, and there were plenty of food and water supplies on board. There was no obvious reason for the sailors to take over the ship. Was there something going on that we don't know about?

Mutiny on the *Bounty*

One of the most famous mutinies of all time – which had nothing at all to do with a chocolate-covered coconut bar – happened in 1789 in the Pacific Ocean. HMS *Bounty* was a British ship which sailed to Tahiti in 1788 on a voyage to collect breadfruit plants. Her captain was William Bligh, a brilliant and experienced sea man – though some say he was a harsh and difficult captain to work for.

After ten tough months at sea, the crew were delighted to spend some relaxing months on the beautiful island of Tahiti. So much so that, when the time came to start the long voyage home, most of the men decided that they would rather stay. This wasn't an option – and that's when the trouble started.

Life on board ship was always hard and the months at sea could seem never-ending. The diet of maggot-ridden 'ship's biscuit' (a kind of rock-hard bread, sadly; nothing at all like a custard cream) and harsh punishments of flogging didn't make the trip any more appealing. It was too much for some of Bligh's men.

On 28 April 1789 the captain's second-in-command, Fletcher Christian, along with twelve others, burst into Captain Bligh's cabin and dragged him up on deck. According to his log book, the men 'came into my cabin while I was fast asleep, and seizing me, tyed my hands with a Cord & threatened instant death if I made the least noise'.

They set the captain adrift in a seven-metre boat, along with eighteen of his loyal crew members. The merry mutineers then sailed straight back to the good life on Tahiti.

Now, things weren't looking too good for Captain Bligh and his men. They knew that they had very little chance of surviving on the open sea without any supplies. But incredibly – despite being chased by cannibals and stoned by the locals when they finally found an island – most of the sailors *did* survive. It was tough – they had to catch fish to

eat and find rainwater to drink. But they eventually made it to the island of Timor (east of Indonesia). It had taken them seven weeks and they had travelled more than 3,600 miles. Whatever you think of Captain Bligh, it was an incredible achievement!

5. A Curse?

Some superstitious people think that the *Mary Celeste* was cursed. From the moment she was launched in 1861, the *Mary Celeste* (who was originally called *Amazon*) seemed to have nothing but bad luck. In fact, even being renamed is supposed to be bad luck for a ship!

A few examples:

- Her first captain, Robert McLellan, was taken ill and died
- Under the command of her second captain, John Parker, she ran into a fishing boat, was badly damaged and had to return to the shipyard for repairs
- A fire broke out on board while she was at the shipyard
- The *Mary Celeste* later collided with another ship in the English Channel and needed further repairs
- In 1867 she ran aground during a storm off the coast of Nova Scotia
- In 1872 she was found empty and all ten people on board had disappeared (our mystery)

After she was found abandoned, the *Mary Celeste* sailed for a further twelve years. She had many different owners during this time and, unfortunately, lost money for most of them. She came to a sad end when she was run aground off the coast of Haiti. Her final captain, Captain Gilman Parker, had loaded her with a worthless cargo of rubber boots and cat food, then tried to sink her, hoping to claim the insurance money. He died three months after his trial.

David Cartwright, one of her owners, said:

> Of all the unlucky vessels I ever heard of, she was the most unlucky.

Could the *Mary Celeste* really have been cursed? And if so, what happened to the people on board?

Abandon Ship!

Captains only abandon their ships for a very good reason. What kind of emergency could have forced everyone off the ship?

6. A Sea Quake or Spout?

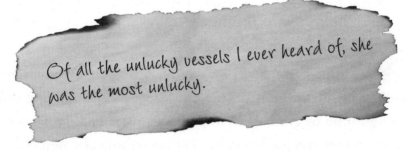

A sea quake is an earthquake that happens underneath the sea. One theory is that a sudden sea quake hit the *Mary Celeste,* dislodging the ship's stove and some of the barrels of alcohol, which leaked as a result. (Remember from the evidence that the stove had been moved and nine barrels were found empty?) As you probably know, fire – in the form of sparks from the stove – combined with alcohol would have a very 'explosive' result! The crew knew this too. Might they have panicked, jumped into the yawl (a small boat) and left as quickly as they could?

Another strange sea phenomenon is called a waterspout. This is the result of a whirling tornado moving over the sea, which pulls a long slim 'spout' of water many metres up into the sky. If a waterspout had suddenly hit the ship, it would explain why there was water sloshing between the decks. It could also be the reason why the two hatches blew off.

In either case, Captain Briggs would probably have thought that staying on the ship was too dangerous. He might have had enough time to grab a few important things like the sextant, chronometer and log book, but left everything else behind.

7. A Potential Explosion?

Now I didn't know this – and I'm pretty sure you didn't either – but apparently barrels for holding liquid are usually made from white oak. Why? Because white oak is watertight and keeps liquid intact. If you were a half-decent barrel maker, you'd *never* use red oak for a wine barrel because it's, quite frankly, useless for the job.

All the barrels on board the *Mary Celeste* were made of white oak – except for nine, made of red oak. For some reason, the wrong wood had been used. All very interesting, you might think, but what does it matter?

It matters because it explains the mystery of the empty nine barrels of alcohol on board, which were not, as many people at the time thought, drunk dry by the crew. What's much more likely is that the alcohol leaked through the red oak. In any case, raw strong alcohol is not at all drinkable and would have made the crew very ill if they'd tried it!

The leaking barrels would have begun to smell quite strongly. Is this why the deck hatches were removed – to get rid of the smell and the fumes coming from the cargo?

Alcohol is highly flammable – it catches fire incredibly easily – so with the strong smell of alcohol in the air, perhaps the captain and crew were worried about an explosion or fire breaking out – not a barrel of fun (sorry) on a wooden ship! Maybe they decided to get everyone to 'safety' in the yawl.

So let's imagine that all ten of them *did* get into the yawl. What became of them?

The fact that the halyard (rope) was broken might have been because they had used it to tie the yawl to the ship, and the rope snapped under the strain. The yawl may have capsized and they were drowned, or perhaps it drifted away and they eventually died of hunger and thirst. But nothing was ever found – no yawl and no bodies.

8. Alien Abduction!

Some have suggested that, because everyone vanished without trace, the ten people on board must have been kidnapped by aliens. This sounds like a crazy idea, but there are certainly people out there who believe that aliens visit our planet. They also believe that aliens sometimes kidnap the occasional human for further inspection. So far, no one has actually proved the existence of aliens or UFOs (Unidentified Flying Objects) and there is no concrete evidence that human beings are being spirited away by creatures from outer space. But that doesn't mean it's not happening!

Do you think it's possible that a group of aliens swooped down in their spacecraft to capture the crew and passengers of the *Mary Celeste*?

YOU DECIDE

It's a tricky one – maybe the only people who will ever know what really happened are the ten people on board the ship?

In the meantime, you need to make a decision. Which do *you* think is the most likely explanation?

Turn to the back of the book to record your findings!

MYSTERY 3

Mythical Mermaids

THE MISSION . . .

. . . to find out if mermaids really exist.

© HULTON ARCHIVE/GETTY IMAGES

A painting of a mermaid by John William Waterhouse.

BURNING QUESTION

Are mermaids just characters in fairy tales and myths?

MISSION DETAILS

No sailor's tale would be complete without a beautiful mermaid.

We all know what mermaids look like – they're a cross between a human and a fish, with the upper half of a woman and a large scaly fish's tail.

According to legend, mermaids live in the ocean and swim like fish. Though lovely to look at, in many stories, mermaids are sinister creatures who bring nothing but trouble to humans.

Tales of mermaids are told around the world and go back for many hundreds of years. So is there any truth in the mermaid myth?

THE LOCATION

Only one condition – it's got to be wet. Mermaids live in oceans and seas all over the world. Stories from some countries say that their mermaids live in rivers, lakes and pools.

When not in water, mermaids can usually be found sitting on rocks, combing their long hair and singing. They swim off quickly if they think they're in danger, so they are pretty impossible to catch. Slippery as a fish, one might say! (A group of fisherman said they once managed to catch a mermaid, however – read their story on page 55.)

THE EVIDENCE

Stories about mermaids appear as far back as 1000 BC.

- The ancient Assyrians told tales of a goddess who fell in love with a human, but accidentally killed him. She tried to hide in a lake and became half fish, half human – the first mermaid
- In Greek and Roman mythology, evil sea nymphs called sirens lured sailors to their deaths on the rocks. The sirens were half bird, half woman, the daughters of the sea god Phorcys. They had such sweet voices that anyone who heard their singing couldn't help themselves – they had to go closer. The Greek hero Odysseus got round this problem by making all his sailors plug their ears with wax so that they couldn't hear a thing. A great tip for any upcoming rounds of *X-Factor* auditions!

Grab your ear plugs, the Sirens are coming!

The evil side of mermaids is well-documented. Even Blackbeard, the legendary and not-very-easily-scared pirate, told his crew to avoid certain waters in case there were mermaids around. Mermaids were thought to bewitch sailors, take their treasure and then drag them down to a watery death.

Mermaids appear in the folklore of China, Japan, Africa, Scandinavia, Britain and many other places. One of the most famous stories about mermaids – 'The Little Mermaid' – was written in Denmark by Hans Christian Andersen in 1837. You'll probably know this one as it was made into a famous movie of the same name. In the story, the mermaid of the title falls madly in love with a human. She is so desperate to join him on land that she uses a witch's spell to exchange her mermaid's tail for human feet. Unfortunately, the feet are incredibly painful and she feels like she's walking on knives. That must have been a stabbing pain . . .

The statue of the Little Mermaid – as seen in Copenhagen Harbour.

Mermaids have since featured in countless books, films and TV programmes. But has *anyone* actually seen one? Well, there are certainly a few people who think they have.

Here are some of their eyewitness accounts:

- In January 1493 the explorer Christopher Columbus saw three mermaids playing together in the sea, just off the coast of Haiti. He said the mermaids had human faces, though he was surprised that they were not as pretty as he had expected – in fact, he said that their faces were 'more like a man's'! A group of mer*men*, perhaps, Christopher?

- In 1608 explorer Henry Hudson set out for the chilly waters of the Arctic in search of a north-east passage. During the voyage, two of his crew shouted that they had spotted a mermaid in the water. All the men hurried to the side to see the mermaid, who had long black hair and white skin. In the log book, Hudson described her as having the 'tail of a porpoise and speckled like a mackerel'. A bit of a fishy tale, maybe?

- A 1947 sighting took place on the Scottish island of Muck (great name!). An 80-year-old fisherman called Alexander Gunn said that he had seen a mermaid sitting on a lobster trap quite close to the shore, combing her hair. When the mermaid realized she was being watched, she immediately disappeared into the waves . . .

- In the summer of 1833 six fishermen sailing off the Isle of Yell (another great name!) in the Shetlands said that a mermaid had got caught up in their fishing lines. They hauled her aboard and kept her on their boat for several hours before returning her to the sea. Apparently, she had bristles running from her head to her shoulders, which she could raise or lower, like a crest. Hair-raising stuff! The creature 'offered no resistance nor attempted to bite, but she moaned piteously'

- A much more recent encounter also describes the sad sound of a mermaid. In 2008 newspapers reported the experience of a man and his family in the Western Cape area of South Africa. They were walking by a local river when they spotted what they thought was a mermaid in the water. She had black hair, strange hypnotic red eyes and made a sound like a woman crying. The family believe it was a South African Kaaiman, a legendary creature, half fish, half human, that is supposed to live in deep pools

- In the summer of 2009 the people of a town in Israel reported seeing a mermaid jumping out of the water like a dolphin and performing stunts! Despite a $1 million reward for finding the mermaid, the aquatic acrobat has never been seen again

There are many, many more accounts of mermaid sightings, from ancient times to the modern day. Could all these people be mistaken? Or are they making it all up?

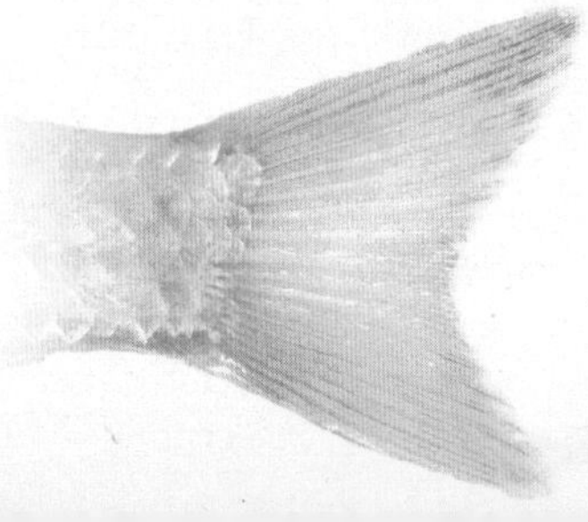

Freaks and Fakes

The famous 'Fiji mermaid' was exhibited as part of P. T. Barnum's Travelling Show in the nineteenth century.

Other oddities in the show included:

- Tom Thumb – the smallest man on earth (about 60cm tall)
- A bearded lady
- A dog-faced boy
- A giant mummified man called the Cardiff Giant

Now, you probably haven't seen many bearded ladies or dog-faced boys in your neighbourhood recently (if I'm wrong, please let me know) – but in those times, travelling circuses and 'freak' shows full of weird and wonderful characters were pretty common. Thankfully, television was invented in the 1900s, so the freak shows gradually died out.

Just as well – many of Barnum's exhibits were later exposed as fakes. The Fiji mermaid was found to be the upper half of a monkey sewn to the lower half of a fish! But despite its weird appearance, the Fiji mermaid became one of the show's biggest attractions. Proving that people would believe anything in those days . . .

In 2004 a similar photo circulated on the internet, claiming to be that of a mummified mermaid body. It convinced a lot of the people who saw it – but it too was a fake. Proving that some people will *still* believe anything!

MY MISSION

So how does a person go about finding a mermaid? Go on a mer-mission, of course! All you have to do is set sail for a few years, hang around some rocks and wait to hear the sweet sound of singing . . .

Hmm – rather than spend years sailing the seas (I'm a busy man, you know – people to see, TV programmes to make . . .) I've decided to keep a careful eye out for all kinds of merpeople while I'm investigating the oceans for the other mysteries in this book. Here's what I'll be taking along on all my missions:

EXTRA KIT

- EAR PLUGS – in case the singing starts! I really don't want to be mesmerized (or should that be mer-smerized?) by an evil mermaid
- A VERY BIG NET – mermaid-sized, of course
- A HUGE WATER TANK – to be filled with fresh sea water, for keeping a captured mermaid in
- A SET OF HAIRBRUSH AND COMBS – to keep her happy; I might even throw in a few hair slides

MISSION COMPLETED

While I've been travelling around the oceans, lakes and rivers of the world, I've collected many more tales and sightings of mermaids. However, the same 'explanation' keeps cropping up again and again – and it involves a creature which definitely isn't a mermaid. Intrigued? Here's more:

WHAT DO YOU THINK?

1. Mermaids Are Sea Cows

Is it possible that the whole mermaid idea is a mistake and that, for hundreds of years, sailors have been seeing an animal in the water? We are talking about a creature called a dugong – also known as a 'sea cow'.

So what is a dugong? It's a mammal that lives in warm coastal waters from East Africa to Australia, including the Red Sea, the Indian Ocean and the Pacific. Dugongs look a bit like big-nosed sea lions. They can live for up to 70 years and they are powerful swimmers. They spend much of their time alone or in pairs, though they occasionally gather in larger groups.

Here's one:

Now, a dugong doesn't look much like a mermaid to me – but you can see how the shape of the body and the tail swimming through murky water might confuse people (especially extremely short-sighted sailors).

But what about the mermaid's beautiful singing voice? Dugongs make a kind of weird high-pitched chirping – I've heard it on my travels – and, to be honest, it's not exactly tuneful. As well as this, you may have noticed that sea cows *don't* have long flowing hair.

So why the mix-up? Perhaps it's because of the dugongs' unusual behaviour? As they are mammals, they have to breathe air (though they can stay underwater for several minutes before surfacing). Sometimes they 'stand' on their tails in shallow water, with their heads above the surface to breathe. From a distance, a dugong's head could arguably be mistaken for a human one.

What do you think? Could all those mermaids really be sea cows?

2. Mermaids Are Real

Many people say they have seen a mermaid – so why would all these stories be around if mermaids didn't exist? The trouble is, we're lacking hard evidence – probably because those pesky merpeople just don't want to be caught! If only we could actually capture one to prove their existence, once and for all. But, as far as we know, no fish-tailed female has ever been brought to shore. And to this day, not a single photo or video has ever been taken of a real living and breathing mermaid. Maybe one day, a sailor will finally bring home a fishy friend.

3. Mermaids Are Made Up

The only other alternative is that all the stories and tales over the years are just that – fictional stories and tales. Perhaps they're a leftover from the days when many cultures believed in sea gods and other powerful water spirits. Or maybe the stories were just a way for sailors to entertain themselves during those long, boring sea voyages?

YOU DECIDE

After reading this, do you still believe in mermaids? There are only three choices and it's up to you to pick one . . .

MYSTERY 4

The Bermuda Triangle

THE MISSION . . .

. . . to find out about the mysterious disappearances of ships and planes in the Atlantic Ocean.

BURNING QUESTIONS

- Why have so many people disappeared in this particular area?
- What other weird stuff happens here?

MISSION DETAILS

The 'Bermuda Triangle'. What could it be?

An exotic three-sided shape?

A new kind of musical instrument?

The real Bermuda Triangle is much scarier than either of these. It's a large area of sea. Nothing too nerve-racking about that, you may think. But this stretch of ocean is a weird place; a place where large numbers of planes and boats seem to vanish into thin air. And nobody knows why . . .

Some think strange and mysterious forces are at work – aliens, time warps, even death rays emanating from Atlantis have all been suggested. Others put the disappearances down to more rational reasons like bad weather, mechanical failure or poor piloting.

Whatever's going on, weird happenings go back to the time of Christopher Columbus, who sailed across the Atlantic from Spain in 1492. He reported seeing strange dancing lights on the horizon and a ball of fire falling into the sea. He also said that the ship's compasses wouldn't work properly – a phenomenon which has been widely reported by captains and pilots ever since.

A painting of the Santa Maria – which Christopher Columbus captained in 1492.

Stories of unexplained disappearances in the Bermuda Triangle started to circulate widely in the 1950s and '60s. Since then, it has become one of the most talked-about mysteries in the world. There's even a song about it! (If you're a fan of good music, don't bother downloading it.)

Time to find out more about the so-called 'Devil's Triangle' . . .

THE LOCATION

You won't find the Bermuda Triangle on any map. The Triangle in question is an imaginary one that is pinpointed on an area of sea in the Atlantic Ocean. There are three 'points' to the Triangle: the island of Bermuda, the island of Puerto Rico and the city of Miami in Florida, USA.

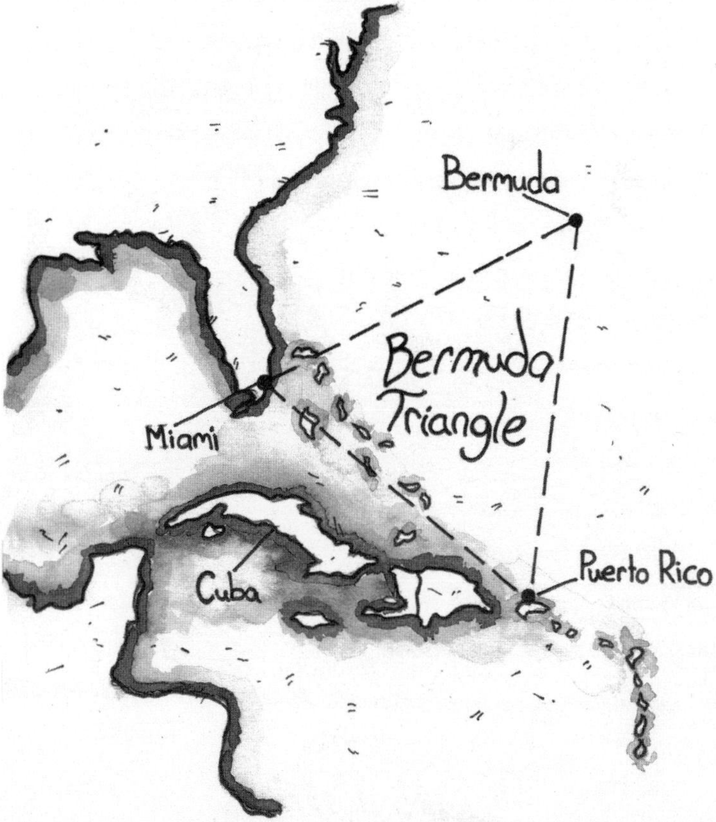

THE EVIDENCE

Though it's hard to put an actual number on the craft that have run into trouble in the Bermuda Triangle, some reports say that as many as 100 ships and planes have vanished in the last 25 years.

Very often, no distress or SOS signal is sent out before the disappearance. The plane or ship just goes right off the radar.

Of all these, Flight 19 is the most well-known and -documented disappearance.

The Mystery of Flight 19

On 5 December 1945 five Avenger torpedo bombers took off from Fort Lauderdale, Florida, on a standard training mission. There were fourteen men on board the five planes. After two hours of flying, a series of panic-stricken radio messages started to come through to HQ.

According to the chief pilot, Lieutenant Taylor, the in-flight compasses had stopped working and he wasn't sure of his location. Remember, this was long before the time of GPS, and pilots relied heavily on compasses for directions.

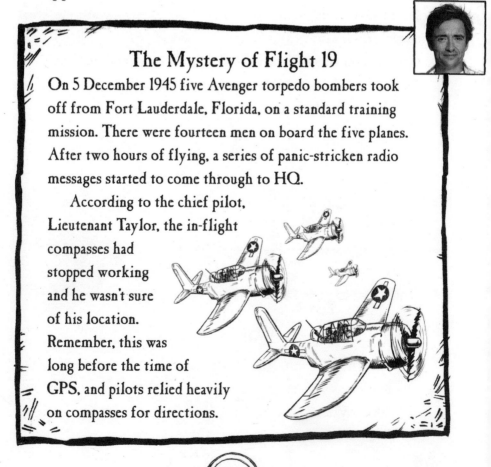

Part of the conversation between the pilots and crew and the military base went like this:

'We can't find west. Everything is wrong. We can't be sure of any direction. Everything looks strange, even the ocean.'

After some confusion, the last message was heard:

'It looks like we are entering white water . . . we're completely lost.'

Soon afterwards, contact was lost. A rescue plane was quickly sent out to find the bombers. Unbelievably, it exploded in mid-air and was also never seen again. (Let's not blame this on the Bermuda Triangle, though – the plane was apparently faulty.)

The bombers of Flight 19 were never heard from either. No trace of the five aircraft has ever been found.

There was a full investigation, but in the Navy's final report, the disappearance was put down to 'causes or reasons unknown'. Clearly, they didn't have a clue what had happened.

What could have happened to five planes to make them vanish completely?

Equally puzzling are these well-known disappearances:

- A huge ship called the USS *Cyclops* went missing in March 1918 after leaving Barbados. She was heavily loaded with cargo and had a crew of more than 300. When she failed to arrive at her destination

(Baltimore in the United States), a huge search was conducted but not a thing was found. As this was towards the end of the First World War, people thought that the *Cyclops* could have been torpedoed by a German submarine. However, no SOS signal was ever sent, and no debris or wreckage was found. Spooky . . .

- In 1963 the *Marine Sulphur Queen*, a large carrier ship with a huge cargo of – take a guess . . . sulphur! – disappeared near the southern coast of Florida. Some items were eventually found from the missing ship – these included a few life jackets (some were ripped; by sharks, it was thought), a piece of oar, a fog horn and a piece of broken board with part of the ship's name on it. To this day, no one knows if the ship's disappearance was down to leaking sulphur causing an explosion – or something more sinister

- In January 1948 a British South American Airways plane called *Star Tiger* – containing 25 passengers and six crew – disappeared during a flight. No bodies, debris or wreckage were ever found and no emergency message was sent. The investigation said ' . . . no more baffling problem has ever been presented'. Yep, definitely baffling

- Spookily, in the same month of the following year, January 1949, the *Star Tiger*'s sister plane, the *Star Ariel*, also vanished, somewhere between Bermuda and Jamaica. Again, there were no emergency messages or calls for help – it just seemed to disappear in mid-air. Weird . . .

- A Douglas DC-3 aircraft containing 32 people went missing in December 1948. It took off from Puerto Rico, headed for Florida – right into prime Bermuda Triangle territory. The pilot sent a routine message when he was about 20 minutes away from landing. After that the plane was never heard of again. No one in the area heard or saw an accident and, again, searches found no wreckage in the water. This is beginning to sound very familiar!

- In the spring of 1974 a large luxury yacht called *Saba Bank* sailed from Nassau in the Bahamas on a test navigation. She and her crew never arrived at their destination

- In October 1991 a Grunman Cougar jet heading to Tallahassee vanished and has never been found. The pilot made a request to increase his altitude – nothing unusual in that – and soon afterwards the plane disappeared from the radar. Guess what? No debris was found

- The *Genesis* cargo ship disappeared on its way from Trinidad to St Vincent in April 1999. Before she vanished, a radio message was sent out, saying there was a problem with one of the pumps. Despite extensive searches, the ship and crew were never seen again.

There are many similar stories. However, before you make the mistake of thinking that the *Mary Celeste* could also have been a victim of the Bermuda Triangle, let me put you straight. The *Mary Celeste* was not sailing anywhere near the Triangle – she was many hundreds of miles away.

Back to the main story. Just what on earth is going on in the Bermuda Triangle?

More Strange Stuff . . .

Not only do things seem to vanish into thin air, there are other kinds of freaky phenomena occurring. All these weird things have been reported by people travelling through the area:

- Disturbances and turbulence happening mid-flight
- Unusual-looking fog and cloud – sometimes yellowish in colour
- Compass and instrument failure or machinery behaving strangely
- Being unable to see the horizon properly
- A sense of weightlessness, or other strange physical feelings

A Near Miss

In 1966 a tug called *Good News* was heading towards Florida from Puerto Rico. Weather conditions were good and everything seemed normal until the crew noticed that the compass was spinning around crazily – in their words, 'going bananas'. Nobody could understand why. Then the captain, Don Henry, noticed something really odd. He couldn't see the horizon (the line between the sea and the sky). It seemed as if the ocean and the sky had blended together and were the same colour.

If that wasn't weird enough, when he checked a cargo barge (which was attached to the ship) he couldn't see it – the barge was completely immersed in a strange cloud of fog! At the same time, the ship felt as if she was being pulled backwards by a very strong force. The shaken captain quickly ordered the engine on full power and the boat sailed on. Five minutes later, the fog cleared and the compass began behaving normally again. No one on board could explain what had happened. To this day, the captain and crew think they almost became victims of the notorious Bermuda Triangle. A close shave . . .

Lost in Time?

December 1970. Bruce Gernon and his father were mid-flight in their small plane, headed for Miami. They flew into some unusually dark clouds, which seemed to move and change shape around them. The clouds quickly formed a huge tunnel! Meanwhile, all their electronic equipment stopped working and the pair began to experience an odd feeling of weightlessness. When Gernon glanced behind the plane, he was stunned to see that the tunnel walls were collapsing in on them! He flew out of there as fast as he could . . .

The plane eventually came out the other side of the cloudy 'tunnel' into a blue sky with the familiar sight of Miami beach below them. After landing, Gernon realized something very strange. It had taken them just 47 minutes to make what was normally a 75-minute flight. Where did the missing 28 minutes go?

To this day, Gernon is convinced that his plane travelled through time, flying through some kind of time warp or time slip. He has even written a book about his experience.

The 'Dragon's Triangle'

In the Pacific Ocean, not far from the coast of Japan, is another strange area of sea where ships, boats and planes are said to disappear. Like the Bermuda Triangle, this region doesn't appear on any maps – but it does have a scary reputation. So much so that the Japanese have named it *Ma-no Umi* or the 'Sea of the Devil'! It is also known as the Dragon's Triangle.

In 1989 a writer called Charles Berlitz (famous for his books about the world's mysteries) said that five Japanese military vessels, and a total of 700 people, had disappeared here during the 1950s. He also said that the Japanese government had declared the whole area a danger zone after 100 scientists on a research boat had vanished in the Triangle. Others have scoffed, putting the disappearances down to the high level of volcanic activity and earthquakes in the area.

Interestingly, both the Bermuda and the Dragon's Triangle are said to be among the world's 'Vile Vortices'.

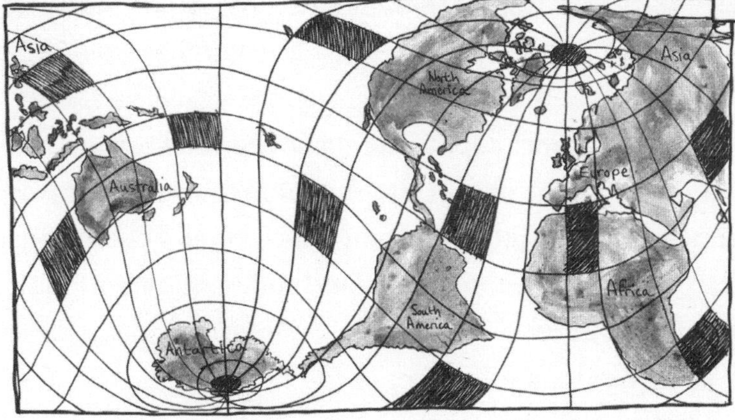

Electromagnetic fields

These are twelve points on the Earth's surface where mysterious disappearances are said take place. If these are marked on a map, you can see that they are spread out equally in twelve parts across the Tropic of Cancer, the Tropic of Capricorn, and the North and South Poles. Some people think the vortices are the sites of ancient energy lines or unusual electromagnetic fields.

Sounds convincing. But is it true . . . ?

WHAT HAPPENED?

Things just don't disappear, do they? OK, my socks frequently do, but I'm fairly sure that there isn't some kind of invisible force over my house, sucking them up. Well, actually, you never know . . . perhaps there's a 'Bermuda Sock Triangle', a place where all the odd socks of the world end up?

OK – back to the real Triangle. What are the logical explanations?

One possibility for Flight 19 – and perhaps other missing planes – is that the planes simply got lost and were forced to ditch in rough seas after running out of fuel. Poor navigation by the pilots could be to blame, and their equipment may also have been faulty.

In the case of Flight 19, Lieutenant Taylor admitted that he was completely lost. From the garbled conversation he had with HQ, we know that he saw an island below the plane. He assumed that the planes were flying over a group of islands called the Florida Keys, so he decided to head north to the Florida peninsula, where the planes could land.

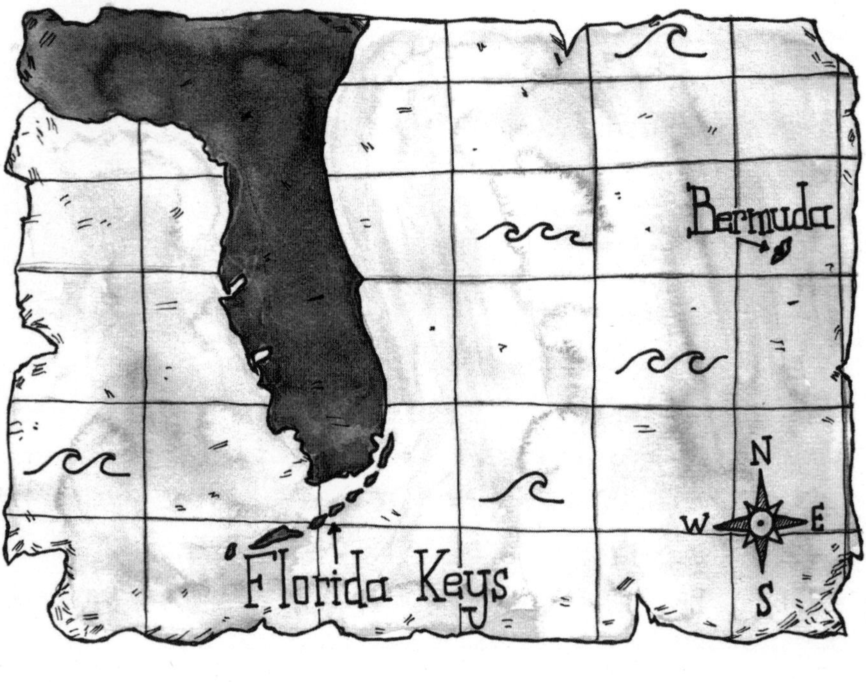

However, many people think that he was mistaken and his aircraft were actually *north* of Bermuda. If so, his decision meant they would have flown *further out* into the Atlantic Ocean. Eventually, the planes would have run out of fuel. The bombers were old-fashioned heavy military craft. If they ditched into the sea, they would probably have sunk very quickly.

Could this explanation account for all the missing planes on record? And what about all those missing ships and boats?

MY MISSION

Venturing into the Bermuda Triangle zone is a pretty nerve-racking experience. Even though thousands of people fly or sail through the 'danger zone' every year with no problems (as I keep reminding myself), I'd rather not take any chances.

So, in order to keep my name off the 'vanished without trace' list, I've got a strategy. Rather than zooming across the Triangle in a small plane or boat, I've decided to super-size all my modes of transport – in the hope that, the larger the craft, the less chance there'll be of it disappearing. So I'll be flying through the Triangle on one of the largest passenger planes in the world – a massive Airbus A380, which seats more than 500 passengers.

I've got a window seat, and my nose will be pressed against the window looking out for weird fog and any other strange goings on. I'm headed for Miami, Florida, a buzzing city and holiday destination. On the way back, I'm taking to the water and boarding a huge cruise ship – another massive craft that accommodates around 3,000 passengers. Try making that vanish into thin air, Bermuda Triangle!

EXTRA KIT

I'll be taking along:

FLUORESCENT YELLOW LIFE JACKET – so if anything happens I will hopefully be spotted by rescuers

WHISTLE – to attract attention in the above scenario

VOICE RECORDER – I'll be recording my thoughts along the way, like a captain's log. If anything goes wrong, maybe they'll find the recorder and work out what happened

EXTRA COMPASSES – so if anyone's compasses start playing up, I will have several back-ups!

MISSION COMPLETED

Phew – back on dry land at last. I survived the Bermuda Triangle! To be honest, apart from being constantly on the look out for alien spaceships, strange fog and compass mishaps, the cruise was very relaxing. There was a great show every night, as much food as you could eat and . . . Sorry, I'm going off the point! But I'm relieved to say that I didn't see any sign of a spaceship, or fog and all my compasses worked fine. The outward flight was uneventful too. Seems like my 'make it big' strategy worked . . .

It was eerie at times, though, peering over the edge of the ship as we sailed through the ocean, and thinking about those watery depths and what they might hold. Are there hundreds of wrecks of ships, boats and planes down there?

And now, after reading piles of books and talking to lots of people on my journey, I've collected all the theories that might explain the Terrible Triangle:

1. Electronic Fog

Some of those who have experienced 'Triangle Terror' describe a strange greyish or yellow mist surrounding their plane or ship. It isn't like normal fog. This cloudy mist seems to have a spooky life of its own. It is said to move along with the craft and to make electronic equipment malfunction. Could this fog be the reason why so many pilots and captains lose their way – and does it eventually swallow them up?

In the 1970s a man called John Hutchison tried to prove that the spooky fog was real. He did various experiments to show that a force called electromagnetism was causing the fog. His theory (and it is just a theory) was that if electromagnetic fields of different wavelengths bounced off each other, it could cause objects to behave strangely – even ships.

Hutchison claimed that he had recreated the mysterious 'electronic fog' cloud at his home – and that it had produced some incredible results. Apparently, the fog caused everyday objects to literally defy gravity. A copper pipe was said to rise up and disappear, a bar of steel levitated (rose on its own), and samples of tough aluminium fell apart like jelly.

I'd pay good money to see a show like this, but unfortunately, very few people have been able to witness this amazing phenomenon. And no other scientists have been able to produce the so-called 'Hutchison Effect'. In fact, the existence of the fog has never been proved in a proper lab test. Some in the scientific world have even accused Hutchison of faking his experiments using wire and magnets.

Others think that powerful electromagnetic storms could be the cause of the frightening fog. Bruce Gernon (see page 71), a 'fog survivor', came up with the idea that storms from within the Earth could penetrate the atmosphere in the form of electronic mist. According to Gernon, there is scientific evidence that the magnetism (a force which occurs all over the Earth) is weaker in the Triangle area than anywhere else. He thinks there is a connection.

If the fog *does* exist, does it cause people to lose their way, ships to sink and planes to crash into the sea? Or does it hold some other weird secret? The electronic fog theory lingers on . . .

2. Aliens!

Another suggestion is that aliens have discovered a passageway to Earth via the Bermuda Triangle and are using it as a kind of 'collecting station' for human beings. Are creatures from another planet capturing our planes and ships? And taking these interesting, possibly valuable, objects back to their planetary homes?

The alien theory would tie in with the fact that this area does seem to have a large number of UFO sightings (Unidentified Flying Object – another way of saying 'flying saucer' or 'alien spacecraft'. You can read more about these later, in the Alien Encounters section of the book).

In 1971 members of the crew of USS *John F Kennedy*, an American aircraft carrier, witnessed something very strange: a glowing circular object hovering above their ship . . . It was large, about 60–90 metres in diameter, and yellowy-orange in colour. Whatever the thing was, it hovered silently for about 20 minutes, then *ping!* Disappeared. The strange thing was that during the entire time the UFO was above the ship, the ship's compasses stopped working . . . Sound familiar?

This is just one of many strange sightings in the area. No one knows if aliens are responsible or if the UFO sightings are caused by natural phenomena, such as ball lightning.

Did this spaceship enter through a Star Gate?

Some alien believers think that the Bermuda Triangle is a 'Star Gate' – a doorway used by aliens for intergalactic space travel. This leads us on to another popular theory. That the Bermuda Triangle is what's called a portal to another world . . .

3. A Time Portal

There has been plenty of speculation that the Bermuda Triangle area contains some kind of unknown opening or passageway. Another idea is that the opening is a 'rip in time', where planes and ships are transported to another dimension, time or place. Or they are caught up, trapped in a kind of weird no-man's-land between different worlds. If you're thinking this all sounds like an episode of *Doctor Who*, you'd be right – it does!

People who believe this idea think it explains some of the strange variations in time reported by Triangle survivors, such as Bruce Gernon's lost 28 minutes. He could have experienced what's called a 'time slip' – when people are said to have moved backwards or forward in time.

A more scientific explanation is that these openings in time are things called wormholes. We're not talking about the little pink creatures that burrow through the soil, by the way, but something much, much bigger.

In physics, a wormhole is a passage in space-time – like a short cut between two regions of space or time. It's a big, big idea (and entirely theoretical at the moment), but world-famous brainy scientist Professor Stephen Hawking takes the idea of wormholes very seriously indeed. He has spent years working on the physics behind wormholes (I've got a GCSE in Science, but this is a just a tad more advanced).

Put very simply, if wormholes did exist – and if humans could work out a way of travelling through them without being flattened like a pancake – they could potentially act as time machines. That could be incredibly useful. Especially for those times when you've done or said something silly – imagine being able to go back in time and change it!

Wormholes, time slips, portals – whatever you call them . . . is time travel the explanation for the Bermuda Triangle?

4. Wild Weather

The disappearances could be down to something very simple, yet completely beyond our control – that favourite subject of the British, the weather. The Caribbean-Atlantic region is well-known for violent storms, hurricanes and tornadoes. They can be very sudden and very unpredictable – so sailors and pilots can easily be taken by surprise. Any of the following weather-related events could sink a ship, or even crash a plane . . .

Destructive hurricanes

Massive swirling storms that gather up heat and energy from warm sea water, hurricanes usually begin in the Atlantic (near the Equator) and move north into the Gulf of Mexico and the Caribbean. A hurricane can spell disaster for both pilots and mariners as it is probably the most destructive weather event that exists. Boats can be capsized and planes very badly damaged

© STOCKTRECK/GETTY IMAGES

A satellite photo of a hurricane from above.

Rogue Waves

Satellite research has shown that a single wave can reach as high as 35 metres in open ocean areas. A wave like this could damage or destroy even the largest ship

Waterspout

A tornado (a whirling mass of air) at sea can create a waterspout, a kind of water twister. It travels over the water like a long funnel, sucking up water from the sea. The spouts vary in size and speed, but they can be huge, spiralling hundreds of metres into the sky and moving at up to 80 miles an hour. The spout usually disappears on reaching land – but can cause huge damage at sea

© IMAGEBROKER.NET/SUPERSTOCK

A whirling waterspout in action . . .

Lightning

During a storm a lightning bolt can contain up to a shocking one billion volts of electricity! No wonder it can damage planes or ships or set fire to their fuel supplies. The electric current can also produce a magnetic field, which causes problems with communications and compasses. A phenomenon called ball lightning is a circular mass of light which can move around on its own. Could this explain some of the UFO sightings reported in the Triangle – and the 'dancing lights' that Columbus once saw?

Add into the mix the effects of fast-moving currents, like the Gulf Stream, which can whisk debris away very quickly, some would say, is it any wonder that planes and ships disappear leaving no trace behind them?

5. A Flatulent Ocean?

Did you know that the ocean suffers from gas? Methane gas is created by ancient forests and organisms that have slowly rotted away over hundreds of years. It is trapped under the ocean floor and occasionally, such as during an underwater earthquake, the methane gas erupts violently into the water. (A bit like a fart in a bath, but a lot, lot bigger!)

These large bubbles of gas can hit ships and cause huge problems. They can also cause a temporary dip in the water, which can sink a ship.

And it gets worse. As gas is lighter than air, it continues moving upwards and could affect the lift of aircraft flying above the sea. The gas mixes with the atmosphere and changes the gas-to-oxygen ratio going into the plane's engine. It could be enough to make the engine stall and crash the plane.

How often does this kind of gas eruption take place? No one knows for sure.

6. Death by Atlantis?

Some people believe that the lost city of Atlantis is located deep underwater in the Bermuda Triangle – and that it is having a strange effect on the surrounding area. (See pages 7–27 for more on Atlantis and other possible locations.)

The writer Charles Berlitz wrote a famous book about the Bermuda Triangle in 1974. He thought Atlantis could be near an island called Bimini, to the west of the Triangle. In 1968 a 'road' of stones was found on the sea floor close to Bimini. Some scientists, however, think it is a completely natural stone formation, rather than a man-made Atlantean relic.

Atlantis, if it existed, was supposed to be an incredibly advanced civilization – and some think that the Atlanteans may have created a weapon that ultimately destroyed their own city. Could this unknown weapon, if it ever existed, still have the power to destroy modern-day planes and ships? Is there some kind of technology under the sea whooshing out harmful death rays or laser beams?

Another Atlantis theory is that the ancient people harnessed the power of energy crystals. Some claim that these crystals still rest on the seabed, sending out waves of energy that destroy ships and planes or, at the very least, confuse compasses and other instruments. Is there any evidence for this? As far as we know, no one has yet found any ancient weapons of destruction.

7. Accidents Will Happen

One very simple explanation is that the Bermuda Triangle area is incredibly busy – in fact, one of the busiest shipping lanes in the world goes right through it. It is also a major flight route for aircraft heading towards Florida, the Caribbean and South America. Perhaps there is absolutely nothing weird going on at all – simply that there are bound to be more accidents where there is more traffic?

It's also interesting that many of the big Triangle disappearances happened some years ago. In the 1950s and '60s planes and ships were not as reliable as they are today, and their fuel tanks weren't as large. Could this account for the higher number of disappearances in the past?

It's estimated that the Bermuda Triangle took more than 1,000 lives in the twentieth century. That averages about ten people per year. Some would say that is pretty normal for an area of such busy traffic.

Perhaps it's down to a combination of factors. Could faulty or old-fashioned planes, bad weather and poor navigation together form the big answer to the mystery of the Triangle?

8. The Environment

The environmental conditions in and around the Bermuda Triangle are unusual, to say the least:

- A huge current called the Gulf Stream moves through the Triangle. The Gulf Stream is an incredibly strong, swift current that moves warm water from the Gulf of Mexico north into the Atlantic. The movement can throw boats hundreds of miles off course, and sailors need to be aware of it when they are navigating. The Gulf Stream can also quickly carry wreckage away from a disaster, making it impossible to find

- There is also a strange area of water within the Triangle called the Sargasso Sea. It is the only sea in the world without a shoreline, bounded by sea currents on all sides (including the Gulf Stream). Christopher Columbus was one of the first to note the area, which is covered by a kind of thick mat of floating seaweed (called *sargussum*). The seaweed can cause problems for boats, as well as the fact that the Sargasso Sea is incredibly flat and still. Many sailing ships entering the

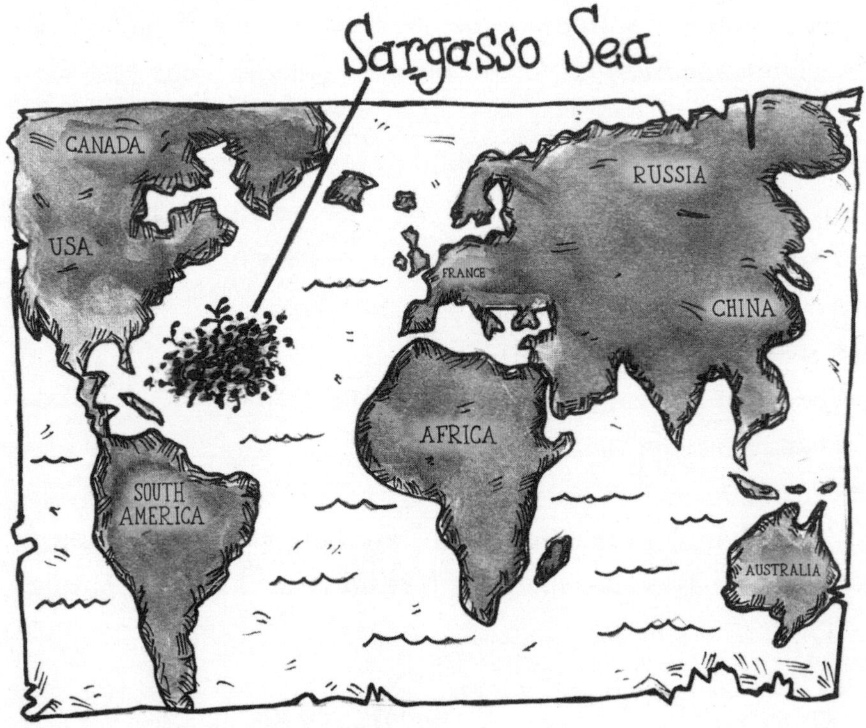

area become completely motionless. In fact, Columbus got stuck here for so long that he thought he might have a mutiny on his hands!

- The sea floor under the Bermuda Triangle contains some of the deepest underwater trenches in the world. One is called the Puerto Rico Trench and dips at one point to a whopping 8,229 metres below sea level. Anything heavy sinking into the sea would fall a long way down, never to be seen again

- Did you know that there are *two* North Poles? (Yep, news to me too!) Apparently, the needle of a compass will always be drawn to the *magnetic* North Pole, which isn't fixed, and moves over time. The *geographic* North Pole, however, is several hundred kilometres away from the Magnetic Pole and is always in the same place. Interestingly, the Bermuda Triangle area is one of only two places on Earth where true north and magnetic north line up together on a compass. (The other place is the Dragon's Triangle, off the coast of Japan – see page 72.) Some people think that this phenomenon is what's causing compass confusion and making instruments malfunction. Others disagree. Could there possibly be a connection?

- Another reason for compass confusion could be the effect of magnetism in this area. In some areas of the world there are super-strong magnetic fields, created by magnetic rocks, electrical storms or magma flowing near the surface of the Earth. The magnetic fields can have a chaotic effect on compasses and other equipment

Does this environment have anything to do with the weird goings-on? Many people believe so.

YOU DECIDE

Which do you think is the best solution to the Bermuda Triangle? Make your choice, then answer my next big question – having read all these stories, would *you* be brave enough to travel through the Bermuda Triangle?

Don't forget to record your thoughts at the back of this book!

MYSTERY 5

The Philadelphia Experiment

THE MISSION . . .

. . . to find out if the ship, the USS *Eldridge*, was actually made invisible.

BURNING QUESTIONS

- Can objects be made to vanish into thin air – and then return?
- Was the experiment a cover-up?

MISSION DETAILS

There are two things immediately obvious about the Philadelphia Experiment. One, it was an experiment. Two, it took place in Philadelphia. Other than that, details are a little thin on the ground. Some think this is because the whole incident was covered up by the government (who didn't want anyone to know what had happened). Others think it is because it never actually happened. So who is right?

The experiment was supposed to have been performed by the United States Navy, back in 1943. So why are people still talking about it now? Well, what happened made everyone who heard the story *very* excited. It still does. Because unlike the cases of the *Mary Celeste* and the Bermuda Triangle – where things that disappear are put down to mysterious forces beyond our control – it seems that the Navy actually made a ship disappear. It's more mind-boggling than Harry Potter's cloak!

The idea of being invisible is very appealing. I'm sure we could all think of some useful ways to deploy everyday 'invisible technology'– you could make your annoying sibling or super-strict teacher vanish whenever you fancied, for example!

The US Navy, however, denies everything.

Let's find out more . . .

THE LOCATION

The place where the experiment was supposed to have taken place was a naval shipyard in Philadelphia, Pennsylvania, USA.

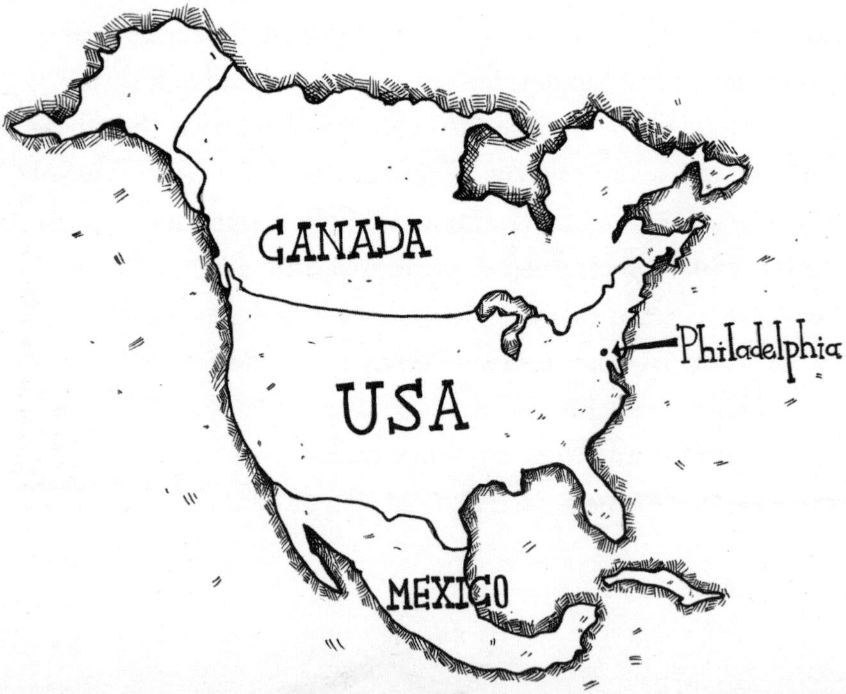

What Happened?

October 1943. It's the time of the Second World War, and the United States government, one of the Allied powers (which include Britain, France, the Soviet Union and China), is looking for new ways to help defeat the enemy.

The USS *Eldridge* is a large destroyer, built earlier in the year to escort soldiers and supplies to important locations around the world. With 1,000 Allied ships torpedoed and sunk in 1942, it's vital to improve defences against enemy submarines and ships.

The US Navy need the best brains in the country. So they employ the brilliant physicist Albert Einstein to work on developing ammunition and explosives.

But some think Einstein was working on a different project for the Navy . . . a top-secret one. And, let's face it, making your whole ship invisible would be the perfect solution for avoiding wartime attacks.

The Incredible Mr Einstein

Do you recognize this man? Underneath that wild hair is one of the finest brains of the twentieth century – it's Albert Einstein.

One of the most famous scientists of all time, Einstein was born in Germany in 1879. At the age of five, his interest in science was sparked when his father showed him a pocket compass. Albert was fascinated by it. Why did the needle always point in the same direction, whichever way the compass was turned? He realized that an unknown force was acting on it. This interest in forces continued throughout his life, as Einstein's most important work is about energy, the speed of light and gravitational forces.

In 1905 – his 'wonderful year' – Einstein rewrote Newton's laws of gravity when he came up with his theory of relativity, probably the most famous scientific equation ever known.

Here it is:

e = mc2 (in case you didn't know, that's energy equals mass multiplied by the speed of light squared!)

Apparently, it shows that matter and energy are different forms of the same thing. Matter can be turned into energy, and energy into matter. When his theory was proved correct in 1919, Einstein became incredibly famous, and in 1921 he received the acclaimed Nobel Prize for Physics.

In 1933, when Adolf Hitler became Chancellor of Germany, Albert Einstein left the country and emigrated to the United States. He never returned to Germany and in 1940 became a US citizen.

Einstein famously said: 'Imagination is more important than knowledge.'

There's no doubt that Einstein *did* work for the US Navy during the war – but was he responsible for the Philadelphia Experiment? This is what is supposed to have happened:

- Using large generators, naval scientists unleashed a powerful electromagnetic force around the USS *Eldridge*, creating a kind of 'force field'. The ship disappeared!
- The invisible vessel was then 'teleported', in true *Star Trek* style, from the naval yard in Philadelphia to a place called Norfolk, in Virginia. Then it reappeared back again in Philadelphia – all in all, 'travelling' a distance of about 350 km!
- Some say the men aboard the ship were also made invisible, with disastrous consequences. Some were never seen again, while others suffered terrible side effects – such as constantly disappearing and reappearing! Later, others went completely mad. (No wonder!)

THE EVIDENCE

So how do we know about the experiment if it was all so top secret? It wasn't until twelve years after the incident that the Navy were contacted by a man called Carlos Allende. He said he had witnessed the whole thing while he was a deckhand on board a nearby ship. Allende claimed that he had seen the USS *Eldridge* surrounded by a greenish fog (sound a bit 'Bermuda Triangle'?). He had felt a terrific jolt of energy, then the ship disappeared.

A man called Morris Jessup, who had written a well-known book about UFOs, then got involved. Allende had written notes all over a copy of Jessup's book and had sent it to the Navy. The UFO book described Jessup's idea that there was a connection between electromagnetism and flying saucers. Allende read this and thought that electromagnetism could have been used in the Philadelphia Experiment too.

People who believe Allende's extraordinary story think that the Navy, shocked by the results of their weird experiment, stopped all research immediately. They then produced a cover story for the missing men on board, saying they were lost at sea.

What do you think? Do you believe Allende's story? Let's bear in mind that Allende also said that Albert Einstein himself had discussed subjects such as invisibility and faster-than-the speed-of-light travel with him. Likely – or not?

MY MISSION

A particularly tough one on this occasion. Why? Because there really isn't anything for me to investigate. Here's the reality:

- After years of naval service the USS *Eldridge* was eventually sold as scrap in 1999. So – no ship
- The naval shipyard in Philadelphia was closed in 1995. It was renamed the Philadelphia Naval Business Center, and is now home to various private companies and shops. So – no shipyard

- As the Navy flatly denies that anything happened, we can't talk to them about it
- Carlos Allende, the only witness, died in 1994. He did, however, give a last interview in the 1980s about his involvement in the experiment. He said some interesting things. He described how he had leaned over some railings and actually reached into the force field surrounding the ship. It apparently looked like an ultraviolet glowing haze and felt very strange – 'It kicked,' said Allende. Einstein then saw Allende touching the force field and came over to ask him how it had felt. Einstein then spent the next two weeks with Allende teaching him about the 'physics of invisibility'. Allende remained convinced the USS *Eldridge* was radiated with an energy beam that day in an experiment performed by Einstein. Could any of this be true?

MISSION COMPLETED

When it comes down to it, there are only two positions to take on the Philadelphia Experiment. You either believe it, or you don't. Let's look at the arguments for and against:

1. It Happened – But How?

Now for the tricky science bit. To be convinced of this story, you need to know how it could have happened. It's all down to Einstein's work. But – as I'm no Einstein myself – I'll try to keep it as simple as possible.

Einstein spent many years of his life working on an idea

called a single unified theory – sometimes called the *Theory of Everything*. It seems that he was basically trying to unify the laws of physics, bringing gravity, electromagnetism, and subatomic phenomena together into one set of laws. If you think that sounds difficult, you'd be right! Even Einstein had to admit defeat in the end, and no other scientist since has managed to finish his work.

As we're not brainiac physicists, the most important thing we need to know is that if Albert *had* cracked this theory, the results would have been astounding. It could have made incredible things possible, like travelling through time and finding new sources of energy.

So was the explosives job just a cover for Einstein? Was he trying to test out his unified field theory? Some think that if Einstein had managed to make a connection between gravity and electromagnetism, he might have been able to literally bend light. If light had been bent *around* the ship and not across her, could she possibly have been made invisible?

Others think that Einstein used his unified field theory to make the ship 'teleport'– when all the particles that make up an object are transported to another place. Is this how the ship managed to appear in a completely different location? The whole idea of 'beaming' things elsewhere sounds a bit *Star Trek* – but could science fiction actually be science *fact*?

2. It Never Happened

Many others believe that the Philadelphia Experiment is just a massive hoax – a made-up story. They say it simply never happened and that Carlos Allende didn't see anything that day. They argue that, if it is true, why hasn't the experiment been repeated in the years since? If the ship experiment had worked all those years ago, by now we'd all be making things invisible! There are some other good points on their side too:

- There is no evidence that Einstein was involved in research on invisibility or teleportation
- The Office of Naval Research has stated that the use of force fields to make a ship and her crew invisible does 'not conform to known physical laws'
- There is only one witness that we know of (Allende) – so just one person's word
- Despite all the work done by physicists since Einstein's time, there is still no evidence that it is possible to unify gravity with the other forces – or make a ship disappear

YOU DECIDE

The Philadelphia Experiment is one of those 'hush-hush' mysteries that it's exciting to believe in. But was it all a hoax? Turn to the back and make your choice!

WANT TO KNOW MORE?

If you want to find out more about some of these intriguing mysteries, try these books and websites:

Herbie Brennan's Forbidden Truths: Atlantis and other Lost Civilizations – Herbie Brennan (Faber & Faber)

Can Science Solve? The Mystery of the Bermuda Triangle – Chris Oxlade (Heinemann)

Unsolved! Mysteries of the Bermuda Triangle – Kathryn Walker (Crabtree)

The Mary Celeste: An Unsolved Mystery from History – Jane Yolen and Heidi Elisabet Yolen Stemple (Aladdin)

Unexplained: An Encyclopedia of Curious Phenomena, Strange Superstitions, and Ancient Mysteries – Judy Allen (Kingfisher)

www.nationalgeographic.com – Great for all kinds of information about the world, you can search the site for their views on the mysteries in this book. Also there are some interesting National Geographic TV investigations e.g. *Finding Atlantis* at http://channel.nationalgeographic.com

www.unmuseum.org – An investigation into all things unexplained and paranormal

www.sciencekids.co.nz – Great for science facts, you can also search the site for facts relating to the mysteries in this book

CREEPY CREATURES

MYSTERY 1

The Loch Ness Monster

THE MISSION . . .

This is a big one, so hold onto your hunting hats . . .
. . . to find out what – if anything – lives in the murky depths of Loch Ness.

BURNING QUESTIONS

- Is there a monster in Loch Ness?
- If so, why has it never been found?
- Do other lake monsters exist?

MISSION DETAILS

Loch Ness is the most well-known loch in Scotland. A loch, by the way, is the Scottish name for a lake. And there are a lot of lochs in Scotland.

Every year tourists flock to Loch Ness in their thousands, and it is famous all over the world. Is this because the loch is stunningly beautiful? Well – it is – but there's an even bigger reason. People visit the loch to see if they can catch a glimpse of the massive creature that is supposed to live in its waters – the Loch Ness monster. Otherwise known as 'Nessie'. (Which is how I'll be referring to the Loch Ness monster from now on, as it's much easier to type).

Hundreds of people swear that they have seen Nessie. Some have taken photographs and even made films – though most are pretty blurry, to be honest. And it's not just holidaymakers hoping to solve the mystery: scientists have used special scanning equipment to search the dark waters. But still no one has found the monster.

And it seems that Nessie is not the only creature of its kind. There are many more strange and wonderful creatures thought to be living in deep lakes all around the world.

Could these creatures have survived for years without ever being discovered? Read on . . .

THE LOCATION

You can find Loch Ness in the mountainous north of Scotland, in a region called the Highlands.

If you ever visit, you'll see that Loch Ness is no ordinary lake – it's huge!

- 37 kilometres long and extremely deep, a whopping 230 metres at its deepest point. Compare that to the height of the London Eye, a mere 135 metres tall . . .
- The loch is the largest body of fresh water in the whole of Britain – there is more water here than in all the lakes of England and Wales combined

© ANDRE GONCALVES / AGE FOTOSTOCK / SUPERSTOCK

The incredibly large Loch Ness

No wonder it's been so hard to find the Loch Ness monster . . . This is NOT like looking for the soap in the bath.

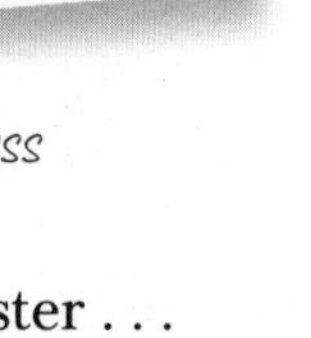

Hidden Monsters

Did you know that Nessie is the most famous cryptid in the world?

(It's OK – I didn't either!) Let me explain.

The word 'cryptid' means 'hidden creature'. (It comes from the Greek word kryptos which means – no points for guessing – 'hidden'!)

People who study the Loch Ness monster – as well as other creatures whose existence hasn't been proved – are called 'cryptozoologists'. A pretty long name for a person who's interested in things that might – or might not – exist. (A bit like you and me, really. Hey, we're cryptozoologists! Do we get a badge?)

All the creatures you'll read about in this book would be fascinating to a cryptozoologist. But you can't do a GCSE in this subject, as it is not seen as a 'proper' science. Maybe someone needs to prove Nessie exists for cryptozoology to be taken seriously? Then we'd get a badge...

THE EVIDENCE

There's no shortage of tales about a mysterious creature living in Loch Ness. Some of these go back many, many years.

Strange Stories

Locals once told of the kelpie – a magical and malevolent water monster, also known as a water horse. On land it could apparently turn itself into a real horse. But if someone rode it, it would gallop straight into the loch and the unsuspecting rider would meet a watery death. Was this story a way of warning local children to stay away from the dangerously deep water – or was there any truth behind it?

Spooky Sightings

The earliest sighting of the Loch Ness monster happened way back in the sixth century. The story goes that a monk called St Columba came across a group of men burying a mauled and mangled body. They told the monk that the man had been attacked and killed by a horrible creature in the loch. St Columba ordered one of his (terrified) followers to swim across the loch and fetch the dead man's boat. But the monster was lying in wait for its next victim and it rose to the surface with a terrible roar, its mouth open wide. St Columba raised his hand and made the sign of the cross, exclaiming, 'Stop! Go no further nor touch the man!' The saint was so scary that the monster fled! Maybe he wore a terrifyingly huge hat or something.

St Columba stands up to the Loch Ness Monster. The big bully! (The monster, I mean. And note: no hat. Must've had a REALLY loud voice.)

A Monster Year

Sightings of the monster increased dramatically during one particular year – 1933. A husband and wife, Mr and Mrs McKay, were driving along a new road next to the loch when they noticed a strange disturbance in the dark waters. Going for a closer look, they were amazed (and just a little freaked out) to see a huge creature rolling around in the middle of the loch, creating quite a splash.

Later that year, the creature was spotted again. Another couple driving along by the loch apparently saw 'a most extraordinary form of animal' crossing the road in front of their car. They described the creature as being about 12–15 metres, with a long thin neck like an elephant's trunk. The driver, a Mr Spicer, said, 'I am certain that this creature was of a prehistoric species.' Whatever it was, it soon disappeared, lumbering back into the loch. His comment was interesting though – as some think that Nessie may well be a descendant of a prehistoric creature. More on that later.

Back to 1933 – when in November a man called Hugh Gray also spotted a large object splashing around in the loch. Luckily Mr Gray had his camera with him, so managed to take the first ever photograph of the monster. Some people scoffed at it, saying that whatever the blurry shape was, it didn't prove the monster's existence.

Following these sightings, people began talking about the monster. Visitors came to the loch to look out for the creature and the newspapers soon got wind of the news. Monster mania had begun!

There have been hundreds of sightings of Nessie since then – far too many to list here. Many more photographs have been taken too, but quite a few have been proved to be either fakes or mistakes – objects such as logs or boats.

Photos from the Past

Looking at the photographic 'evidence' of Nessie (and the yeti coming up on page 133), some of the older snaps seem to have been taken by a visually challenged zombie with incredibly shaky hands. They are blurry, out of focus and really not up to today's standards. But if you're thinking you could have taken a better shot, the answer is – no, you probably couldn't.

When it comes to photography, we really have got it easy these days. Digital cameras are so small and simple to use compared to some of the clunky equipment that used to be around (just check out the size of the camera on page 113 to see what I mean!).

In the early twentieth century, things were very different for photographers. Your camera would probably have looked a bit like this:

And worked like this:

No prizes for guessing this was called a 'box camera'.

The Brownie camera was one of the most popular cameras of its time. And it would have been exactly the kind of gadget a keen monster hunter would have used because it was more portable than all the other cameras around.

But even using a Brownie would be tricky for many of us today.

- To take a shot, you held the Brownie at waist-level and looked down into the finder (see the picture above). Because you had to hold the camera for much longer than today's models, the manual advised you to hold your breath when shooting to make sure the camera stayed still!

- You only had a small number of shots too. Vintage cameras needed to be loaded up with film, so you would usually get 12 or 24 shots. Once you'd used up your film, that was it. And if you accidentally took a pic of your hand, you were stuck with it – no deleting
- Producing a simple photo took much, much longer. The film had to be wound onto a reel before it could be taken out of the camera and put in an envelope. Then on to a dark room for developing. Any exposure to light would destroy all your precious shots

So, try to imagine being on a monster hunt and spotting the most exciting find of your life. As Nessie swam by, you'd get yourself in position with the camera at your waist and wind the film on with a small handle, before you could push the shutter and take the photo. All this while holding your breath! Add into the mix a fast-moving object and all the technical problems of shooting on moving water (the sunlight bounces off it and makes your subject very dark), and it's really a wonder people in the past managed to get any decent photos at all.

Modern-day monster hunters can use cameras with really fast shutter speeds to capture objects moving quickly. Vibration Reduction (VR) helps get rid of any 'shake' – and polarizing filters reduce reflections on the surface of the water. We have the technology – now all we need to do is find the monsters . . .

It's a Hoax!
Monster Footprints . . . ?

Following the sightings of 1933, the *Daily Mail* newspaper decided to send a team of professionals to Loch Ness. The team was led by a man called Marmaduke Wetherall, a well-known game hunter whose expert tracking skills had helped him hunt down all kinds of creatures in far-off places, like Africa. But he'd never tried to find anything as big as this before.

Marmaduke dreams of photographing a monster – but with the largest camera in the world and a monkey for an assistant, will he succeed? Wise choice of assistant, though – he works for peanuts.

There was great excitement when Marmaduke actually found the monster's footprints! Plaster casts were taken and sent for scientific assessment. But they turned out NOT to be prints from a mysterious lake monster – they had been made by a stuffed hippopotamus foot, probably the base

of an old-fashioned umbrella stand or lampshade. (Yes, readers – sadly, in those days, people thought nothing of shooting a hippo or an elephant and making its limbs into a household accessory.) Cue red faces all round!

Photographic Evidence . . . ?

Probably the most famous photo of Nessie was taken in 1934 by a surgeon called Robert Kenneth Wilson. He and a friend had stopped for a driving break when, suddenly, a sinister shape broke through the surface of the loch. Wilson ran to get his camera and took this picture, which clearly shows the neck of the monster emerging from the water. The surgeon's photograph became a global sensation! For 60 years it was the proof needed of the monster's existence. But, yet again, things were not as they seemed . . .

© KEYSTONE/GETTY IMAGES

The world-famous 'Surgeon's Photo'. People wondered if it had been 'doctored'!

In 1994 the 93-year-old stepson of Marmaduke Wetherall (yes, the very same Marmaduke who had been fooled by those footprints years ago) admitted that the photograph was a fake. He had made the monster in the surgeon's photograph – by sticking a cut-out wooden neck onto a toy submarine! It was, apparently, in revenge for his stepfather being made a laughing stock all those years ago.

The 'monster' was nothing more than a toy and a piece of wood – would you have been taken in by it?

Incidents like these show us why trying to find the truth about Nessie is so difficult. Quite a few stories and photos over the years have been made up. Why do people pretend to have seen the monster? Sometimes to make money out of selling their story, sometimes to get attention, and sometimes – just because they can!

Nessie – the Movie

The most famous piece of film showing what seems to be a creature in the loch was taken in 1960 by monster hunter, Tim Dinsdale. It shows a mysterious hump-like shape crossing the water at high speed and changing direction several times. In 1962 the film was shown on television and was examined by experts. No one has yet proved that it is a hoax. But some believe that Dinsdale was mistaken and all he filmed was a boat.

Whatever was swimming in the loch that day, Dinsdale's film made everyone get more serious about searching for the monster. Brainy students from Oxford and Cambridge universities did the first proper scientific investigation in the summer of 1960, using boats, cameras and echo-sounding equipment. The data they got back was unclear but showed that there may have been 'something' under the water.

In 1962 the grand-sounding 'Loch Ness Phenomena Investigation Bureau' was launched, an organization determined to get to the bottom of the mystery. One of its members was Sir Peter Scott, the grandson of the famous explorer Captain Scott.

The bureau organized volunteers to watch the loch with cameras but, though sightings were made, nothing definite was found. Later, they went underwater and used mini-submarines, sonar technology, and even old-fashioned baiting to investigate the murky waters. (Not sure what they dangled in the depths to attract the monster – a very big fish, perhaps?)

Something was detected moving up and down, possibly diving to the bottom of the loch. Whatever it was seemed to be about six metres in length.

Fast forward to the early 1970s, when a man called Robert Rines decided to set up another array of equipment (the most sophisticated stuff around at the time, including underwater cameras and sonar scanners) to try and find Nessie. In 1975 four of his photographs were made public and there was huge excitement around the world. The photos showed what appeared to be a long-necked creature swimming underwater – they even showed a flipper! This was probably the most exciting discovery yet made.

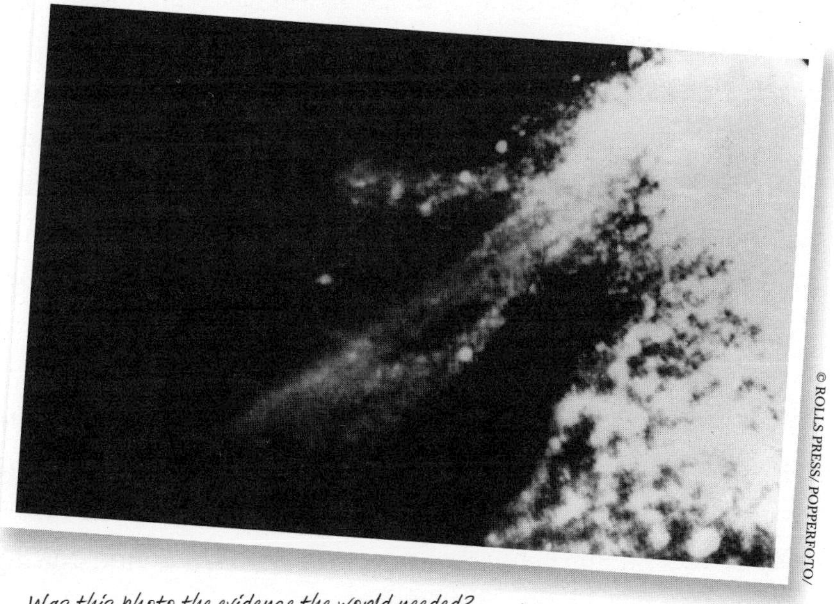

Was this photo the evidence the world needed?

Sir Peter Scott, who was also a skilled artist, painted a picture of two imaginary Nessies coasting along the loch, based on Rines's photographs (see one of them on page 119). Scott was clearly convinced by the photos – but the scientists were less sure. Those who examined them thought they were definitely authentic photos – but that they still did not prove the existence of the monster.

Following the flipper frenzy, several more 'monster missions' were organized. It was clear that many people were convinced enough to spend their time and money trying to find Nessie.

Other expedition findings:

- One search heard strange noises being made by something deep at the bottom of the lake. The noises stopped every time a boat passed overhead – evidence of a living creature?
- In 1987 Operation Deepscan was launched: 24 boats spent a week on the loch using £1million worth of equipment to scan the lake. They thought that they had found something 'larger than a fish' in the waters but could not identify it. Could it have been a monster – or was it perhaps a seal?
- In 2003 the BBC carried out the most extensive search of the loch ever made, using 600 sonar beams and the very latest satellite navigation technology. They found nothing

Does all this mean that there is no monster – or is it just very, very good at hiding from investigators?

Nessie Features

Let's try and get a clearer idea of what the Loch Ness monster could actually look like.

According to eyewitness accounts and photographs, Nessie could have:

- A long snake-like neck
- A longish tail
- Flippers – maybe two, maybe four
- A hump – which could be part of its body, protruding above the surface of the water; some descriptions say the creature has two or more humps

The most popular image of Nessie – the one you'll find on T-shirts and souvenirs – is of a creature with humps. Like this:

Could Nessie have humps *and* flippers? Is the monster like a giant snake or more like a dinosaur? More coming up . . .

Global Lake Monsters . . .

Nessie isn't the only creature thought to be lurking in the deep. Here are just a few other mystery monsters from around the globe . . .

- **The cute and cuddly one . . .**

Is there a monster lurking in the depths of Lake Ikeda, Japan? Like Nessie, the creature has a nickname – 'Issie'. There are other similarities too. No one has yet taken a decent picture of the Japanese monster.

- **The horrible humpy one . . .**

Lake Okanagan in British Columbia is said to be the home of an aggressive monster called Ogopogo. It is described as having a snake-like body and humps – sound familiar? The native Okanakane Indians definitely believe in the monster – they protect themselves by throwing meat for Ogopogo into the lake whenever they cross it!

- **The weird whiskery one . . .**

A weird-looking 'worm monster' is said to live in Iceland's Lake Lagarfljot. It has been described as a pale, humped animal, about fifteen metres in length, with a long neck and, bizarrely, whiskers! The most recent sighting was in 2012

MY MISSION

So, what's the best way to find a super-shy monster in a very large lake? Most visitors just watch and wait, hoping that if they hang out at the loch for long enough, Nessie might make a surprise appearance. Almost all leave disappointed.

Professional teams of 'monster hunters' are another thing altogether. These guys have got all the equipment – the scanners, the radars, the latest technology and gadgets. Over the years, many scientific research expeditions have scoured the loch in the hope of finally getting proof of the monster – but most have also come away disappointed . . .

As for me, I'll be driving up to the Highlands and camping out by the loch for a few nights. During the day I'll be observing the loch and sailing out in a small boat – with a few gadgets, of course:

KIT LIST

- HIGH-POWERED HUNTING BINOCULARS – to survey the loch and watch out for any mysterious ripples or splashes; fully sealed with a nitrogen gas filling – and waterproof too
- A TOP-OF-THE-RANGE CAMERA WITH OPTICAL ZOOM LENS – for long-distance shots
- A VIDEO CAMERA WITH NIGHT-TIME INFRA-RED – in case Nessie pops up in the dark

- AN OUTBOARD MOTORBOAT – small and speedy to whizz around all parts of the loch
- A SONAR SCANNER, ECHO-SOUNDERS & HYDROPHONE – on board I'll have a sonar scanner, echo-sounders and I'll be using a hydrophone – an underwater mike (these gadgets will help detect anything large moving through the water, while the microphone should pick up any underwater 'Nessie noises')

MISSION COMPLETED

It has to be said, this monster-hunting business is really quite boring. They should really call it 'monster waiting'. You need a lot of patience – and a lot of snacks – to keep going through the long days and nights of watching and waiting.

I've been camping out on the banks of the loch for a week with all my cameras set up, watching the waters with binoculars for any suspicious movements. I haven't spotted the famous humps – but I have seen quite a few mysterious splashes and ripples (plus a lot of tourists on boats).

However, my scanning equipment did come up with some images of large unknown objects – about two or three metres long. They are really dark and blurry, like most of the photos taken in the loch. The problem is that the water here is really murky. I don't know if these images are logs, seals, schools of fish – or maybe Nessie?

WHAT DO YOU THINK?

There are a lot of theories that people have come up with about Nessie, from prehistoric plesiosaurs to overgrown eels! If you're a Nessie believer – and there are many of you out there – take a look at the two possible explanations below and decide which you think fits best.

Nessie Exists

1. Nessie is a Plesiosaur

Some people believe that Nessie is a prehistoric creature, one that has survived undiscovered in the loch for many thousands of years. If this is true, Nessie could be a plesiosaur, a meat-eating reptile that existed alongside the dinosaurs around *65 million years ago*. Of course, dinosaurs – and plesiosaurs, as far as we know – are extinct. But could Nessie be the exception – a living example of a species that we believed once died out?

Extinct – or Alive?

You see, we've been proved wrong before about a creature that we thought was extinct. In 1938 a fish called a coelacanth (pronounced see-low-canth) was found alive and well swimming around in the waters of the Indian Ocean. This was an absolutely amazing find. Why? This scary-looking fish – which can grow up to 1.5 metres long – was thought to have become extinct 60 million years ago! Some think that the extreme coldness of the deep water in which

the fish was found, and the fact that it has few predators, helped it survived all these years. The coelacanth is living proof that a prehistoric creature can be found living in the modern world. So, why not Nessie?

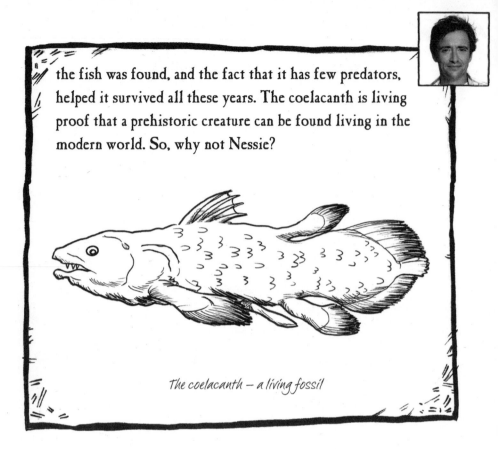

The coelacanth – a living fossil

There are a few problems with the plesiosaur idea, though:

- If Nessie has been living in the loch for thousands of years, scientists say there would have to be more than one monster. There would need to be a whole population of plesiosaurs giving birth to new little Nessies. And so far we haven't seen any sign of a big monster family
- What would the monsters eat? Scientists don't think there is enough food in the loch to feed a group of large creatures. There are salmon, plankton and various fish, but there would need to be an enormous amount to feed just one plesiosaur, let alone an entire family
- Loch Ness wasn't actually formed until the end of the last Ice Age, about 10,000 years ago. So where did the

plesiosaurs live until the time they entered Loch Ness? The whole of this area was covered in thick ice for hundreds of years, so it's hard to see how they could have survived

- Plesiosaurs are thought to be aquatic reptiles, and reptiles are cold-blooded creatures. A reptile couldn't survive in the freezing waters of Loch Ness – it's just too cold. Also, reptiles breathe air – so Nessie would have to surface in order to breathe. Wouldn't the monster have been found by now if it was regularly coming up for air?

2. Nessie is a Giant Eel

Some people think that Nessie is actually a mammoth, oversized eel. Could those mysterious humps be those of a giant fish writhing around in the water?

However, there are a few 'buts' to this idea:

- If you look at the behaviour of a normal eel, you'll see that they swim with a 'side to side' winding motion, not by making 'humps' arching out of the water
- If Nessie *was* an eel, it would have to be an absolutely massive one. 'Eely' huge! The largest eel that has ever been discovered is a conger eel weighing a whopping 160kg (350lb), found off the shores of Iceland. Conger eels live in the seas of Great Britain and other parts of northern Europe and can grow up to three metres long. However, they are *not* found in Loch Ness because it is a freshwater lake – and conger eels live in salt water. No eel has ever been found that matches up to the alleged size of the hulking Loch Ness monster . . .

Nessie Doesn't Exist

Those who don't believe in the monster point to the fact that we've been searching for many, many years and, still, nothing has ever been found – even with the latest technology. They believe that it's a story that's got out of hand. And that all the sightings, photographs and films are either fakes or mistakes. So have a look at these Nessie 'mistakes' and see what you think.

1. Nessie the Elephant?

This is one of those ideas that sounds so unbelievable, it might even be true. Recently a man called Neil Clark (who is a museum curator of palaeontology and therefore knows what he's talking about) suggested that early sightings of Nessie were not of a monster at all – but of an elephant! Now, you don't often see a group of elephants having a swim in your local lake, but I promise you, there is a logical explanation to all this. Here goes . . .

Years ago, there were no TVs, computers or DVDs to while away the time. People had to make their own entertainment – perhaps playing the piano, having a sing-along or going to see a show. (Fun!) One popular outing was a visit to a travelling circus, where you could see wild animals and human performers doing tricks and stunts (fortunately, this kind of animal show no longer exists).

Circuses would tour the country, visiting towns and villages to entertain the locals and make some money. They often had lots of exotic animals to transport. Those animals needed a wash now and again. And what better spot for a refreshing bathe than the cool waters of Loch Ness – an ideal stop-off point en route to the city of Inverness?

Neil Clark believes that many of those 1930s sightings could have been the upper part of a bathing elephant and its trunk sticking out from the water. It would certainly account for the 1933 descriptions of the monster's neck being like an elephant's trunk!

But how could this explain so many hundreds of monster sightings since the 1930s?

2. Mistaken Identity

Maybe there's nothing weird living in the loch at all. It is simply a case of people mistaking one thing for another. And, just as importantly, people seeing what they *want* to see. For example, people who spot a seal splashing in the distance might really believe they are seeing a monster – because that's why they've come to Loch Ness!

Other things that have been commonly mistaken for Nessie in the past are:

- Boats
- Pieces of wood/dead trees
- Waves
- The wake of a boat
- Deer swimming across the loch

The loch is incredibly misty too – and swirling fog can make you think you see all sorts of strange things. So, do you think people have been spotting monsters that aren't really monsters for all these years?

3. Nessie is Tree Gas!

Farting trees? Whoever would have thought it?

If you ever visit Loch Ness, you'll see that there are a lot of pine trees growing close to the water. As the pines die, they fall into the water, and it's possible that the floating logs get mistaken for the monster. But eyewitness accounts often describe seeing an object that is moving along at speed and causing a lot of disturbance in the water. Now dead trees are exactly that – dead! Meaning that they don't usually move around much – or cause disturbances. Come to think of it, even living trees don't swim very fast. So how could a log behave like a moving monster?

Someone came up with the idea that 'tree gas' propels these dead logs along. This is how it works.

- As the pine trunk slowly becomes rotten, it fills up with gas. It is covered with a layer of tree resin (a sticky substance produced by trees) which effectively seals the trunk and stops the gas from coming out
- Eventually the trunk gets so rotten that it suddenly breaks and all that gas shoots out of a gap, causing the log to pop up to the surface and whoosh along like a jet-propelled rocket! Imagine that one of the log's branches is sticking out of the water, just like a monster head, and you've got yourself a super speedy Loch Ness monster!

4. Weird Waves

Could a combination of wind and water create the effect of a swimming monster? There is an unusual event that occurs in some very long, very cold lakes, just like Loch Ness. It is called a *seiche* (pronounced 'saysh'). It's caused by the action of wind on the surface water, which suddenly forces a lot of water to one end of the lake. When the wind stops, the water begins to move back and forth – a bit like the movement of the water when you get out of a bath. All this movement – which can go on for as long as a week – causes strange disturbances in the water that may not look natural. It could even cause a log caught up in the seiche to look as if it is moving around and alive.

Would this phenomenon account for the many Nessie 'sightings'? If it is the reason, this could also very well explain similar 'monsters' found in other large lakes around the globe.

YOU DECIDE

In the end, the only way of proving that the Loch Ness monster exists is to actually catch it – or at least take pictures that show it clearly and unarguably to be a monster.

So where do *you* stand on Nessie? Turn to the back of the book to review your findings.

MYSTERY
2

The Yeti

THE MISSION . . .

. . . to find out if a mysterious ape-like creature lives in the mountains of the Himalayas.

BURNING QUESTIONS

- Does the yeti really exist – or is it just a myth?
- If it's real, what kind of creature is it?
- Is the yeti dangerous?

MISSION DETAILS

The soaring mountains of the Himalayas are remote, beautiful – and dangerous. Many have lost their lives here, attempting to climb Everest, the highest mountain in the world.

Despite the harsh, freezing conditions, it is said that a huge, hairy creature lives high up among the snow and ice. A creature that is unknown to humankind.

The locals call it the yeti; westerners sometimes call it the 'abominable snowman'.

Whichever name you prefer, the yeti has been the subject of all kinds of investigations, TV documentaries and horror movies.

Those who have seen the beast say it is a hulking hairy figure, about two to three metres tall. With a cone-shaped head and the face of an angry gorilla, it's not the kind of thing you'd want to come across on a dark night (or even a sunny afternoon, for that matter!).

Even scarier is the stinky smell that accompanies the beast. According to eyewitnesses – or should we say *nose*-witnesses – your average yeti is about as whiffy as your dad's trainers filled with warm cheese and left in the sun . . . *pee-ew!*

But, despite many sightings – of the beast itself and also of many huge footprints – still no one has captured an abominable snowman or proved beyond doubt that it really exists. So, when you've seen the evidence, will you be a yeti believer?

THE LOCATION

The Himalayas are a truly spectacular range of mountains in Asia. Incredibly high, they are often called the 'roof of the world'. And no wonder. They include Mount Everest, the highest peak on Earth, standing at 8,848 metres (29,029 feet)!

The Himalayas are made up of two mountain ranges, separated by a wide valley. The mountains are a mammoth 2,500 kilometres long, spanning parts of northern India, Nepal, Bhutan and Tibet. At the higher parts, thick snow covers the mountains all year round and the temperature rarely rises above freezing point. *Brrr*. . .

The yeti is supposed to live in the higher regions, where conditions are really extreme. If it exists, it must be an incredibly tough creature to survive in the ice, wind and savage storms that frequently batter the mountains. But in many ways the Himalayas are the ideal place for a creature that doesn't want to be seen. As it's so inaccessible to humans, it's easy to hide . . .

THE EVIDENCE

The peoples of the Himalayas have told stories about the yeti for centuries. The name itself comes from the Tibetan words *yeh-teh* which mean 'man-bear'. (Though most witnesses say that the yeti looks more like a human crossed with an ape.)

Different cultures living in the Himalayas tell different stories – some are terrified of the yeti and see it as a dark and magical creature. Others don't seem too bothered. Some of the more frightening tales tell of:

- The yeti appearing in local villages to attack and kill yaks (and occasionally a human – see page 144)
- Yetis kidnapping people
- A belief that if you look a yeti in the eye, you will become paralysed with fear, get sick and die (my old headmaster could do something similar)

The yeti legend came to the western world during the twentieth century. Reports of a weird furry creature roaming the mountains began circulating in the late 1800s, but it wasn't until the 1920s that many more sightings began to be reported. This was because western explorers and climbers began to visit this remote area more often.

One of the earliest accounts comes from 1921, when an expedition team to Everest was scaling the north face of the mountain. Looking up, they noticed some mysterious dark figures moving about in the snow, high above them. Who – or what – could be up there?

By the time the mountaineers reached the spot, the figures were gone. All they could find was some large, human-like footprints.

The team leader, Bury, thought they might have been made by a wolf, but the local guides disagreed. They said the prints were from a wild man of the snows – *metoh kangmi.* This was later – and wrongly – translated by a reporter as the abominable snowman. The name stuck, even though the creature looks *nothing* like a snowman. But looking at this illustration – it is 100 per cent abominable!

Definitely hairy – definitely scary!

A few years later, in 1925, a famous incident occurred when a photographer on a British expedition reported seeing a creature near the world's largest glacier, the Zemu. From a distance of around 200 metres, he watched the creature for about a minute, as it wandered around uprooting bushes (presumably for a snack). He said:

'Unquestionably, the figure in outline was exactly like a human being, walking upright . . . It showed up dark against the snow and, as far as I could make out, wore no clothes.'

The creature soon disappeared and the photographer (who hadn't had time to take a picture – *duh*) later found fifteen footprints, similar to human ones, in the snow.

'The marks of five distinct toes and the instep were perfectly clear, but the trace of the heel was indistinct . . .'

Fascinating footprints

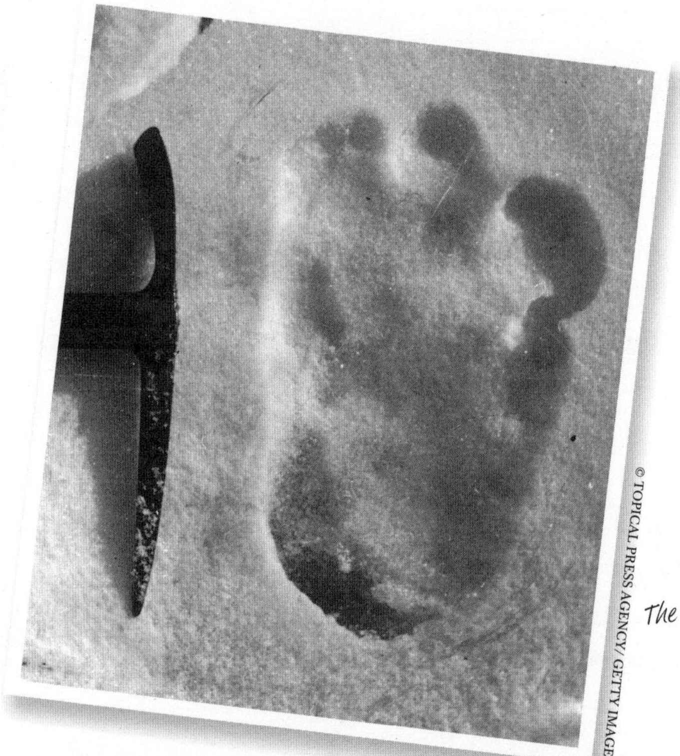

The real footprint of the Yeti?

This incredible footprint, and others like it, were found and photographed by British climbers Eric Shipton and Michael Ward in 1951. They formed part of a long trail of prints that eventually disappeared into the ice. The prints had certainly been made by a creature that walked on two feet, like a human. (All creatures that walk on two feet are known as bipeds.)

'What it is, I don't know, but I am quite clear it is no animal known to live in the Himalaya, and that it is big' – Eric Shipton

Each footprint was 33cm wide and 45cm long – much bigger than a normal human foot, as you can see from the photograph. It was also very deep, so whatever made the print was something large and heavy.

Many people believe that these unexplained prints are still the best evidence we have that the yeti exists.

Not Yeti?

Legendary mountaineers Sir Edmund Hillary and Tenzing Norgay broke all records when they made the very first ascent of Mount Everest in 1953. There was huge excitement all over the world. And more excitement still when the pair found mysterious footprints on the way up . . .

Hillary became fascinated by the yeti stories and returned to the Himalayas in 1960 on a quest to find the abominable snowman. He was shown a 350-year-old cone-shaped scalp at a remote monastery which was said to be

that of a yeti. The scalp was brought back to England for closer inspection. Was this the evidence needed to prove its existence? Sadly, the scalp was examined and thought to be a fake made from the skin of a Himalayan goat. (Not everyone agrees with this, though – some still believe it could be a yeti's head.)

© POPPERFOTO/GETTY IMAGES

Sir Edmund Hillary puzzles over the scalp

Hillary also brought back some small samples of fur, but these were later found to be from the rare Tibetan blue bear, which lives in the Himalayas.

Anyway, after all his investigations, Hillary eventually decided that the yeti was mythical and that the footprints he had seen on his ascent of Everest were probably human ones that had been melted by the sun.

The Hunt Goes On . . .

One of the biggest searches in yeti history happened in 1954 when a research team was sent to the Himalayas by the *Daily Mail* newspaper. A huge number of footprints were discovered, followed and photographed. Some were found to be human – but others were larger and could not be identified.

Sightings and hearings have continued over the years. In 1970 Don Whillans, a British climber on Mount Annapurna, heard strange and eerie cries in the distance, like nothing he'd ever heard before. His Sherpa guide immediately identified it as the call of a yeti. Later that night, Whillans saw a dark, ape-like figure moving around near their camp. Bet he didn't sleep very well . . .

The next day, Whillans's sighting was proved true when large deep footprints were found in the snow. But the most exciting part came later that day. Whillans was in his tent when the dark creature returned. He watched the strange figure through binoculars for about 20 minutes as it rooted around for food and pulled branches from a tree, before running off. To this day, he remains convinced that the animal was neither a human nor an ape . . .

Secrets of the Shrivelled Hand

Why would anyone keep a crusty, brown, shrivelled-up old hand for years? Perhaps they thought it might come in 'handy' one day?!

Well, the monks of the remote monastery of Pangboche in the Himalayas kept a hand just like this. They believed that it was the hand of a yeti, and that it would protect them from bad luck.

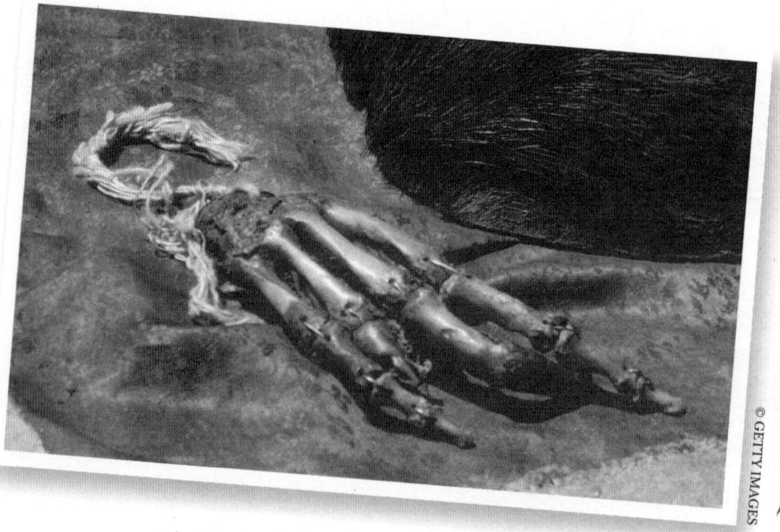

© GETTY IMAGES

The hand, all shrivelled and brown. Eeew!

In 1958 an explorer called Peter Byrne was shown the hand while on an expedition to search for the abominable snowman. Naturally, he was keen to find out if it really did belong to the famed yeti. But it would need a proper scientific analysis and it would need to be taken to a lab.

The monks didn't want to let the hand out of their sight. But, on a second visit, Byrne managed to persuade them to let him have just one of the fingers in return for a sum of money. (The remainder of it was later stolen from the monastery – clearly a very popular hand!)

The finger was 9cm long, 2cm at the widest part, curled and black at the end with an extended nail. The hand itself was said to be about the size of a human's.

The 'yeti's finger' was smuggled out of the country into the UK, but what happened after that is a mystery. Many years passed. In 2008 the finger was finally found nestling in the vaults at the Royal College of Surgeons in London. Not such a strange thing when you consider some of the other items here. Its most famous collection – the Hunterian Collection – includes:

- pickled organs from soldiers who fought in the Battle of Waterloo
- Winston Churchill's false teeth
- the skeleton of Charles Byrne, the 2.31m tall 'Irish giant'!

In 2011 DNA from the finger was analysed – and it was found to be 'of human origin'. So, if the finger is from a yeti, then the mysterious beast is even more like a human than anyone thought! But it's more likely to be from a real human – maybe one of the monks donated it?

Yeti Attack!

In 1974 a savage attack took place in the remote Machermo Valley. A young Sherpa woman called Lhakpa Dorma was found wounded and unconscious, while around her lay the bodies of several yaks. They had been killed and half eaten by an unidentified, ferocious creature . . .

When Lhakpa recovered, she described how she had been herding her yaks when she was attacked by a creature she thinks was a yeti. It came up from behind her, grabbing her round the neck and throwing her down some distance away. She then watched in terror as the creature began to attack and kill her yaks. According to her description, the yeti had huge teeth, a wrinkled face, long nails and moved incredibly fast.

All these years on, the old lady is still alive – and still convinced that she had a lucky escape from the yeti. What could have attacked her and her livestock? Was it a bear – or the real abominable snowman?

The Sherpas of the Himalayas

Despite the harsh conditions, thousands of people live in the Himalayas. Of these, the Sherpas are probably the most well-known in the western world. They live high up in the mountains in the north-eastern part of Nepal. Many Sherpa villages are found perched in precarious positions on terrifyingly high ledges and slopes, some as high up as

4,267 metres. There are no roads or cars – hiking is the usual way of getting around. Some Sherpa children climb the equivalent of a skyscraper just to reach school every day! Nobody 'pops to the shops'. It is tough; really, really tough. But great snowball fights . . . if you've got the energy after hiking home from school.

Sherpas are often employed to help trekkers and mountaineers on their expeditions to Everest, as they are used to the high altitude and can usually carry much heavier loads than western visitors.

Sherpas keep herds of yaks – a kind of shaggy-haired ox with horns that is perfectly adapted to living at high altitude. Yaks are incredibly important to the people of the Himalayas – they provide milk, meat and cloth, and are a very useful method of transport.

You looking at me? An unfriendly yak

More Yeti Hunters

In 2008 a team of Japanese yeti hunters photographed footprints, about 20cm long, on snow in the Dhaulagiri mountain range in western Nepal. The expedition leader, Mr Takahashi, believed them to be prints of the yeti.

In fact, Mr Takahashi also believed that he had seen a yeti on a previous expedition in 2003. He described his sighting as follows:

'It was about 200 metres away in silhouette. It was walking on two legs like a human and looked about 150 centimetres tall.'

Reinhold Messner, one of the world's most famous, record-breaking mountaineers, also returned to the Himalayas after he caught sight of a yeti in 1986. He described his yeti as 'big' and 'stinking'! And he was determined to get to the bottom of the mystery.

Messner spent years visiting the Himalayas and talking to the locals about the yeti. He eventually came to the conclusion that the yeti was probably a large brown Tibetan bear, rather than a mysterious unknown ape.

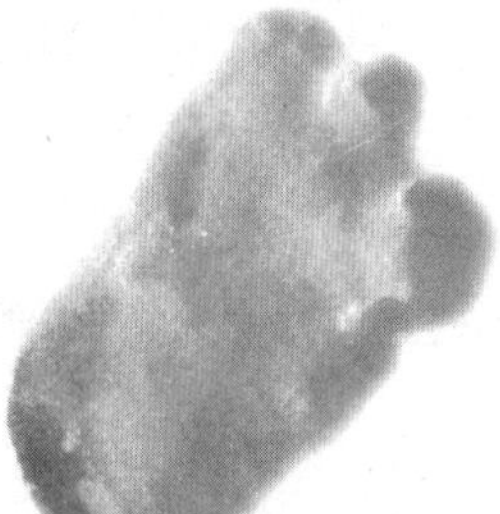

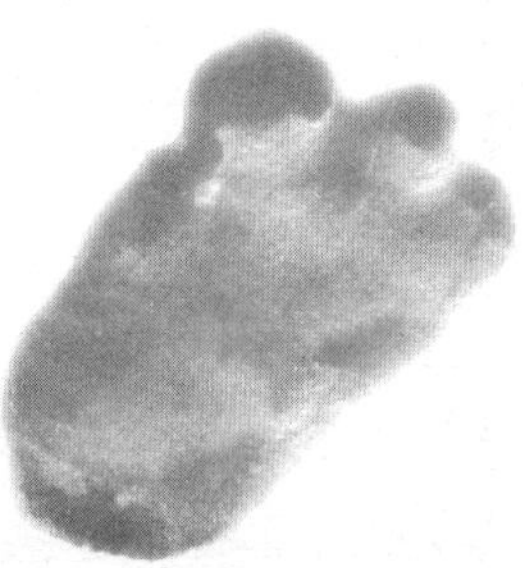

Yetis Around the World

The legend of an ape-man creature does not only appear in the Himalayas. Mystery beasts resembling the yeti have been reported in many other parts of the world. They include:

- The Sasquatch of North America
- The Yowie in Australia
- The Hibagon in Japan
- The Almasty of Russia

and many others . . .

Probably the most famous of these is the Sasquatch – more commonly known as 'Bigfoot' – who is said to roam forests and woods in parts of North America.

There are many similarities between the yeti and Bigfoot. Both are tall, hairy, ape-like creatures that walk on two feet and have long arms and short necks. Both are feared. Both have big feet. Like this:

This is why the creature isn't called Smallfoot.
Print found in Bridgewater, Massachusetts, USA.

Bigfoot sightings began to be reported in the 1800s (when large footprints were found near the Rocky Mountains in Canada) and they have continued ever since.

In 1995 a forest patrol officer in the Snoqualamie Forest of Washington heard something moving about and making a splashing noise. He leaned over a ridge to see a hulking ape-like animal staring at him.

One of the most famous pieces of 'evidence' comes from northern California where, in 1967, two men called Roger Patterson and Bob Gimlin actually captured Bigfoot on film. Their footage showed a hairy ape walking across a clearing, then looking around – almost as if he knew he was being watched. Some people think the film is a hoax and that Bigfoot is actually a man dressed up in an ape costume. Others are convinced the film is genuine. No one has proved it either way.

Roger Patterson had a cast made of the footprints left by the creature – they were 37cm long with five toes. Just like the yeti.

Whatever you believe, there's no doubt that Bigfoot is big news in North America.

Identify the Yeti

Just in case you ever come across a yeti, here's what to look out for, according to eyewitness reports:

- It is an extremely fast mover. Not one has been seen standing still
- It walks standing upright, like a human
- It is covered in dark reddish-brown hair
- It makes a weird high-pitched whistling noise
- It is tall and looks like a combination of a man and an ape
- It is very good at avoiding being seen or photographed!

MY MISSION

I'll be travelling to the Nepal region of the Himalayas to see if I can spot the yeti – or at least its footprints. I'll be trekking at high altitude, and camping out at night. It's going to be really, really cold – so I'll need some serious cold weather kit.

KIT LIST

- DOWN JACKET, WOOLLY HAT, SKI GLOVES AND BALACLAVA – to keep me toasty warm
- TREKKING BOOTS WITH EXTRA ICE GRIPPERS ATTACHED – there's a lot of ice and snow up here
- SUNGLASSES AND SUN CREAM – the sun is really strong even though it's cold
- WALKING POLES – to help get a grip on the slippery ground
- MAP AND COMPASS – it would be easy to get lost in these mountains)
- WATER BOTTLE, CAMPING STOVE AND EASY-COOK FOOD SUPPLIES
- HIGH-ALTITUDE TENT, EXTRA-THICK DOWN SLEEPING BAG
- ICE AXE – to help me get across any icy slopes
- LONG-LENS CAMERAS, VIDEO CAMERA AND BINOCULARS

Taking it easy

At very high altitudes (anything above 2,500 metres) the amount of oxygen in the air begins to decrease. And the higher you climb, the lower it gets. This can have a huge impact on your body. Some people are unlucky and get altitude sickness – which makes you feel sick and dizzy, with headaches and breathlessness.

All trekkers and climbers to high mountains need to take things slowly, spending a couple of days at each level to let their body adjust as they climb higher. This process is called 'acclimatization'.

Everyone reacts differently to high altitudes, but I'm hoping I'm not going to suffer too much. Unfortunately, when venturing above 3,000 metres, 75 per cent of people will experience 'mountain sickness' . . .

The scariest airport in the world

First of all, I have to get to the Himalayas. And I have a feeling that the journey is going to be even worse than bumping into the most ferocious yeti. The first part is easy – simply fly to Kathmandu, the bustling capital city of Nepal. The yeti myth is everywhere in Kathmandu – I could stay at the Yak and Yeti Hotel, then fly up to the mountains on Yeti Airlines!

But next is the bit I am dreading. Why? I will have to get into a tiny twenty-seater aircraft and land at what is supposed to be *the most dangerous airport in the world.* This is the place where most climbers arrive before they attempt Everest. Welcome to Lukla Airport . . .

© BEN PIPE / ROBERT HARDING PICTURE LIBRARY / SUPERSTOCK

It's not even an airport really; more of a tiny – and scarily short – strip of tarmac, only 450 metres long. This 'runway' has been built right on the edge of a steep valley, 2,860 metres up, with a sheer drop on one side. The landing is nerve-racking – very fast and very bumpy – and you often have to descend through dense cloud. Which is never good when you're in a small plane.

MISSION COMPLETED

I made it into (and out of) the world's most dangerous airport. I almost lost the entire contents of my stomach, but not sure if that was due to the bumpy flight or altitude sickness . . .

It was cold, lonely and a bit spooky. I saw a lot of yaks (yak-loads in fact) – but most importantly, I saw these.

Yes, my very own yeti footprints!

They were big – about 40cm long – and deep. The fresh prints went snaking around in a trail into some trees, then disappeared. No funny smells, no weird whistling or anything else. Just footprints. But big ones. Bigger than mine, anyway.

So I'll be adding my bit of evidence to the many others from over the years.

WHAT DO YOU THINK?

Is the yeti a real creature? It's 'make your mind up' time . . .

The Yeti Doesn't Exist

Some think that the 'yeti' is just a regular mountain creature that has been mistaken for something more sinister. It's true that many animals do live in the Himalayas – though very few are found above 550 metres because of the intense cold, snow and ice.

Animals living at high altitudes need to have thick skins and fur to keep warm. Many will hibernate during the winter months, when there isn't much food around, or move down to the lower levels.

Here are a few examples of Himalayan mountain wildlife:

- ***The Tibetan blue bear***: incredibly rare and almost never seen; shaggy fur, greyish black, walks on all fours
- ***The Black bear***: can grow to almost two metres long, but does not generally attack other mammals; lives on ants, grubs, nuts and leaves
- ***The Brown bear***: heavier and larger than the black bear, it lives in the higher parts of the mountains, eating plants, goats and sheep
- ***Snow leopard***: very rare and hardly ever seen, snow leopards have thick spotted fur and prey on deer, birds and tahrs (see below)
- There are also ***wolves***, ***martens***, ***foxes***, ***langur monkeys***, ***red pandas*** and ***Himalayan tahrs*** – a cross between a mountain goat and sheep.

It's unlikely that someone could think a goat or a wolf was a yeti – but a bear standing on its hind legs is a possibility. Different types of bears live in forests all over the world too, so this could explain many of the sightings in other countries.

But what about some of the strongest evidence there is for the yeti – the many footprints that have been found? These prints have been studied by experts who've agreed that:

- they are not from an ape or a bear or other forest creature
- they don't come from any animal that we know of

How can they be explained? One suggestion is that the yeti prints are just normal tracks, made by animals or perhaps by local people. But something has happened to them to make them look unusual . . .

A Trick of the Sun?

Imagine an ordinary animal track in the snow with the sun shining down on it. The warmth melts the snow and, depending on the angle of the sun's rays, completely alters the shape of the print. It can become bigger, longer, more dramatic looking – and it could end up appearing like that of some weird, unexplained creature. Could this be the reason for all those mysterious tracks?

Famed mountaineer Reinhold Messner thinks so. And after years of exploring the Himalayas he believes that the 'yeti' is actually a brown bear, one that sometimes walks upright on its hind legs, as well as on all fours. The bear is known locally as *chemo* and lives at altitudes of 3,500–5,500 metres. Because it is nocturnal, it isn't often seen by humans, so he thinks this has added to the mystery over the years.

But if it is just a bear, where did the idea of the yeti come from? Perhaps the yeti is the 'bogey-man' of the Himalayas – a figure of fear talked about in stories to frighten locals (and make their kids behave!) and to explain away the occasional yak attack.

The Yeti Exists

But if the yeti does exist, what *is* it exactly? There are two schools of thought:

1. It's a Giant Ape

Some believe that the yeti may be a descendant of a prehistoric ape that lived in parts of Asia hundreds of thousands of years ago. This extinct giant ape is called *Gigantopithecus*. Its existence was only discovered in 1935 when remains of its (incredibly large) teeth were found in China.

Gigantopithecus was supposed to have been the largest ape that ever lived, a kind of real-life King Kong. It is estimated to have been a massive three metres (nearly ten feet) high and to have weighed up to 540 kilograms (1,200lb) – that's two or three times more than a gorilla!

Many scientists believe that this giant ape roamed South-east Asia for nearly a million years before becoming extinct roughly 100,000 years ago. No one knows why it died out.

Or did it? Some yeti enthusiasts believe that the yeti is a direct descendant of *Gigantopithecus*. They think that the species could have survived unknown in the rugged mountains for thousands of years, adapting as time passed by.

However, there is no evidence of this ancient ape anywhere but Asia – so how would this account for sightings of Bigfoot and other similar creatures in other parts of the world? Tricky . . .

2. It's a Man (Sort of . . .)

Some people have another idea. They point to the fact that the yeti looks a bit like a man to say that it might be something human. They think that it could have evolved from Neanderthals – an extinct species of human. Neanderthal humans lived in Europe but disappeared completely about 25,000 years ago. This was 10,000 years after the arrival of modern humans in Europe (that's us), so for many years, two 'types' of human lived at the same time. No one knows why the Neanderthals died out, but our species lived. One theory is that we were just better equipped for survival.

Is this what Neanderthal man looked like?

The theory is that Neanderthals may have retreated to mountains and forests thousands of years ago and lived completely apart from modern humans. As the years went by, they became wild – and the yeti is the result!

However, very few (if any) scientists think this is possible. One of the problems with this idea is that Neanderthal man used tools – and the yeti has never been seen doing a spot of DIY! Would he/she really have lost this useful skill?

YOU DECIDE

Scientists know for a fact that we haven't discovered all the species of animal in the world, not by a long shot – and there are definitely new creatures out there waiting for us to find and classify them. There are also creatures like the coelacanth (see page 125) which have amazed experts because they were thought to have become extinct millions of years ago. Could the yeti be another creature that defies scientific belief?

Make up your mind! Turn to the back to record your verdict.

MYSTERY 3

Vampires

THE MISSION . . .

. . . to find out if bloodsucking vampires really do exist.

BURNING QUESTIONS

- What is a vampire, exactly?
- How do you know if someone is a vampire?
- How can you get rid of one?

MISSION DETAILS

Think of a vampire – what springs to mind? A fanged man dressed in black lying in a coffin? A pale-faced high-school student who is in love with a human? A flying monster with extraordinary strength and super-senses?

These days, a vampire could be any one of the above. There are even vampires who are vegetarians (they try to avoid blood – but I hear it's fangtastically hard . . .).

The vampire myth goes back for centuries, but nowadays vampires are more popular than ever. You can't move for yet another blockbuster movie, TV series or bestselling book featuring flocks of fanged fiends.

These days vampires are so popular, they even get fang mail! (OK, I promise I'll stop with the 'fang' jokes. Well, I'll try. Sometimes there's not a fang I can do about it . . . Sorry!)

But what exactly *is* a vampire? He or she is a member of the 'undead'. In other words, the vampire is neither dead nor alive but exists in a kind of limbo between the two states. A vampire exists for ever (unless some brave person manages to destroy it – more on that later) but must drink human blood in order to survive. It does this by catching a human – any human will do as long as he/she has got a decent blood supply – and biting their neck with its sharp fangs. The vampire can then drink the human's blood and feel a whole lot better. The human, however, feels considerably worse. Following the bite, the victim turns into a vampire too.

Fictional vampires are everywhere – but what about in real life? Could there be one living down the road from you? 'Necks' door, perhaps? Oops. That's worse than the fang fing. Sorry!

My mission is to investigate the fictions and realities of the vampire world and find out if the vampire stories have any truth in them . . .

THE LOCATION

Myths and legends about bloodsucking creatures are told all over the world, from Asia and Africa to the Americas. But the best-known vampire story of all comes from Europe – Eastern Europe to be exact. It is the story of Dracula.

The famous Count Dracula of Transylvania

Though Dracula is a fictional character, he was based on a very real person called Vlad the Impaler (the name's a bit of a clue to the horrible things he did). Vlad came from a spooky-sounding place called Transylvania.

Transylvania is a region of a country called Romania. Its name literally means 'beyond the woods', as much of Transylvania was at one time covered in forest. It has been taken over by different countries and empires during its history, including the Roman Empire and the Hungarian Empire. But the name Transylvania will always be associated with haunted castles, dark forests and, of course, vampires . . .

THE EVIDENCE

Tales of the undead have been around from ancient times, in many different cultures. One of the oldest images ever found is on a vase from ancient Persia (founded in the sixth century BC), which shows a man struggling with a creature that is trying to suck its blood. Roman and Greek myths feature horrifying tales of creatures such as the blood-devouring lamia and the striges, an evil bird that feeds on human flesh and blood. In fact, most countries have myths and legends that feature evil spirits or creatures that drink blood.

Vampires as we know them today – dressed in black, blood-red lips and deathly pale white skin: you know the kind of thing – are the type found in Eastern European folklore in the late seventeenth and eighteenth centuries. In Eastern Europe, the threat of vampires was taken very seriously indeed. Transylvanians believed in 'strigoi' (their name for the undead). These ghastly creatures walked the earth because they hadn't been buried properly or had led an evil life. The thought of a vampire being on the loose struck terror into people's hearts. They might have dug a grave to try and find the offending corpse and get rid of it. Driving a stake through *its* heart was one way of doing this (and still the most effective way to wipe out a vampire, according to the experts).

In the 1700s stories of vampires began to circulate in Western Europe too. Bram Stoker, an Irish author who lived in London in the 1800s, researched these legends and was inspired to write his famous horror story – *Dracula*. The most influential book in vampire history was published in 1897 and made Mr Stoker famous all over the world.

© BUYENLARGE / SUPERSTOCK

Bram's bloodthirsty bestseller

The Dreaded Dracula

In the story of *Dracula*, a young English lawyer called Jonathan Harker travels to Transylvania to meet the mysterious Count Dracula on a business matter. Ignoring the bad omens along the way – garbled warnings from terrified villagers, his carriage attacked by wolves (a bit like when those Scooby Doo guys say, 'Let's split up,' and don't

see trouble coming) – Harker finally arrives at Dracula's very large and very spooky castle. He is relieved to find that Dracula is a polite and intelligent gentleman. However, as the days go by, things get nasty. Harker realizes that the count is no gentleman, but an evil vampire who wants to suck his blood and make him a member of his 'undead' gang. Though he is trapped in the castle, Harker manages to escape from Dracula's clutches by climbing the castle walls, and eventually makes it back to the safety of England.

But England isn't safe for long . . . Dracula soon turns up – in a small seaside town called Whitby, in the north-east. He attacks Harker's friend Lucy, who becomes a vampire too. But in true vampire-hunter style, Harker gets his revenge on Dracula when he returns to Transylvania to get rid of the evil vampire once and for all. Hurrah!

Today, in Whitby, there are Dracula mementoes everywhere – there's even a 'Dracula Experience' for tourists where the entire story is re-enacted and you can watch a model of Dracula slowly rising from his coffin!

Dracula is a great story, but it is just that – a story. However, Count Dracula was said to have been inspired by two ghastly real-life characters. The first is:

Very Bad Vlad

'Vlad the Impaler', as Vlad Tepes was known, was born in Transylvania in 1456, though he actually ruled a region called

Wallachia, south of Transylvania. If you'd been unlucky enough to live here in the fifteenth century, you would have done well to avoid Vlad. A ruthless and violent man, he used his power to have thousands of people killed, often by being impaled on long spikes (hence the nickname). No wonder his name struck fear into people's hearts . . .

Like Count Dracula, Vlad lived in a spooky castle, and rumour has it that he drank his victims' blood. He was also known locally as 'Vlad Dracul' because *dracul* means 'devil' in Romanian – which, of course, is where Bram Stoker got the idea for Dracula's name.

Vlad sports a Transylvanian trend – the horizontal moustache

This charming man was killed in 1476 during a battle against the Turks. It is said that his tomb was later found to be empty. People took this as a sign that Vlad was a vampire, who had left his grave to go in search of more blood.

The Blood Countess

Another equally horrible figure was the Countess Elizabeth Bathory, aka the 'Blood Countess'. She came from Eastern Europe too, living in Hungary in the seventeenth century. The countess had a barbaric beauty regime which consisted of killing young girls so she could bathe in, and drink, their blood. For some reason, she thought that this would keep her looking young and beautiful! Fortunately, the Blood Countess was arrested in 1610 and locked up in a tower for the rest of her life. The local girls could now breathe a sigh of relief – phew . . .

The Countess takes time to pose for a portrait – in between blood baths . . .

Modern Day Vampires

You'd find it hard to come across two more unpleasant people than Bad Vlad and the Blood Countess, but were they really vampires – or just very evil people?

There have been many reports of vampire activity since those times, but let's fast forward to the twentieth century, where some very interesting real-life accounts have taken place. Both happen to be in good old London town . . .

The London Vampire

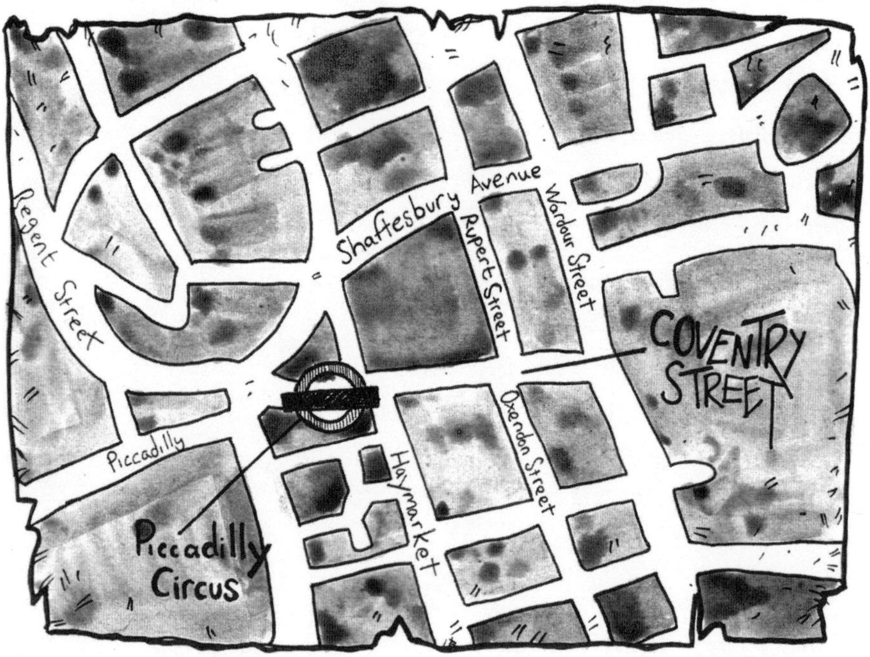

Daytime. A quiet street in London, 1922. Not the most likely location for a vampire attack – but that is exactly what is supposed to have happened. On 16 April 1922 a man was admitted to London's Charing Cross Hospital with a mysterious deep wound in his neck. He had no idea how he had got it. All the man could remember was that he had been walking down Coventry Street (near Piccadilly Circus) on his way to work when he felt an agonizing, stabbing sensation in his neck. He passed out. When doctors examined him, they said that he had been stabbed with some kind of 'thin tube'.

Just a few hours later, a second man was brought into the hospital – also with a strange wound on his neck. Exactly the same thing had happened to him, also in Coventry Street . . .

Unbelievably, a third patient later turned up at the same hospital. And guess what? He too had suffered a deep wound in his neck. The place? Coventry Street, of course.

The newspapers soon got hold of the strange story, and rumours began to spread that there was a dangerous vampire on the loose in the capital. Some said that the police had hired a vampire hunter, who was supposed to have chased the vampire and stabbed it through the heart. While no one knows if this is true, the attacks never happened again.

What do you make of this story? Could a real vampire have attacked the men in broad daylight? Did the victims themselves become vampires after they were attacked? These questions remain unanswered.

The Highgate Vampire

One of the spookiest places in London is a place called Highgate Cemetery. It is a large burial ground that dates back to Roman times, full of overgrown gravestones and scary-looking crypts.

Highgate Cemetery has always had a reputation for being haunted, but from the 1960s onwards, it was rumoured that a vampire stalked its ivy-strewn grounds . . .

© DARIO MITIDIERI, GETTY IMAGES

Highgate Cemetery – wonder if there's a 'scaretaker' around?

It all started in 1963, when two schoolgirls taking a short cut through the cemetery reported seeing dead bodies rising from their tombs. A few weeks later, a terrified couple said they had seen a hideous face hovering behind some iron railings.

Later, someone said they had found the bodies of dead foxes – completely drained of blood – in the cemetery. Victims of thirsty vampires? It was rumoured that a member of the 'undead' had been brought to England from Wallachia (south of Transylvania) in a coffin during the eighteenth century and buried here. The legend of the Highgate Vampire was born.

More scary incidents occurred there over the years. A young woman described how she was attacked and thrown to the ground by a tall figure dressed in black with a deathly white face. The spooky man apparently vanished when a car stopped to help her.

The last recorded sighting was made in 2005 by a person returning to his home near Highgate Cemetery. A dark figure whispered to him as he passed the cemetery gates – 'Good evening, sir'! Not sure if the person hung around to reply . . .

Since then Highgate Cemetery has gone very quiet. Has the vampire gone elsewhere – or was there anything there in the first place?

Everything You Need to Know About Vampires

Is it obvious that someone is a vampire? Would you know for sure if you came across one in everyday life? Vampire hunters – here's a checklist of what to look out for:

- Vampires sleep in a coffin, or a grave, during the day
- They have very pale skin and pointed fang-like teeth

Their lips are red (all that blood), and apparently their breath stinks. (Is that what's known as 'bat' breath?)

- Vampires can't bear sunlight – they can only go out in darkness, as light either burns or kills them
- They don't sleep or eat food – only blood will do
- A true vampire has no reflection when looking in a mirror and casts no shadow
- They have hypnotic powers and can use mind control with humans to get what they want
- Many have 'super-senses' giving them ultra-sensitive hearing, smell and vision
- Vampires are shapeshifters – they can change into other forms, mostly bats, wolves and also clouds of gas. That means they can get under cracks in doors and around windows . . . *eek*!

Vampires do differ slightly in different parts of the world: Russian vampires are supposed to have purple faces (should make them 'berry' easy to spot, then?). But one thing we're agreed on is that vampires everywhere are scary and it's best not to mess with them. Especially when they fancy a quick bite . . .

Where Do Vampires Come From?

When a person dies, many people believe that their 'soul' passes on into the next world. The 'next world' might be heaven, hell or some other form of afterlife, depending on your beliefs.

Vampires are said to be created when a person's soul can't pass on to the next world, and it is forced to stay inside the body of the dead person. But why? Perhaps the person has done something wicked or has upset the Church in some way. Some cultures think that a vampire is created when a body isn't buried properly or because the Devil has taken over the body. They have even come up with some ways of preventing a dead body turning into a vampire – for instance:

- Nailing the corpse down inside the coffin – to stop it getting out in the night in search of blood
- Burying the body with lots of smelly garlic or 'holy bread' (bread which has been blessed by a priest)

Evidence of this kind of practice was recently unearthed in Bulgaria, when archaeologists found old skeletons with iron rods inserted through their chests – clearly done to prevent the bodies from becoming vampires. Or had the ghost of Vlad the Impaler been at work?

How to Get Rid of a Vampire

There's no doubt that having a vampire around can be a real pain in the neck! So how do you get rid of one that's breathing down yours? There are a few ideas about this. Some believe that a whiff of garlic usually sees them off, while others think more drastic measures are called for.

So should a Dracula-like figure turn up on your doorstep, the first rule is – *never ask them inside.* Vampires can only come into your house if they are invited. And once they're in, they can come back as many times as they want!

Here are a few other tips for getting rid of an unwanted bloodsucker:

- Expose it to sunlight – maybe keep the vampire talking till dawn so it's too late for it to get back to its coffin?

- Fill your house with garlic – vampires hate it! Garlic has long been prized for its pure, medicinal qualities and many believe that it can drive evil away
- Ward off the vampire with anything holy, such as a crucifix, holy water or an object that has been blessed by a priest. Some believe that vampires cannot walk over the ground of a church or temple either
- Find a mirror and hang it on the door – as you know, vampires don't have a reflection and they really don't like facing up to it!

- Get close to a stream or river – vampires apparently can't cross running water
- And finally – if all else fails – the ultimate solution is to find the grave or coffin of the vampire and hammer a wooden stake or dagger through its heart. (In some cultures, a suspected vampire corpse is burned and beheaded instead.) Obviously, you would need to do this during the day when the vampire is sleeping. And you would need to be pretty brave. Because there'd be a lot at 'stake' . . .

Bats and Blood

Whether or not you think vampires are real, there is one real-life creature that does a very good impression of one. It drinks blood, has sharp teeth, comes out at night – and it's called a vampire bat. Actually, in many movies and books, vampires take on the form of a bat at night – a very handy way for them to get around and into places to find victims.

The vampire bat lives mainly in Central and South America. Like all bats, it is nocturnal and emerges at dusk. It uses its own radar system, called 'echolocation', to move about and to find prey in the darkness. Talking of prey, in the case of the vampire bat, any warm-blooded mammal such as a cow – or a human – will do.

The vampire bat doesn't exactly have fangs but it does have very sharp front teeth, which it uses to make a tiny hole in the victim's skin. There is a special substance in the bat's saliva that prevents the blood from clotting so that it

can keep drinking. As it operates at night, its victims are often sleeping when the attack happens – the person may not even realize they've been 'bloodsucked'. The bat meanwhile can drink up to half its body weight in blood! But if it can't get blood for two nights in a row, it will usually die.

You wouldn't want to 'hang around' with this 'bat' boy!

A Beastly Bat Bite

In the seventeenth century, Spanish explorers – 'Conquistadores' – journeyed to the Americas in search of gold and other glittering treasures. But they soon began to suffer from an unknown and terrifying sickness. Many of them died – and no one knew why. But over time, it dawned on the explorers that those who were getting ill also seemed to have small bite marks on their bodies. What was happening to them?

At night, the explorers slept in local caves, which seemed a good place to shelter. But the cause of the sickness was finally discovered when someone noticed that bats living in the caves were landing on the men at night – and biting

them! In fact, what the vampire bats were actually doing (while they were drinking the men's blood) was passing on a fatal disease called rabies – but the Spaniards had no idea of this. They thought that the bats were draining them of their precious blood. Still, the men did stay out of the caves from then on, which helped prevent many more deaths.

In real life, vampire bats don't drain their victims of blood but, as the Conquistadores found out to their cost, they can pass on some very nasty diseases. They are best avoided!

MY MISSION

The only way I'll know for sure if vampires exist is to actually see one for myself. So my mission will happen at night, when vampires are supposed to come out in search of victims . . .

And, as vampires live in graves or coffins, the most obvious place to look for them would be a graveyard. Highgate Cemetery, once the home of a suspected vampire, sounds perfect, so that's where I'll start. I'll be sitting up all night with my camera (that shouldn't be difficult – could *you* manage to doze off in a graveyard?), ready to capture whatever emerges from the shadows.

The only drawback is – I'm scared. Really scared. It's going to be incredibly creepy in a graveyard at night on my own. Forget about vampires – what about ghosts – or even zombies? I'm not sure which is worse . . .

And if I do see a real vampire, the chances are that the vampire will be even more delighted to see me. A human victim ready and waiting – without having to travel!

I definitely need to protect myself. I've decided to dress completely in black to try and conceal myself in the darkness. Maybe then the vampire won't see me.

And I'll have an extensive supply of objects to ward off any Draculas who might feel like a drink.

KIT LIST

- NIGHT-VISION GOGGLES – these infrared stealth goggles attach to the head so that I can quite literally see in the dark (and have my hands free to ward off possible attacks)
- CAMERA WITH FLASH – mounted on a tripod (in case my hands are shaking!)
- DARK TROUSERS, JUMPER AND BALACLAVA (to blend in)
- HIGH-INTENSITY ALUMINIUM TORCH (for shining into those dark corners)
- COMFY CUSHION TO SIT ON (gravestones can be a bit hard and cold, I find)
- VERY THICK, VERY LONG SCARF – not because of the cold, but to wrap around my neck several times. Try and get your fangs through that, Dracula!

For protection

- As many bulbs of stinky garlic as I can carry – I'll hang a few around my neck as well, to be on the safe side
- Around my neck will also be a large crucifix; actually, several crucifixes – you can never be too careful . . .
- A hand mirror – I'll keep it in my pocket so I can get it out quickly if necessary and shove it in the vampire's face
- Most importantly – and this could be a lifesaver – a wooden stake and hammer: I've got a piece of old fencing from my garden and a mallet that I normally use for hammering tent pegs (I'm hoping these will do if things get serious)

MISSION COMPLETED

The night spent in the graveyard was indeed scary. And tiring. And dark. I didn't sleep a wink. At about four a.m., something caught my eye and I looked up to see a dark, cloaked shape moving across the corner of the graveyard. Then I heard harsh breathing close by – then felt cold breath upon my face! I clutched my garlic even harder and reached in my pocket for the mirror as a black shape loomed closer – then disappeared into the darkness. Was it a vampire – or just my imagination? I have no idea . . .

WHAT DO YOU THINK?

Vampires Don't Exist

While there are plenty of fictional vampires in movies, we've never actually caught a real one – alive or on film. Is this because they simply don't exist?

Many people think that this is the case – and that all the stories and legends about vampires stem from fear. Take a look at these two possible explanations for vampires.

1. Fear of Disease

Could the vampire myth be rooted in illnesses? In the past, when we didn't know much about medicine, many diseases seemed mysterious and frightening. People had no idea where diseases came from and how to treat them properly. Some illnesses – which we now know to be explainable and treatable – made victims appear or behave really strangely. And because people didn't understand why, they might have looked to vampires as a convenient explanation.

Take TB (tuberculosis), for example, a common disease in eighteenth- and nineteenth-century Europe. TB, if untreated, would make people very pale and thin over time. They would cough up blood and literally waste away – exactly what is supposed to happen if you become a vampire's victim (before you turn into one yourself). So it's likely that some victims of TB were believed to be victims of vampires.

Another 'vampire disease' is called *Erythropoietic Protoporphyria.* Try saying that with a pair of plastic fangs in your mouth . . . You'll be pleased to hear that this disease of the blood is incredibly rare. However, it was quite common among the rich families of Eastern Europe from the Middle Ages onwards. Which is exactly where many vampire legends circulated from.

Sufferers of this disease get reddish eyes, mouths and teeth. They become sensitive to sunlight, and if they go out in the light it can make their lips crack and bleed. Their lips also tighten and pull back from their mouths, so it looks like they're baring their teeth. As if all this didn't make them look vampire-ish enough, the poor victims were locked up during the day and let out at night.

So – what we've got is a bunch of desperately ill people – perhaps wearing dark cloaks – wandering about at night with red eyes and bared teeth. Well, you can see why people might have assumed that a bunch of vampires were on the prowl . . .

Another disease that can produce vampire-like symptoms is rabies, which is usually spread by animal bites. The Spanish explorers (see page 179) caught rabies from bats. Sufferers are sensitive to light and can become really aggressive. Symptoms can include making hoarse sounds, baring the teeth, frothing at the mouth and biting others.

It's interesting to note that vampire stories began circulating in Europe around the time that certain areas were experiencing rabies. In Hungary between 1721 and 1728, for example, there was a terrible outbreak of rabies which killed dogs, wolves and humans. Not just a coincidence?

2. Fear of Death

People everywhere have always been fearful of death and of the 'dark side'. Some think that the vampire is an imaginary product of all these fears. If you think about it, having a fear of vampires was a useful thing for societies in the past. It made people stay faithful to the Church and encouraged them to lead good lives – so that there'd be less chance of them coming back as vampires after they'd died.

Another explanation related to death could be the strange behaviour of dead bodies. Corpses are creepy, no doubt. And they can sometimes do strange things. Muscles and tissue contract and tighten, which can make a corpse twitch suddenly and appear to move! Weird! It has even been reported that dead bodies can sometimes sit up suddenly on their own. This kind of thing was reported much more in the past, when dead bodies commonly used to be laid out in coffins in people's houses for days at a time, so that people could say their goodbyes.

One explanation for the movement is that gases in the stomach expand when the body decomposes. The stomach inflates like a balloon, which pulls the body upright. Whatever the explanation, if you were the person near the corpse you'd be pretty freaked out if it unexpectedly sat up! You could see why someone might think it was one of the 'living dead' – a vampire. Dead spooky!

Vampires Do Exist

This is going to be short. Because, as yet, there's no solid evidence that vampires are out there, stalking unwilling human victims at night. Sure, there are loads of stories, even eyewitness accounts, but no one has yet been on the news reporting sightings (or bitings) from a Dracula lookalike. There's only one night every year when vampires are guaranteed to be seen out and about – and that's Halloween!

Yet vampires have been around for so long, they are not going to go away, judging from the number of bestselling books and movies out there. Does this prove that there must be some truth in the vampire myth – or that humans are just fascinated by the idea of these chilling, bloodsucking creatures?

YOU DECIDE

So do you think vampires are mythical beings? Or that they are real? If it's the second option, I have one thing to ask you. Do you have a plan of action in case you are attacked by a vampire? If not, start thinking about it now . . . and perhaps note it down at the back so that you don't forget!

MYSTERY 4

Werewolves

THE MISSION . . .

. . . is to find out if a human being can be transformed into a wolf . . .

BURNING QUESTIONS

- Are werewolves just monsters in horror movies?
- Does the full moon have a magical effect?

MISSION DETAILS

You are alone in a dark forest. Through the branches you can see a full moon glowing in the night sky.

You hear a bloodcurdling howl behind you, and nervously turn to see – a gigantic, snarling wolf with fangs bared, about to pounce . . .

You are – a character in a werewolf movie! *Eek!*

A werewolf in a movie – probably made in 'Howlywood'!

Our mission is to find out more about werewolves – to really get inside their hairy skins. Could a person actually become a wolf in real life? Hunt down innocent people, then change back into a human with no memory of the terrible things they have done? Read on . . .

THE EVIDENCE

What is a werewolf? It looks like a much larger, scarier version of a real wolf. It has incredibly sharp fangs and can run incredibly fast. Victims have little chance against such a super-strong, powerful and vicious creature.

Werewolves are supposed to be humans who have undergone a weird shapeshifting process. The word itself comes from the Saxon word *wer* which means man – 'manwolf'.

If you've ever seen a human change into a werewolf in a movie, you'll know it's a terrifying transformation. As the moon shines down, the person screams in pain as their bones creak and extend painfully into the hulking form of a wolf. They stare down at their limbs in horror, as long brown hairs begin sprouting. Finally their face changes, becoming elongated and hairy, with pointed ears and yellow, staring eyes. They are 100 per cent werewolf and there's nothing they can do! Although, to be honest, I've never seen this end bit in a movie; I'm always behind the sofa by then.

This is no 'furry tale' ending

The werewolf goes out on a killing spree to satisfy its cravings. Unsurprisingly, it likes to 'wolf' down its food! But when dawn breaks, the werewolf returns to its normal, human form. It may or may not have any memory of the chaos it has caused during the night . . .

Changing Shape

Stories of 'shapeshifters' – creatures that can take the form of other animals – are found all around the world. Among them are:

- The Aswang of the Philippines – a creature that turns itself into a dog to eat human flesh
- The Kitsune of Japan – foxes that can turn into humans
- The Icelandic Hammrammr – can change into any animal that it has just eaten, getting more powerful each time

- The Nahaul of Mexico – can turn itself into a wolf, bull, eagle or big cat
- The Russian Wawkalak – surprisingly friendly werewolves, who lick hands instead of biting them!

But of all the shapeshifters around, the werewolf is the most well-known. Legends and stories go way back in time. In ancient Greece some doctors believed that people could change into wolves. The famous Greek historian Herodotus (480–425 BC) wrote about a tribe of people in north-eastern Europe called the Neuri who, he said, could change themselves into wolves once a year. In Greek myth, Zeus, the ruler of all the Greek gods, decided to punish King Lycaon by turning him into a wolf.

King Lycaon gets barking mad . . .

The legends persisted. In the Middle Ages, people had very strong beliefs in the power of witchcraft, magic and the Devil. It was commonly thought that those humans who were secretly werewolves had hair on the *inside* of their skin. The idea was that the person somehow turned themselves 'inside out' when they changed into a wolf! People could quite easily be accused of being a werewolf and sent to trial. It might sound silly to us now, but a few hundred years ago, it was nothing to laugh about. Mainly because the only way to find out for sure if someone was a secret werewolf was to cut open the person to see if they were hairy on the inside! That's a 'furry' bad result for the suspect!

Those people thought to be werewolves often endured horrible fates. In France in the sixteenth and seventeenth centuries, thousands of people were sent to trial, tortured and burned at the stake. Many were innocent of any wrongdoing – though some did admit to committing crimes as 'wolves'.

Wolves or Men?

In 1521 two men called Burgot and Verdum were sent to their deaths after they confessed to rubbing themselves with 'magic ointment' (see page 193), turning into hairy wolves and killing several people. In another incident, in 1603, a man named Jean Grenier admitted that he had killed several people while in the shape of a wolf. He had a special wolfskin that apparently turned him into a beast.

Similarly, in Germany, a man called Peter Stubbe was executed in 1589 when he was found guilty of killing hundreds of people. He also said that he had turned himself into a wolf by putting on a wolfskin belt.

Was there any truth in all this shapeshifting – or was it just an excuse for murder? These cases happened so long ago we will probably never know.

But can belts and skins turn people into wolves? Some legends say so – and there are many other reasons why you might accidentally become a werewolf. To help you avoid them, I have compiled a handy checklist.

How to become a werewolf:

- Have you been bitten by any furry, ferocious beasts recently? According to just about every book, movie and TV programme made on the subject, the most common way of becoming a werewolf is to get bitten by one
- Have you ever slept outdoors under a full moon?
- Were you born on a Friday when there was a full moon?
- Have you ever drunk water from a footprint made by a wolf?
- Are you the youngest of seven children?
- Do you ever wear a skin or a belt made of wolfskin?
- Do you ever rub magic ointment onto your body? These special ointments are thought to contain magical plants like belladonna and henbane
- Have you ever been cursed?

If any of the above sound familiar, then watch out (or perhaps your family and friends should)!

The Beast of Gévaudan

A well-known story from France describes how, in 1764, about 40 people were savagely killed and more than 100 injured by an unknown wild creature, or creatures. The attacks happened over several years in the mountainous province of Gévaudan. Those who saw the beast said it was a reddish wolf-like creature, as large as a cow and a very fast runner.

A woman tries to fight back against the beast.

Three years after the first attack, a massive wolf was found and shot by a hunter, using a silver bullet. The wolf's body was paraded through the village, but rumours flew around that the beast was *not* actually the real killer. People thought that the guilty creature had been hidden by the authorities – because it had turned back into its human form, and they didn't want anyone to know who it was! Meanwhile, the attacks stopped and the people of Gévaudan could breathe easily again. Today a statue remembering the beast's victims still stands in the town but the mystery remains, well, a mystery.

Fewer werewolf sightings seem to be reported these days. However, a couple more modern stories might give you something to think about . . .

The Bray Road Beast

In the quiet countryside of Wisconsin, USA, several sightings of a large hairy wolf-like creature walking on its hind legs were reported in the late 1980s. According to those who saw it, the 'Beast' had long claws, yellow eyes and a terrifying stare. It was rather whiffy too – whenever it was spotted there seemed to be a nasty smell around! One witness – a young lady who saw it loping down the road – said it was a 'very powerful, fast runner'. And as yet no one has identified the mystery monster . . .

The Morbach Monster

Stories say that the town of Wittlich in Germany is haunted by a werewolf, who is supposed to be the ghost of a soldier from the time of Napoleon. He deserted the army and killed a farmer and his wife. Before she died, the wife cursed the soldier and now, at every full moon, he becomes a werewolf. But the villagers keep a shrine and a candle lit just outside the town to protect them. Legend has it that if the candle ever goes out, the werewolf will return . . .

In 1988 a group of men working for the US military were on the way to their jobs at Morbach (an air force base just outside the town) when they noticed that the candle had gone out. They all joked about the monster then went about their work.

Late that night, an alarm went off at the perimeter fence of the base and the men went to investigate. One of them said he saw a huge 'dog-like' animal stand up on its back legs, stare at him, and then jump directly over the two-metre-high fence. A military tracker dog was brought to the fence and found the creature's scent – but the dog absolutely refused to follow it. Was it fear of the werewolf that stopped him?

Full Moon Madness

Every werewolf story begins with a full moon. So what's so mysterious about the moon?

The Moon: big, bright – and bewitching

A full moon has long been connected with changes in behaviour – even madness. In the past, people suffering from mental illness were said to behave strangely, even violently, when the moon came into its full phase. This gave us the word 'lunatic', which comes from 'lunar' – to do with the moon. (A more recent theory is that the patients behaved strangely because they were exhausted – the moon was so bright when it was full, that they simply couldn't get to sleep!)

Scientists know that something called gravitational pull exists between the Earth and the Moon. This force influences large bodies of water, particularly the movement of the tides on Earth.

Some people believe that gravitational pull must have a similar effect on humans. They think that because our bodies and brains are 80 per cent water, the Moon could influence our behaviour – especially when it is full. There is no scientific proof for this theory – but that doesn't stop lots of people believing it.

MY MISSION

To find a real werewolf! But where? Maybe I should go to places where there are still wolves roaming wild. Many wolf populations have died out over the years but in some parts of the world like the forests of Alaska and the Arctic tundra, wolves do still live in the wild. But what would I do if I found one? I'd better work out how to deal with it . . .

How to Get Rid of a Werewolf

After extensive research, I have compiled this handy – and hopefully foolproof – guide. If you ever find yourself up against a werewolf, do one of the following:

- Stab the wolf three times in the head with a knife
- Kneel in one spot for a hundred years (er – wouldn't you both be dead by then? I suppose that's one way of getting rid of a werewolf!)
- Find a wolfsbane plant. The only problem is that humans can't touch it – it is deadly poisonous to us. But it is hated by werewolves and is thought to act as a kind of 'wolf repellent'. Some think wolfsbane can even kill a werewolf

Wolfsbane – deadly to wolves and humans.

- Throw something made of iron at the wolf
- Some say that you need to get three drops of the wolf's blood. When the blood falls on the ground, the wolf should turn straight back into a human
- And last of all, the best-known and most effective solution – shoot it with a silver bullet. This should definitely rid you of a troublesome wolf

KIT LIST

I know exactly what I need to get – but buying these items from my local shops is proving tricky. There's not a silver bullet to be found anywhere. The local garden centre doesn't sell wolfsbane – and I can't touch it anyway. I'm not keen on doing 100 years of kneeling (even with knee pads on) and it's too dangerous to carry a knife. Werewolf hunters in movies don't seem to have this problem . . .

So what am I left with? Something made of iron . . . let me think. How about:

An Iron!

Maybe a household iron – as in, the thing you use to get creases out of clothes – would work!

It's all I've got, quite frankly, which is why I'm lugging a rather heavy carrier bag containing my iron (plus lead and plug). If nothing else, it will certainly make quite a dent in the werewolf's head if I throw it really hard . . .

MISSION COMPLETED

Silly me – I didn't need to go all the way to the Arctic tundra to find a wolf. I simply did the obvious thing – waited for the next full moon. Then it was time to go out on my werewolf hunt, iron at the ready.

At one point while walking nervously along a dark road, I heard a low, growling noise coming from round the corner. Then I saw a shadow looming – a shadow of a hairy beast! I got ready with my iron. Then round the corner came . . . a man walking a large shaggy dog. At that point I gave up and went home. Where's a werewolf when you need one? Perhaps they're all on 'howliday'?

WHAT DO YOU THINK?

Hopefully, by now you will have ruled out the possibility that you are a werewolf (I certainly have) and can turn your mind to the big question. Have werewolves ever existed?

Werewolves Don't Exist

There are several possible explanations for wolf myths – which one do you think is the most likely?

1. Fear of Animals

If you don't believe that werewolves exist, that's fair enough. But why are there so many stories about them? Where did they come from, if not from reality?

Some people think that that the whole werewolf myth springs from fear. Hundreds of years ago, wolves were much more of a threat to people than they are now. Imagine if you were living in a small village near a forest. You (and any livestock you owned) would be under constant threat of attack by roaming packs of hungry wolves. Wolves would have been a hot topic of conversation, creatures to be feared and dreaded.

And it's not just wolves. It's interesting that shapeshifting stories of humans turning into animals such as tigers, bears and foxes seem to exist in every culture. Is this because they are all about the real threat of local animals in times past?

Another theory is that people (deep down, maybe without even realizing it themselves) wish for the power that a particular animal has and want to experience it – hence their desire to change into a powerful tiger or a running wolf or a soaring eagle in flight. Who wouldn't want those kinds of powers?

Could human fears and wishes be at the root of all these

fantastic stories? Let's face it, they are great stories – which is why we're still telling them now!

2. Sickness and Disease

Just as with vampires, some think that the idea of werewolves has grown out of hideous diseases that have affected people over the centuries. The most obvious 'wolf sickness' is called lycanthropy. This is a weird one.

Lycanthropy is a mental illness in which a person believes that he/she has actually turned into a wolf (though they haven't actually grown any fur or sprouted big teeth). The disease was first noted in the seventh century, when victims were seen running about on four legs, barking and howling . . . literally 'barking mad'! It could certainly explain many of the past strange cases of people believing they have changed into wolves and killed people.

Another disease that could make people behave like a wolf is rabies, a virus which attacks the brain and nervous system and which could also be an explanation for vampire-like behaviour (see page 183). The disease makes people very feverish and aggressive and they can behave like crazed wild animals. They don't, however, grow fur . . . unlike the final 'wolf sickness' (also the strangest) – a rare condition called hypertrichosis.

Sufferers of hypertrichosis grow hair pretty much everywhere, even all over their face and hands. This can make someone look like a living wolf-man! In fact, years ago, the victims of this hair-raising condition were often forced to make a living by becoming part of a freak show, for people to gasp and stare at (once they'd paid their money, of course).

A wolf-like appearance – but just the results of a rare condition

Could the idea of werewolves have come from seeing people who had some of these conditions?

3. Wolf Poison

In Europe, during the Middle Ages, it's fair to say that health and safety wasn't what it is today. You could travel in an open cart without a seatbelt on (gasp!), no one picked up their animals' poo or even cared about the state of playground equipment (probably because there wasn't any at that time).

There were, however, outbreaks of food poisoning. Some of the more serious cases were caused by a fungus called ergot, which grew on a grain called rye. Rye was used to make bread and the people who ate the infected bread were poisoned. The disease – called St Anthony's Fire because of the awful burning sensation it produced – badly affected the brain. Symptoms included grunting, shaking and violent behaviour. It also caused terrible hallucinations which made some of the victims think that they were turning into an animal!

Bread poisoning was quite widespread, affecting whole towns and communities – could its victims have been mistaken for werewolves?

Werewolves Do Exist

So – what is the evidence for the existence of werewolves? There isn't really any. We have no film of a real person changing into a wolf. We have no photographs. And the last time I looked, there weren't a whole lot of werewolves on the loose being reported on in the news.

What we do have, though, are many fantastic stories, myths and legends – plus some very entertaining movies and TV shows. So, if you're the kind of person who believes that myths and legends really do have an element of truth in them, perhaps you do believe that werewolves exist? Or maybe you've actually seen a 'furry fiend' with your own eyes? If so, we need to know about it!

If you're a werewolf believer, you'll probably be keeping an eye out for anyone you know showing signs of 'werewolfness'. According to legend, these signs could be: extremely hairy hands, eyebrows that meet in the middle, hair on the palms of the hands or even hair in the ears. (So probably the best way of protecting yourself is to spend a lot of time with bald people . . .)

YOU DECIDE

So are werewolves a lot of nonsense, or do you shiver and shake on the night of a full moon? Only *you* can decide what you think is the truth about werewolves.

To the back of the book you go!

WANT TO KNOW MORE?

If you want to find out more about some of these intriguing creatures, try these books and websites:

Graphic Mysteries: Bigfoot and other strange beasts – Rob Shone (Book House)

You can't scare me! A guide to the strange and supernatural (Tick Tock Entertainment)

The Vampire Book – Sally Regan (Dorling Kindersley)

Can Science Solve? The Mystery of Vampires and Werewolves – Chris Oxlade (Heinemann)

Beastly Tales: Yeti, Bigfoot and the Loch Ness Monster – Malcolm Yorke (Dorling Kindersley)

My Quest for the Yeti: Confronting the Himalayas' deepest mystery – Reinhold Messner (Pan Macmillan)

www.nessie.co.uk – Lots of information about the Loch Ness monster, including latest sightings, evidence, stories and news

www.nationalgeographic.com – Great for all kinds of information about the world. You can search the site for their view on the creatures in this book

ALIEN ENCOUNTERS

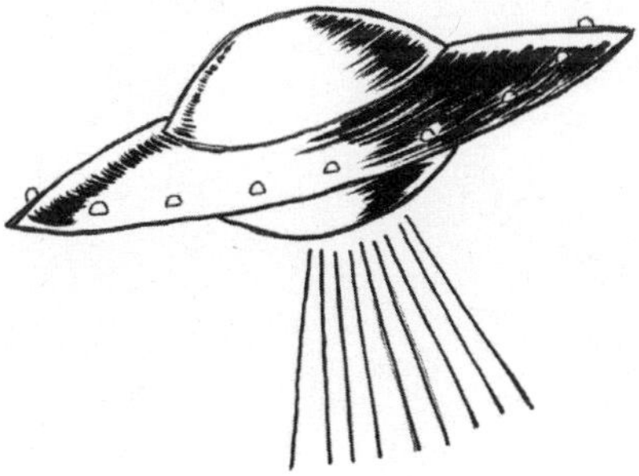

MYSTERY 1

The UFO enigma

THE MISSION . . .

. . . to find out the truth about Unidentified Flying Objects . . .

BURNING QUESTIONS

- Could UFOs be spaceships controlled by aliens?
- Are they natural phenomena?
- Why are they here?

MISSION DETAILS

What is a 'UFO' exactly? It's just what it says it is – a flying object that hasn't been identified. Now, there are a lot of 'objects' soaring around in the skies, and in space. Satellites, aeroplanes, birds, meteors, helicopters, weather balloons, even space junk (that's rubbish which has been left by humans to float around in space). As we know what these objects are, let's call them 'Identified Flying Objects' (IFOs).

But the really intriguing flying objects are the other kind – the UNIDENTIFIED ones. We have no idea what they are – or where they come from . . .

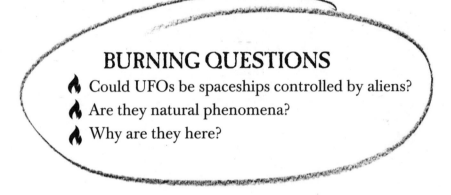

UFOs can appear as glowing balls of light hovering in the air, metallic saucers whizzing through the clouds or triangular vessels blasting through the skies.

The classic UFO – can't think why they're often called 'flying saucers'!

Sightings have been reported by members of the public and by pilots for many years.

THE LOCATION

Anywhere! Just look up into the sky and you've got as good a chance as anyone else of spotting a UFO. They can appear at any time, in any part of the world. So keep looking up at the skies if you want to see one for yourself (but, obviously, try not to walk into a lamppost).

UFOs can come in all shapes and sizes. Saucer-, sphere-, diamond-, cigar- and triangle-shaped objects have all been reported. Some UFOs have glowing lights. All of them fly. Different speeds have been reported, but many are said to move *really* fast – much faster than an aeroplane. Some UFOs hover around for a bit, then whizz away. Others perform impressive moves and turns, almost as if they're showing off to an audience.

THE EVIDENCE

Look back to ancient times and you'll find reports of strange unidentified objects in the skies from all over the world. A fourth-century Chinese manuscript talks of a 'moon boat' that appears every twelve years. In 217 BC ancient Romans saw what they described as shiny round 'shields' flying around in the sky. In 1211 a man called Gervase of Tilbury wrote of a floating ship appearing in the sky and later vanishing. And throughout history, mysterious flying objects have been depicted in great works of art.

It's behind you! This fifteenth-century Madonna has a close encounter with a spiky UFO – or is it a conker? (Madonna with Saint Giovannino – Domenico Ghirlandaio)

During the Second World War, bemused fighter pilots reported seeing glowing balls of light flying close to their planes. They even named them – *foo fighters*. (Years later, a rock group liked the name so much, they 'borrowed' it!)

The weird spheres whizzed and bobbed around and were like nothing the pilots had ever seen before. At first, Allied pilots thought they might be some kind of secret enemy weapons. But when the war was over, it was discovered that German pilots had also witnessed the 'foo fighters' – and they too thought they were enemy missiles! Both sides were wrong. No one ever worked out what the glowing balls were and they remain a mystery to this day . . .

Dancing Discs

Let's go back to 1947, when the world went UFO-crazy. It all started in June, when an American pilot called Kenneth Arnold had a very strange experience. While flying a plane over the Cascade Mountains in Washington, USA, a flash of light caught his eye at a height of about 3,000 metres. Arnold watched, fascinated, as nine shining, disc-shaped objects flew in formation through the clouds, not far from his plane. They were moving incredibly fast. He even timed them, later working out that the objects must have been travelling at a speed of 2,700 kilometres per hour – unbelievably fast and way beyond the ability of any plane that existed at the time!

Arnold was sure that the shiny objects were not made by humans. He said they moved like 'saucers skipping on water'.

It was from this description that the phrase 'flying saucers' began to be used, especially by the newspapers, who were reporting the story all over the world.

So why should we believe Kenneth Arnold? He was inter viewed by US Military Intelligence and found to be a reliable witness and an intelligent, sensible man – not really the kind of person who goes around making up stories about seeing spooky spaceships. To this day, people have tried to find logical explanations for what Arnold saw – raindrops, pelicans, meteors and snowy mountain peaks have all been suggested – but to no avail. The Arnold case is still stored away in a file marked UNEXPLAINED.

Kenneth Arnold keeps a lookout in case more UFOs turn up . . .

The UFO Explosion

Just a few days after Kenneth Arnold's sighting, an airline crew spotted more discs in the skies over Idaho. And in early July, eight circular objects were seen whizzing around in the skies of Tulsa, Oklahoma. They weren't the only ones. All in all, hundreds of UFO sightings were reported across the USA. What was happening? Was the USA being invaded by hordes of alien spaceships – or had people's imaginations been sparked by Arnold's story?

Among all these sightings was the famous Roswell Incident of July 1947, when a spaceship was thought to have crashed into the desert (for more on this mystery, see page 233).

© GETTY IMAGES

The glowing lights of Tulsa – just one of many UFO sightings in 1947.

Since 1947, many hundreds of UFOs have been spotted by witnesses around the world. Here are just a couple of stories that stand out . . .

The Lubbock Lights

This was the name given to some strange lights that were seen in the skies over Lubbock, Texas, in August and September 1951.

These shining lights were seen by many people, over three different nights. They flew in a V-shape and looked like bright, shining pearls. Some witnesses reported seeing eight or so lights, others as many as 30. All agreed that they moved incredibly fast, passing through the sky in a matter of seconds. A teenager called Carl Hart Jr managed to take some photographs of the weird lights (see the next page). The snaps showed eighteen to twenty mysterious objects flying in a neat formation.

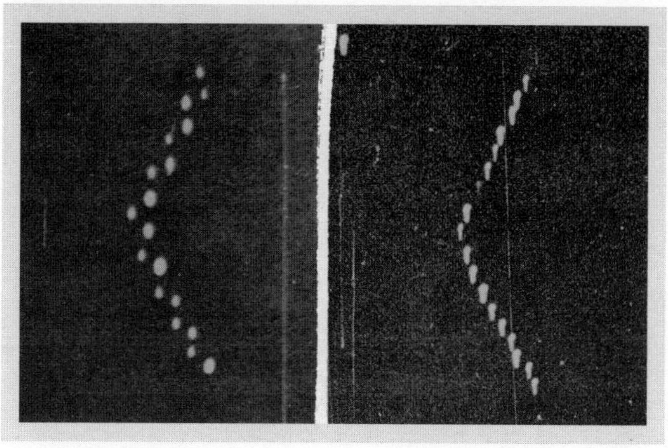

© BETTMAN/CORBIS

Carl Hart Jr's snap of the Lubbock lights – could they be birds – or something stranger . . . ?

To this day, no one has an explanation for the Lubbock lights. At first it was thought they were lights from planes, but investigations at the nearby air-force base revealed that no planes were flying on the nights that the lights were spotted. Strange . . .

A later report said that they must have been birds with 'street lights reflecting from them'. This explanation came from the first ever official UFO report – Project Blue Book.

Project Blue Book

With files literally bursting with UFO sightings, it was time for the authorities to launch a proper investigation. Project Blue Book, as it was named, would look at every report of alien contact and UFO sighting in the USA. It wasn't a small job. More than 12,000 cases were investigated between 1948 and 1969 – 21 years. Well, no one can say that they didn't spend enough time on it . . .

Most sightings were said to be no more than clouds, birds, lightning, weather balloons or similar (boring) explanations. But that still left the cases the authorities *couldn't* explain – a whopping 700 of them. Those pesky UFOs just wouldn't go away . . .

Believe It or Not!

It wasn't just the USA that kept detailed files of UFO sightings. The United Kingdom did the same. And in 2011 these 'Top Secret' files from the Ministry of Defence were opened up to the public for the first time. They revealed 8,500 pages of UFO sightings, photographs and drawings sent in by the public. A staggering 11,000 UFO reports had been logged between 1959 and 2007. Some of the sightings were bizarre – one woman said she had seen a dome-shaped object landing and was then measured by two tall figures dressed in silver!

Others were less than convincing. One man told the authorities that he had seen a cigar-shaped UFO hovering above his house. He was sure that he must have been kidnapped by aliens. Why? Because he noticed that he had gained an extra hour of time and couldn't understand why. (These kinds of 'time-slips' are sometimes described by those who say they have been taken to a spaceship.) However, the report 'deduced' that the clocks had gone back that night! Duh!

Another report described a major 'alien alert' that happened in 1967. On the morning of 4 September the police and RAF were bombarded with calls from members of the public who had seen six saucers flying in a perfect line across southern England

The authorities moved fast. Four police forces, a bomb-disposal unit, the army and intelligence officers were alerted, steeling themselves for a possible alien invasion. A military helicopter was despatched to intercept the possibly hostile flying extra-terrestrials.

It wasn't until the bomb-disposal squad found one of the 'UFO's on the ground and realized it was a fake that the whole thing was revealed to be a massive practical joke. Some engineering students from Farnborough Technical College had made the flying saucers as part of their college Rag Week. I expect the army, police and bomb-disposal squad were rolling about on the floor laughing at that one . . .

But even allowing for silly jokes, hoaxes and mistakes, just like America's Project Blue Book, the British files revealed many cases where no explanation at all could be found. And those cases are still open . . .

TRACKING THE TRIANGLE

Sometimes it's hard to be sure if a person's story is true or not. But when several witnesses see the same thing, it's a different matter.

On 29 November 1989 many people living in northern Belgium reported seeing a large triangular shape with lights underneath it

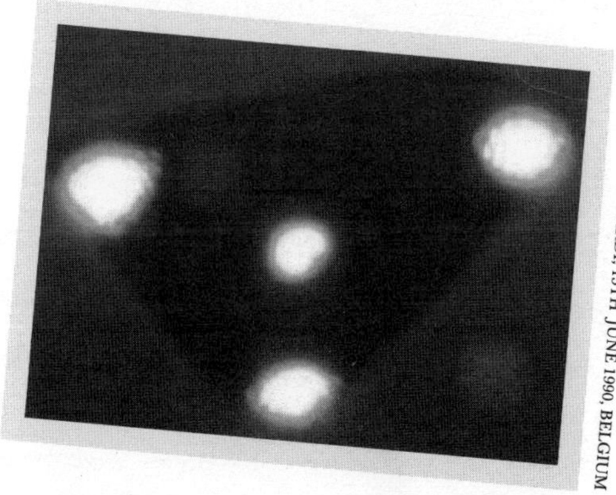

moving across the sky. Its progress was tracked by locals and the police from the Belgian city of Liège across to the borders with Germany and the Netherlands.

Sightings continued up until April 1990, and the low-flying craft was seen hundreds of times. At one point, the mysterious shape appeared on radar screens at Belgian air-force bases. It was chased by fighter planes, but the weird craft kept changing direction and disappeared before it could be properly investigated. The pilots and air-force staff said that it had reached the most incredible speeds. No one has ever got to the bottom of the triangular phenomenon and it remains a complete mystery.

THE RENDLESHAM INCIDENT

On a dark night in December 1980 strange moving lights were seen above Rendlesham Forest in Suffolk, England. US Air Force personnel who were stationed nearby came to investigate the mysterious lights, thinking that a plane might have crashed nearby. They found burn marks on the trees and ground, and broken branches strewn around – but no plane.

The following night, more mysterious lights were seen by several witnesses. One of them, Colonel Halt, has since gone on to say he believes that the lights he saw were 'extra-terrestrial in origin' – in other words, made by aliens. He described one of the lights as looking like a large moving red eye. It apparently separated into several small white objects that flew off in different directions. Would you have hung around to get an eyeful of that?

Later, one of the servicemen who had also witnessed the incident, a Sergeant Jim Penniston, claimed to have seen – and touched – an actual spacecraft in the woods. He even made a sketch of what it looked like – a triangular craft with writing on the side that looked a bit like Egyptian hieroglyphics. However, none of the other witnesses could back up Penniston's sighting, and the spacecraft itself was never found.

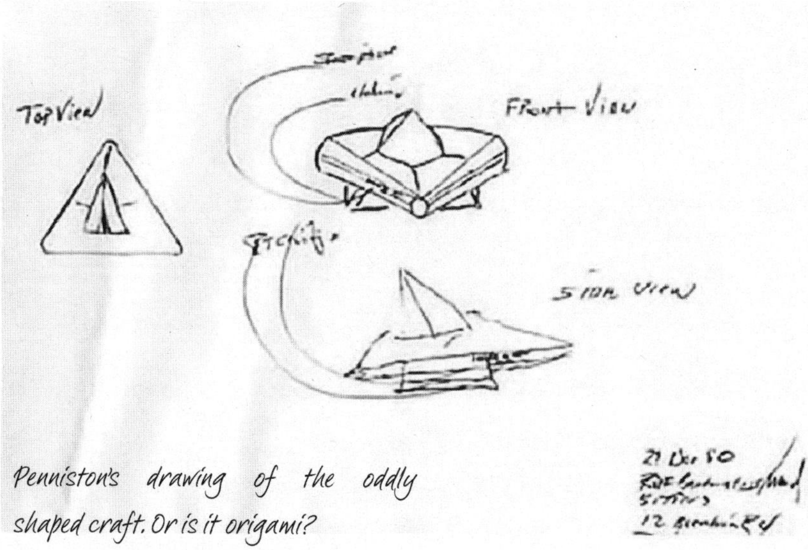

Penniston's drawing of the oddly shaped craft. Or is it origami?

Some UFO researchers believe that the Rendlesham sightings, which took place over two nights, are classic examples of 'close encounters' – real-life encounters with alien spacecraft.

Even stranger, all the files and documents about the Rendlesham incident have since disappeared from the Ministry of Defence Archives. Some believe that the case was covered up by the authorities and the files hidden from the public. In fact, some people believe that the truth about UFOs and aliens is being covered up by governments all around the world . . .

The Men in Black

The Men in Black mystery was around years before Will Smith landed his part in the blockbuster movie. Since the 1950s, stories have been told in the USA of anonymous figures dressed in smart black suits who turn up uninvited at the homes of people who have reported UFO sightings.

Unlike Will Smith, these MIBs don't do funky rapping.

Men in Black – smart but sinister . . .

They are seriously scary. Their job is to 'warn' witnesses to stay quiet about their UFO experiences. But why?

Some people believe that MIBs are mysterious government agents who are being sent out to keep top-secret information, well, top secret . . .

Others think that they are actually aliens sent to Earth to keep humans quiet about alien and UFO activity they have witnessed.

Wherever these sharp-suited figures come from, many UFO believers are convinced that the Men in Black really exist. So if you ever see a UFO and report it, don't be too surprised if you hear a knock at your door . . . and if you do, don't look at their pen; you'll forget everything. Or maybe you already have . . . ?

MY MISSION

Just how will I find a UFO? Well, it's going to be tricky. As I said earlier, you never know where or when an unidentified flying object might appear. The important thing is to be ready and waiting . . .

So I have decided to go on 'UFO Watch', using the loft of my house as a mini space observatory. I'm going to need some gadgets . . .

KIT LIST

LARGE WINDOW – for maximum viewing of the skies

CAMERA WITH SUPER-ZOOM LENS ON A TRIPOD – for capturing the evidence at first hand; a sturdy tripod mount will minimize image shake

CAMCORDER WITH DIGITAL ZOOM – to record a moving UFO

TELESCOPE – a top-of-the range refracting astronomical telescope with slow-motion controls, to help keep any fast-moving UFOs in focus

COMFY SWIVEL CHAIR – well, there's no point being uncomfortable, plus you can whizz around really fast to catch a glimpse of something interesting

PHONE – to contact friends/witnesses

LOGBOOK AND PEN – to make detailed notes of sightings

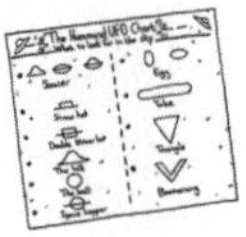

UFO ID CHART – a reference for the various shapes of UFOs

SMALL JAR AND SPOON – for taking soil samples at the site of a suspected UFO landing

I've got a few more ideas to help make my search as effective as possible:

TOP TIPS FOR UFO WATCHERS

1. If you can, ask some friends to join you on UFO Watch – or have them on autocall to get round to your place ASAP. Why? Because UFO reports are so much more believable when there are lots of witnesses to the event. It means you'll get taken seriously, and not laughed at. Which can happen. Trust me.
2. If you do see a UFO, naturally you'll be very excited. But try to stay calm and focused. Get evidence by taking a photograph or a film of the object. Try to include other things in the picture – buildings, planes, people; anything close by that will give an idea of the size, location and scale of your UFO.
3. It's important to make notes of as many details as possible. Directly after you've witnessed the UFO, write down the

exact time and how long you viewed it for. Describe the UFO – its shape, size, colour and estimated speed. Did the UFO have lights? Did it move around in an unusual way or change direction?

All this information is vital, so make notes while everything is still fresh in your mind. Why not draw a sketch of your UFO too?

MISSION COMPLETED

After several nights on 'UFO Watch' I've become something of an amateur astronomer and have spent hours viewing the crater-ridden surface of the Moon through my hi-tech telescope. Fascinating stuff. But did I see any UFOs? Well – I'm just not sure.

At 23:22 hours on the second night I caught sight of a glowing light moving through the night sky. It was fast – and very far away in the distance. The light was a yellowish colour and it left a slight trail behind it, which soon faded away.

I moved quickly, called my friends, but the light disappeared after two or three seconds – not enough time to get that vital shot or for my witnesses to do any witnessing. But I did make those all-important detailed notes in my logbook. (Pat on the back to me.)

So what could my mysterious object have been? It may well have been a shooting star – but there's always the chance that it could have been a genuine UFO. Another case for the MoD files . . .

WHAT DO YOU THINK?

So now it's up to you. What do you think is at the bottom of the UFO mystery? Here are your choices:

1. UFOs are Sent by Aliens

As we've seen, many UFOs do have logical explanations, whether it is a bird, a plane or just a trick of the light. But there are always a small number of cases that just *cannot* be explained. In about five to ten per cent of UFO cases, the flying object remains a mystery. These are the ones that could be genuine UFOs – by that, I mean objects that have come from other planets or worlds.

We've also seen that UFOs are not that hard to fake – all you need is a camera, a home-made 'saucer', a blurry shot, and you've got yourself a pretty convincing photo. There's no doubt that the world of UFOs definitely has more than its fair share of hoaxes. But even so, how can cases such as the Belgian UFO sightings of 1989 be explained? It's difficult to see how hundreds of people – including the police – who all saw exactly the same thing, at the same time, could be fooled.

Let's look at the descriptions of UFOs themselves. They don't seem like anything made by humans. Most of them look unlike any kind of human craft and they move in a completely different way. Often they travel faster than any plane could manage. Is this proof that something non-human is behind them?

Some think that UFOs might be a kind of hi-tech device, remotely controlled by intelligent aliens. Perhaps they are using the devices to study humans and make notes about our strange species? If so, I wonder what conclusions they've come to?

The suggestion has even been made that UFOs are not spacecraft, but some kind of portal or 'wormhole' in our universe – a connection between different areas of space and time. Intelligent aliens – and they would have to be a whole lot cleverer than us – could maybe have worked out how to use wormholes to travel to different parts of the universe. A bit like the Tardis in *Doctor Who*. Which is definitely a VUFO – that's a 'Very Unusual Flying Object'!

But if UFOs *do* contain aliens, why haven't they let us know? Wouldn't it make sense not to be so secretive and to try and communicate with us properly? What are the aliens trying to hide?

Whatever you think, there's no doubt that many people truly believe that UFOs are connected to aliens. Some even spend their time researching UFO evidence. They call themselves Ufologists. They take it extremely seriously, even though Ufology is not accepted as a proper science.

But, as yet, even the Ufologists have not managed to come up with a real UFO, or a part of a UFO, or any other piece of evidence that would prove the link to aliens.

Is it a bird? Is it a plane . . . ? Doesn't look much like either to me. How do you explain this UFO spotted in New Jersey, USA?

2. UFOs are All Explainable

There are many people who think that all UFO sightings can be explained by perfectly rational and logical reasons.

Apart from the usual birds and planes, there is another idea about what could be behind UFOs – and it doesn't involve aliens. It is a natural phenomenon called 'ball lightning'. Ball lightning definitely exists, but for years scientists have found it very difficult to explain.

It isn't like normal lightning. It appears as balls of electricity, fizzing with energy; apparently it looks like glowing tennis balls that dance and spin around in unexpected ways. The balls vibrate, produce sparks, and can even burn or melt nearby objects. They sometimes make a strange hissing noise and often appear during a thunderstorm.

Goodness gracious! Great balls of fire! This 1886 print proves that ball lightning is not a recent phenomenon.

How does it happen? One theory is that when lightning strikes certain surfaces, a vapour is formed. This vapour then condenses and mixes with oxygen in the air to slowly burn – which produces the weird ball effect.

It's easy to see how ball lightning could be the explanation for the 'foo fighters' of the Second World War and the many other strange glowing lights seen by people over the years. But how does it explain the different shapes of craft spotted by UFO witnesses – the ones that don't look like balls of light? Many of these have been seen flying in formation – could ball lightning really form itself into a neat triangle or V-shape?

Other explanations put forward for UFOs include meteors, also known as 'shooting stars'. When tiny rocks burn up in Earth's atmosphere, they create a fast-moving streak of light, which can be seen trailing across the night sky. Meteors are more common than you might think – apparently, on most nights, several meteors cross our skies. Ever spotted one?

Clouds have also been mistaken for flying saucers, particularly an unusual type called a 'lenticular cloud'. (Guess what – it's shaped like a lentil, which is a convenient way of remembering a fancy word!) Take a look at this:

Have you ever seen a cloud like this? It's easy to see why people think it's a flying saucer . . .

There's also the possibility that people are seeing things that aren't there – maybe a trick of the light or a hallucination? It's no coincidence that sightings of UFOs suddenly increased after Kenneth Arnold's famous incident. Were people imagining things because they had read about his story? The human mind can behave in some very strange ways . . .

YOU DECIDE

UFOs definitely exist – but are they being sent by creatures from other worlds? Make up your mind and jot down your thoughts at the back of the book. Don't forget to keep scanning those skies for your own evidence.

MYSTERY 2

The Roswell Incident

THE MISSION . . .

. . . to find out if aliens have ever crash-landed on the Earth . . .

BURNING QUESTIONS

- Were aliens found in the US desert?
- Was the whole thing a cover-up?
- Just who is telling the truth?

MISSION DETAILS

In the summer of 1947 there was an accident in the desert in the state of New Mexico, USA. Nothing too unusual about that, you might think. But this incident was no ordinary one. It involved a speeding vehicle – but it wasn't a car. Many people believe that it was a spaceship. Steered by aliens. Which crashed into our planet. Here's a thought – perhaps they just couldn't find a parking meteor?!

There were witnesses to the crash, but no evidence. Some believe that this was because the military were told to quickly remove all signs of the accident.

Could a speeding spaceship really have hit our planet? Time to investigate . . .

THE LOCATION

This mystery is known, rather unimaginatively, as the Roswell Incident. Why? Because – yawn – it happened quite close to a city called Roswell. You know, just occasionally, I wish they'd think of more exciting names for these kinds of things – maybe the 'Exploding Spaceship Incident' or the 'Disappearing Aliens in the Desert Dilemma'? But for now, we're stuck with 'Roswell'.

Apart from the alien connection, Roswell is a fairly ordinary city located in the south-east of the state of New Mexico. The accident was said to have happened about 120 kilometres outside the city, in a quiet desert area.

Roswell also happens to be home to the New Mexico Military Institute – and the military play a large part in this story.

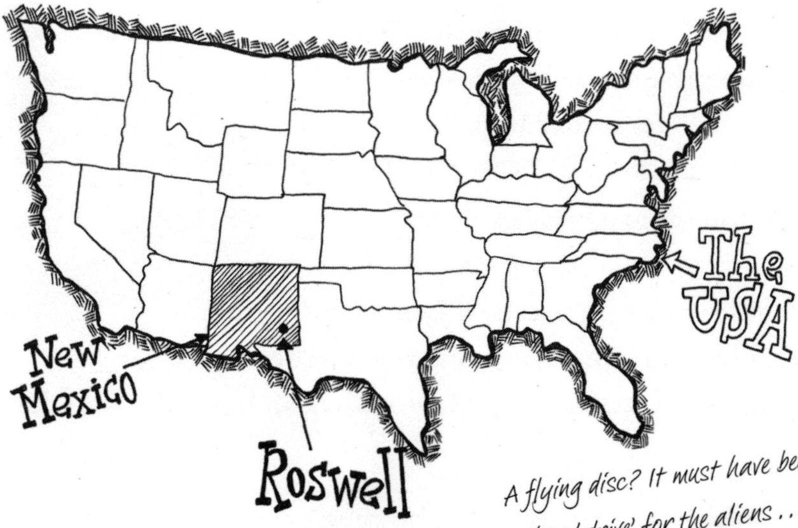

A flying disc? It must have been a 'hard drive' for the aliens . . .

THE EVIDENCE

Step forward our main witness – a rancher by the name of Mac Brazel. In June 1947 Mac rode out on his horse to check on his sheep (as you do if you're a sheep-owning rancher). As he trotted along, he noticed some strange-looking pieces of debris scattered around on the ground. He didn't think too much about them at the time, but later on, he wondered what the unusual bits and pieces might be. A couple of weeks later, he went back, picked some up and took them home.

It was weird stuff. Really strange. Apparently, there were pieces of what looked like thick tin foil – but it couldn't be torn, unlike normal tin foil. There were also what appeared to be pieces of wood with some weird, unknown writing on it. Mac and his family had never seen anything like it before.

There the story might have ended, had it not been for the fact that Kenneth Arnold's sighting of nine flying saucers was widely reported in the papers that week (see page 214). Like everyone else at the time, Mac heard the sensational news and wondered if the stuff he had found was somehow connected to the appearance of those shiny UFOs that Arnold had seen. He decided to show his find to the local sheriff.

The sheriff was mystified too, and together they contacted the authorities. A military investigator called Major Jesse Marcel came to Roswell to take a look at the scene. Soon after, all the debris was cleared away, leaving no trace of the incident.

Making the Headlines

The story didn't stay quiet for long. It was soon reported in the local paper that on 8 July US Military Intelligence had retrieved a 'flying disc' from the desert. This was incredible, world-changing news – a real flying saucer had actually been found! BUT the very next day the military changed their story. They said that it was all a big mistake and what had actually been found was a weather balloon. What a let-down!

How could the military have got this so wrong – surely a weather balloon couldn't be confused with a flying saucer? The sudden change in their story made people suspicious, and to this day, there are those who believe that the real truth was kept from the public.

Note: A weather balloon, by the way, is not your standard party balloon. It is a special kind of large balloon that is sent up into the atmosphere to retrieve information on temperature, wind speed, etc., to help make weather forecasts. It does not have HAPPY BIRTHDAY written on it.

More Witnesses Emerge

Strangely, in the same month, a Mr and Mrs Wilmot had been sitting outside on their porch in New Mexico, enjoying the peaceful evening. It was dark and quiet, but suddenly, out of the sky whizzed a glowing object. The Wilmots said it looked like two saucers glued together. Whatever it was, it had light glowing from inside and was moving incredibly fast (sound familiar?).

The Wilmots were pretty freaked out, and at first decided to keep the story to themselves – after all, they didn't want people thinking they were crazy. But they eventually broke their silence and told people what they had witnessed.

After the initial excitement, the story fizzled out. More than 30 years elapsed. That is, until 1978, when Major Jesse Marcel was interviewed – remember him? He was the intelligence officer who was sent to pick up the debris from the desert after Mac Brazel reported his find. Major Marcel admitted some very interesting things:

- The things that the military had found were like 'nothing made on this Earth'
- He described the 'foil' Mac had found as being like wafer-thin metal but incredibly tough. It was as light as balsa wood, but couldn't be cut or burned. Was it really a unique type of material made by aliens?

Following Marcel's revelations, 'Roswell Mania' erupted – magazine articles, TV programmes and books appeared, full of stories about aliens having visited Earth. More witnesses came forward and were interviewed. For example:

Lieutenant Walter Haut

Haut had been working at the military base in 1947 and he knew a lot about the case. After all, he was the person who issued the press releases following the crash. Haut died in 2005, but he left behind a signed written document –

with strict instructions that it was to be opened only after his death. What secrets did it contain?

As it happens, quite a lot. Among other exciting nuggets of information, Haut said:

- The weather-balloon story was a cover-up
- What had actually been found was an alien spacecraft. Haut had seen it with his own eyes, stored in an aircraft hangar called Building 84
- The craft was made of metal and shaped like an egg, around 4.5 metres long. There were no windows or doors on it
- On the floor were two bodies, partially covered. The bodies had very large heads and were only about 1.2 metres tall

Haut stated that he was convinced that what he'd seen was a craft from outer space and its (not very alive) alien occupants . . .

This was incredible . . .

Glenn Dennis

And there's more: in 1989 a man called Glenn Dennis (who used to be a mortician, so he knew a bit about dead bodies) came forward to say that he had been contacted by the authorities at Roswell shortly after the crash and asked to provide a number of 'child-sized' coffins. Weird . . .

Glenn made his way to the base, where he was apparently told by a nurse that she had seen the bodies of three small alien creatures. The nurse disappeared in mysterious circumstances soon afterwards, though some people have questioned whether she ever existed at all.

Area 51

Roswell isn't the only place where people suspect the authorities of hiding alien evidence. Area 51 is the name of a top-secret military base in the remote desert of Nevada, USA. It's so secret, we're probably not supposed to know it exists. And you can't visit – it's off-limits for everyone except certain military personnel and government officials.

Area 51 – the sign makes it pretty clear that you're not welcome . . .

We don't know what happens here, but UFO and alien believers have long suspected Area 51 of being a place where alien-related activities take place, away from the public gaze. Some theories about this are:

- It's where they hide crashed alien spacecraft
- It's a place where new technologies – such as time travel – are being developed, based on alien technology and information
- Meetings with aliens are held here

Stories about the mysterious Area 51 persist – wouldn't you just love to be a fly on the wall in that place?

THE SPY BALLOON STORY

Back to Roswell. It was time for a full investigation. Which is exactly what happened. In 1995 an official report finally came out. It confirmed that the crashed object definitely had been a weather balloon. So why all the secrecy? Well, this was no normal weather balloon. The report said that it was part of a top-secret government project called Project Mogul. Hi-tech, high altitude – and designed to detect sound waves from Russian nuclear bomb tests. In other words, it was a secret spy balloon! A sort of James Bond of the balloon world . . . having a real-life skyfall.

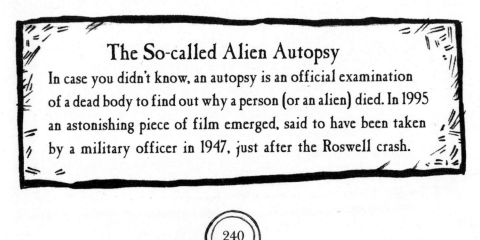

I've really let myself down

This would explain why all the debris was cleared away so quickly and why everything was kept so secret – the Americans didn't want the Russians to find out that they had been spying on them. Was this the real story behind Roswell? But despite this new information, the alien connection just wouldn't go away.

The So-called Alien Autopsy

In case you didn't know, an autopsy is an official examination of a dead body to find out why a person (or an alien) died. In 1995 an astonishing piece of film emerged, said to have been taken by a military officer in 1947, just after the Roswell crash.

It showed the body of what looked like a dead alien laid out on a table. With an over-sized head, large eyes and a small body – and twelve toes on each foot – it certainly looked like something out of this world. A person who looked like a surgeon, dressed in protective clothing, was performing an autopsy on the alien's body.

The film caused a sensation around the world. Here at last was *real evidence* – not only that aliens existed but that the authorities had kept the Roswell aliens secret for years. But questions remained. Why had the film been released only now? And how had Ray Santilli, the man who revealed the film to the public, got hold of it in the first place?

Here's a still from this remarkable movie. What do you think?

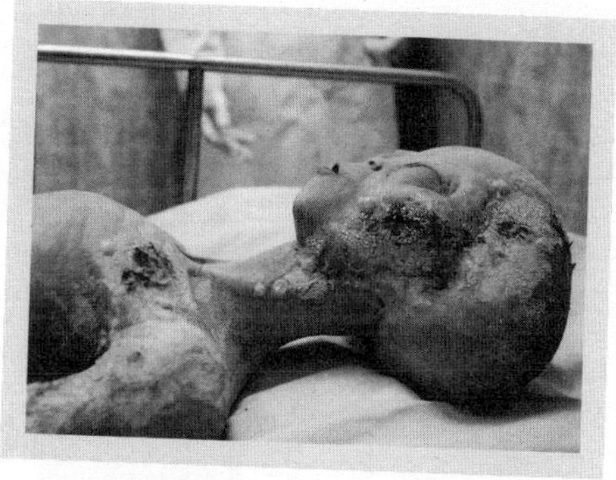

© PHOTO BEARD/ SHUTTERSTOCK

The Roswell alien – not looking in the best of health.

You can breathe out now – after much excitement and controversy, Ray Santilli later admitted that the film wasn't real He said it was supposed to be a 'reconstruction' of what could have happened in Roswell. Looking at it again, there were a couple of obvious signs. Such as:

- The alien looked like it was made of rubber
- The so-called 'surgeons' weren't holding their instruments properly, as real doctors would

Nevertheless, this piece of film remains one of the most convincing alien hoaxes of all time. And for a long time many people believed it was real! (Some probably still do . . .)

All of which proves that, these days, it's really not that hard to fake a piece of film. You just need a camera, some friends and an alien costume from a fancy-dress shop . . .

MY MISSION

A visit to the city of Roswell would be a good start. Roswell also boasts its own UFO Museum and Research Centre, so whatever happens, I can find out more about the case.

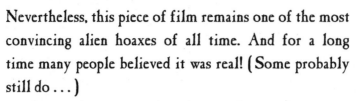

© ALEXY SHOP/ALAMY

Looks like the ideal place to find out about UFOs . . .

KIT LIST

FACTOR-50 SUN CREAM AND SUN HAT – Roswell is in the desert, so it will be hot, hot, hot

PLENTY OF WATER – don't want to dehydrate

WIDE-ANGLE BINOCULARS – for checking out the skies and the desert landscape

TWEEZERS – for picking up any bits of interesting debris

MAGNIFYING GLASS – for close-up examination

COLLECTION BOX – always best to keep any evidence for future use

ROSWELL INFORMATION BOOKS – there are lots of them, so I'll take a few to read on the plane

MISSION COMPLETED

I arrived at Roswell – hot, humid and jet-lagged – to find the entire city overrun by aliens! Had the original crash-landed aliens survived, settled down and had kids?

A closer inspection of the aliens revealed the truth. They were humans – dressed up in some pretty incredible outfits. It seems that, since the events of 1947, the city of Roswell has become the 'alien capital' of the world.

Even the local burger joint looks like a flying saucer!

And every year, in July, the town celebrates 'Alien Month' with a one-week festival. People dress up as aliens, there are parades, concerts, even puppet shows. Here are a few of the locals joining in with the festivities:

© KATHY BURNS - MILLYARD/ SHUTTERSTOCK

Greetings, Earth boy! Take me to your leader . . .

As my visit coincided with this festival, I felt in need of an alien costume to blend in with the locals. There was nothing left to hire so I made do with a pair of deely boppers, some green face paint and a last-minute sheet borrowed from my hotel room. Don't ask why I had the deely boppers and green face paint in my bag, I just did, OK?

Once the festivities were over, I hired a four-by-four, and drove out to the spot where the crash was supposed to have happened. As the site had been so thoroughly cleared all those years ago, I wasn't really expecting to find any debris or shiny foil. And guess what – I didn't. The desert stretched out for miles around Roswell, and there was no sign of any alien activity – just a lot of bushes. But bearing in mind that this all happened in 1947, it's probably not that surprising.

© RABH IMAGES/ ALAMY

The desert landscape – not a UFO, or even an IFO, in sight.

WHAT DO YOU THINK?

Let's look at the facts of the case:

1. Something crashed into the desert that day.
2. The military changed their account of what happened.

So you need to make a decision. Here are your choices:

1. The Object was an Alien Spaceship

There are several witnesses who are convinced that they saw real aliens, and even a real spaceship. But some think that Haut and other witnesses made everything up – perhaps to get attention or to make money from selling their story. But why would someone like Lieutenant Walter Haut, a respectable military man, make it up? And why would he have left his signed document to be read *after* his death? He would have gained nothing from it.

We also need to ask why Haut didn't reveal his sighting of the spacecraft and the aliens earlier in his life. But there's a simple explanation for that – he probably thought that people would laugh at him or think he was crazy. That's why he wanted the truth to come out after he was gone.

There's also the question of the debris that Mac Brazel found – did it come from a spy balloon or a spaceship? If only we had a piece of that 'tin foil', it could be tested to find out its origin. But we haven't, so we can't.

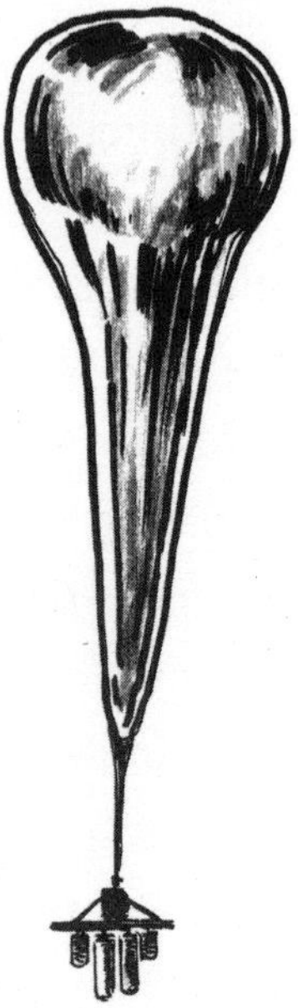

There's no doubt that the authorities have changed their story several times, which makes people very suspicious. And the military were clearly anxious to get rid of any traces of the accident. But were they trying to cover up the fact that aliens had been found or to keep their spying activities secret? Which is more likely?

Ask yourself:

- Do you believe the stories of the witnesses?
- Do you think that the strange debris came from an alien ship?
- Do you think that the authorities were trying to cover up an alien crash?

If you've answered 'yes' to all the above, then you are a Roswell alien believer!

2. The object was a Spy Balloon

The fact remains that no one has been able to come up with actual evidence, such as a chunk of alien spaceship or an authentic photo of one of the alien bodies, to prove that the crashed object was a spaceship. Surely there would still be a piece of the debris that was found in 1947 left to analyse? Or a photo of one of the aliens that isn't a hoax? But there is nothing.

But what about the bodies of aliens that people said they saw? A second US Air Force report in 1997 stated that the witnesses were mistaken. It said what they actually saw was probably human-shaped test dummies that were carried by the balloon for scientific research. Do you believe that people would mistake dummies for aliens?

Is it likely that the object that crashed was a spy balloon, as the government said? It's certainly true that in 1947, both the USA and Russia were keeping their scientists busy by developing atomic bomb technology. Both countries would have desperately wanted to know what their rivals were up to. It's plausible that the spy balloon was a top-secret project that went wrong – which is why the government sent the military in fast to clear up the mess.

Has the Roswell incident been blown up into much more than it should have been? Your call . . .

YOU DECIDE

If you think the alien story is true, then the Roswell crash is one of the most important scientific discoveries ever made. But if you believe the authorities, it's all a big mistake.

Whatever you think, more than 65 years on, it seems that the name 'Roswell' will always be associated with aliens, conspiracy and secrets. Head to the back of the book to note down your theory . . .

MYSTERY 3

The Nazca Lines

THE MISSION . . .

. . . to find out who – or what – drew hundreds of giant pictures on the ground.

BURNING QUESTIONS

- What do the drawings mean?
- Did aliens make them?
- Were they used as runways for alien astronauts?

MISSION DETAILS

I'm going in search of the Nazca Lines – a collection of mysterious lines and drawings which have had archaeologists baffled since they were discovered in the 1920s.

Why Are They So Puzzling?

1. They are really, really old. Experts think they were probably made between 400 and 650 AD.
2. Many of the lines and drawings are absolutely huge – some would fill a football stadium – even two! They can only be seen properly from a very high spot, preferably from a plane.

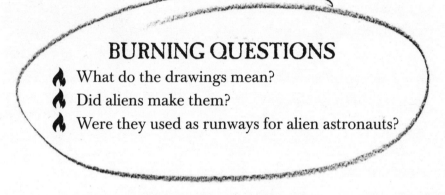

(And, in case you didn't know, planes hadn't been invented between 400 and 650 AD!)

3. No one is really sure who made them – and for what reason.

Actually, the name 'Nazca Lines' is slightly misleading because these amazing works of art are not just lines. There are also geometric shapes, trees, flowers, humans, a monkey, a spider, a hummingbird, fish, a jaguar, a lizard, a dog – even a killer whale! The largest drawing is a 285-metre pelican (I bet you've never seen one of those before!). All are really impressive and beautifully made.

© TRAVELPIX/ ALAMY

A 93-metre-long hummingbird soars across the desert floor.

How did the ancient people – or beings – who made them do such precise drawings on such a massive scale?

Let's go on the Nazca trail . . .

THE LOCATION

Sandwiched between the coast and the Andes mountain range of Peru lies the Nazca Desert. If you ever visit, take plenty of water, as this is one of the driest places in the world. In fact, the very dry atmosphere is one of the reasons why the Nazca Lines have survived intact for so many hundreds of years.

The part of the desert where the Nazca Lines are found is called the Pampa Colorada, an 80-kilometre-long plateau running parallel to the Pacific Ocean. Its name means the 'Red Plain', so called because the area is covered in reddish-brown stones.

THE EVIDENCE

The Nazca Lines are what's officially known as geoglyphs. If you've ever made a picture out of pebbles on the beach, you will have created your very own geoglyph – it's a piece of art made by arranging stones or earth on the ground.

The Nazca geoglyphs were spotted in the late 1920s, around the time that air travel started to become more common.

The lines are an amazing sight, and people come from all over the world to view the ancient wonder. There are hundreds of lines, triangles, quadrangles, zigzags and circles, as well as creatures of land, air and sea.

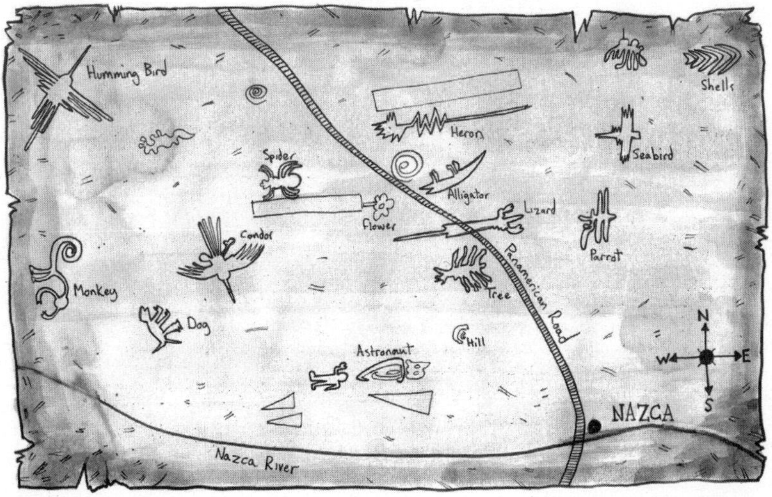

A map showing part of the virtual 'zoo' in the Nazca Desert.

How Were the Lines Made?

No paint or chalk was used to make the drawings – they have literally been scratched onto the ground. A closer inspection reveals that the reddish-brown stones on the desert surface have been skilfully cleared away to reveal the lighter soil underneath. Each line is up to 30 centimetres deep. It's as if the desert has been used as a giant drawing pad!

Now, if you've ever tried to paint a really big picture, you'll know just how difficult it is to get the size and scale right. How did these drawings get made so precisely when they were done so long ago – a time when people didn't have planes or computers or other modern technology to help? This is something that has been puzzling experts for a long time.

And as the best way to see the shapes is to fly above them, this has led to the suggestion that aliens might have been involved with their creation . . .

© KERREN SU/ CHINA SPAN/ ALAMY

Beware of the world's biggest spider!

Great Geoglyphs

The Nazca Lines are the most famous geoglyphs in the world, but there are many others.

- Among them is the 3,000-year-old Uffington Horse in Berkshire, England, a prehistoric drawing that was made by filling trenches with crushed chalk
- The mysterious Marree Man in South Australia was only discovered in 1998. It is massive – 4.2 kilometres high – and no one has any idea who made it or when
- The Atacama Giant is found in the Atacama Desert of Chile, where there are many other geometric and animal pictures – even a giant llama! The giant is 119 metres tall and is believed to have been made between 600 and 1500 AD
- There are also huge geoglyphs in Egypt, Malta, the United States (Mississippi and California) and Bolivia. Perhaps there are more waiting to be discovered . . . check the back garden

Looking into the Lines

Since the discovery of the Nazca Lines, teams of experts have travelled to the desert to investigate. There have been many ideas about what the lines could have been used for, from ancient racetracks to landing strips for aliens – more on all these later!

As you can see from the spider on page 252, most of the drawings are made from one single continuous line. The lines never cross each other, which some think may indicate that they were once used as pathways – perhaps for some kind of procession or ceremony?

Whatever they are, pretty much everyone agrees that it would have taken a very long time, and a lot of people, to plan and make them – possibly many, many years.

MY MISSION

My trip to Peru kicks off with a flight to its capital city, Lima. From there I can drive the 400 kilometres or so south to the Nazca Desert. It'll be very hot and dry, so my desert survival kit will be vital.

I won't be able to walk around the lines because they are now a protected area and a UNESCO World Heritage Site. It's fair enough – even though they have survived in the desert for 2,000 years, hundreds of tourists trampling over them would soon turn the Nazca Lines into 'non-existent' lines.

To see the lines you can climb a special viewing platform or fly over them in a small single-engine light aircraft. The view might be better from the plane, but I hear that the flight can be very turbulent in the hot, strong desert winds. Turbulence is bad – and I really don't fancy spending the flight with my head in a sick-bag. So – the viewing platform it is . . .

KIT LIST

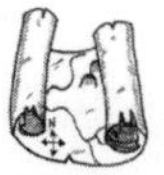

MAP – I really don't want to get lost in the desert

COMPASS – in case I get lost in the desert . . .

WATER – as much 'agua' as I can possibly carry

CAMERA WITH WIDE-ANGLE LENS – for taking the best shots of the lines in the desert landscape

BINOCULARS – for viewing the lines from a distance

SUN HAT AND SUNGLASSES – a 'must' in the desert

SUN-SCREEN – the highest factor I can get

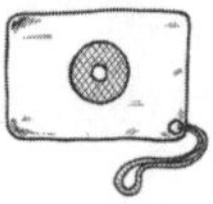

SIGNALLING MIRROR – in case of emergency, I could use the mirror to signal for help: all you need are some sun rays (and there are plenty of those in the Peruvian desert) to bounce off the mirror's surface and you've got yourself a flashing light

SPARE TYRE – having a tyre blowing out in the desert wouldn't be fun

PETROL CAN – running out of petrol wouldn't be much of a laugh, either!

MISSION COMPLETED

After a long drive I eventually found the metal tower called the Mirador, which is by the side of the highway.

© JIM DYSON/ GETTY IMAGES

The Mirador – that's Spanish for 'lookout' – is where you go to, er, look out!

I climbed the steps to the top and had a good look around with my binoculars. From here I could see three of the famous drawings:

- A gigantic lizard
- A figure they call 'the Hands' (see below)
- A tree

They were huge – an amazing sight. The figure, in particular, was really strange. It looked like a weird unknown creature, maybe a bird. The hands were human-like, but one had only four fingers. Could this be some kind of alien creature?

© ILLUKEE/ ALAMY

My trip to the Nazca Lines has made me realize just what an amazing feat it was to create them. And it's left me wondering how on earth humans could have done it . . .

WHAT DO YOU THINK?

1. The Nazca Lines were Made by Humans

Many archaeologists think that this is the case. The artists would have been the ancient Nazca people, who lived in the region from roughly 200 BC to about 600 AD. The driest desert in the world can't have been an easy place to live, but the nifty Nazcas seemed to have managed. They constructed irrigation channels to make the most of their limited water supplies and grew a variety of crops, such as corn, beans and cotton. Nice job, Nazcas!

Nazca Nasties

We don't know a lot about the Nazcas, but over the years, archaeologists have dug up some interesting objects that reveal a number of strange facts about their lives. Things like decorated bowls, patterned textiles, musical instruments – and the largest collection of severed heads in Peru . . .

Most of these skulls have holes drilled through the front of them. Rope was strung through the holes – experts think these were carrying ropes so that the heads could be 'worn', perhaps around the body. Very decorative . . .

At first, the experts thought the heads must have come from those (unlucky) enemies killed during tribal battles, later worn by the Nazcas as 'war trophies'.

This kind of thing was known to have happened in other ancient civilizations. But on closer inspection, they were found to be heads of the Nazca people themselves! Why would they want to wear the heads of people they knew – maybe even those of friends and family? Was it some kind of bizarre fashion accessory or had everyone literally 'lost their heads'?

One theory is that the Nazcas liked to have 'offering heads' as sacrifices to the gods. The heads appear to come from both men and women, but no one knows why a particular person would have been chosen for the special honour of donating their head to a good cause . . .

Drilling holes into the skulls can't have been a 'hole' lot of fun!

Buried Nazca bodies have been found too, with their heads missing. And here's another thing you'll find it hard to get your head around: their heads had been replaced with a 'head jar' – a ceramic pot with a human face painted on it. Even more bizarre – there were small plants growing from the top of the jars! Jar hair, I suppose?

No one knows for sure what all these strange findings mean; all we know is that for some reason heads – and cutting them off – were very important to the Nazca people.

How – or whether – this strange ritual could relate to the Nazca Lines is not known.

© THE ART GALLERY COLLECTION/ ALAMY

Is it a head or a jar? Neither – it's a head jar.

Whatever went on in the Nazca people's heads, creating the Nazca Lines would have been incredibly hard, complicated work – so if they were made by the Nazcas, they must have had a very good reason for making them. Archaeologists have come up with a few possible ideas:

Starstruck

One of the first people to properly research the Nazca Lines was a woman called Maria Reiche. She spent years studying them and became convinced that the lines were created as a huge star chart – a massive map of the sky and its constellations. She thinks this could have helped the Nazcas find important stars and predict planetary events, such as eclipses.

For the eyes of the gods

Think about it. Why is it that the lines are best seen from the sky? Perhaps they weren't made for humans to see at all? The Nazcas may have made them for their gods to look at.

They worshipped nature gods, which they believed helped them in important matters such as the weather, water supplies and growing crops. The drawings could have been made to appease the gods or to ask for their help.

The lines may also be linked to a series of eclipses in Peru, which astronomers think happened around the time the lines were being made. During a solar eclipse, the Moon passes between the Sun and the Earth, eventually blocking out the Sun. Imagine the Sun suddenly disappearing, being in total darkness and not understanding why? It must have been terrifying. Some think that the Nazca people believed that a giant eye was watching them from the sky. They may have thought that this eye caused the eclipses – a kind of giant 'blink' from God. Did they make the lines to please the 'eye in the sky'?

"Do you ever feel like you're being watched?"

Water works

What's really important if you live in one of the driest deserts in the world? Water, of course. One suggestion is that the lines pointed to places where water flowed under the desert floor, acting as a kind of 'water map' to help locate the precious liquid. Agriculture was crucial to the Nazca way of life – without water, their crops would have died and so would they.

Ancient racetracks

Another idea is that the lines were built as racetracks – like a kind of stadium for running races. The lines do look a bit like a series of winding paths. But no one is sure how they would have been used – and whether they were intended for animals or humans.

Probably the most convincing argument for the Nazcas being responsible for the lines is that some of the figures drawn in the desert are very similar to images found on Nazca pottery and art. Take a look at this jar, for example.

Birds and fish were often found on Nazca pottery – can you see any similarities between these and the Nazca Lines?

2. The lines were made by aliens

In 1968 Swiss author Erich von Däniken wrote what was to become a very famous book. It was called *Chariots of the Gods?*. In the book he put forward the idea that the lines were landing strips for alien spacecraft. He thought that they were too complex to have been drawn while standing on the ground – so he argued that they must have been made from the air. But as ancient cultures did not have aeroplanes, he believed that only aliens flying in spacecraft could have mapped out the lines. Some have suggested that the Nazca people could possibly have used hot-air balloons to get up into the sky and map out the pictures – but no evidence has been found that they ever went ballooning.

Many of von Däniken's readers agreed with his idea that alien astronauts visited humans in ancient times. They think that the aliens were welcomed – even worshipped as gods – and that they could have given humans in many parts of the world the knowledge to create wonderful buildings and structures.

How else would so many ancient cultures have achieved such incredible feats – things that should have been impossible? Feats like the building of the Great Pyramids in ancient Egypt, constructing the circle of Stonehenge in Great Britain and, of course, making the Nazca Lines (among many others). The alien believers argue that they must have had help from more advanced, intelligent beings. However, many historians think that there were other, clever, ways in which humans managed to achieve these feats.

Strangely, one of the Nazca drawings shows a mysterious figure that has been named 'the Astronaut'. Take a look. What do you think? Could this be one of the visiting alien 'astronauts' who helped make the lines in the first place?

The Astronaut is 32 metres tall and looks like he might be feeling a bit queasy . . .

Alien ancestors

If you ever visit the Nazca Desert you'll see that there are hundreds of crisscrossing, zigzag and parallel lines going in many directions and extending way out into the desert. They do look a bit like runways or landing strips, though they wouldn't make any sense to a human pilot. But to a creature from another planet – maybe?

Is it a bird, a plane – or a landing strip?

Erich von Däniken thought the lines might also be signals of some kind to alien beings. Others say that the drawings may have been made by the Nazca people to call the aliens back once they had left Earth.

YOU DECIDE

Were the giant drawings in Peru made by humans – or by something out of this world? Only you can decide if the artists were aliens or ancients. Put your own lines down at the back of the book once you've made up your mind!

MYSTERY 4

Crop Circles

OUR MISSION . . .

. . . to work out who – or what – is making incredible patterns in fields of crops.

BURNING QUESTIONS

- Can crop circles possibly be made by humans?
- How and why are they made?
- Are they the work of aliens?

MISSION DETAILS

Imagine you're a farmer. You grow wheat and your current crop is doing very nicely. You get up one morning and do the daily rounds – to discover the weirdest thing: a giant geometrical pattern in the middle of your field. It's very pretty – but not what you were expecting to see wiggling amongst your wheat.

This strange phenomenon has left farmers – and everyone else – scratching their heads in bewilderment. The crop circles, as they've become known, appear most years, come in many different designs, and look too good to have been made by a human in darkness. How – and why – does this happen?

THE LOCATION

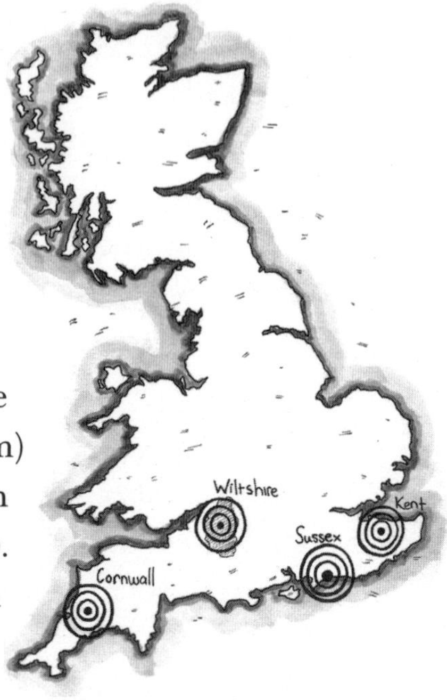

Crop circles have been spotted in Britain for many years, but it wasn't until the 1970s and '80s that they began to get attention – because so many of them began appearing. Most of them were found in the countryside of southern England. The first one (actually there were three of them) that really made the news in Britain was discovered in Wiltshire in 1980. Since then Wiltshire has been famous for its crop-circle activity.

Crop circles have since appeared in many parts of England, including Kent, Sussex and Cornwall. But they have also been found around the world – in the USA, Canada, Europe, Australia and Japan. But, obviously, only in places where there are fields of crops . . .

Crop circle found in Avebury, Wiltshire.

THE EVIDENCE

Crop circles are big news. People talk about them, visit them, take photos of them – there are even people who study them. They call themselves 'cerealogists'.

The circles can measure many metres in diameter and, like the Nazca Lines, they're best seen from the air. Their huge size raises more questions. As you know, it is really difficult to make a very large drawing on the ground, because you can't stand back and see exactly what you are doing. Whoever is making these patterns must be planning out the designs in a very skilful way. And as the circles are usually made at night, they must have brilliant night vision!

The crop circles themselves have evolved over time. They started off as simple circles but seem to become more detailed and impressive with every passing year. All kinds of shapes have been found, including rectangles, claws, and really complex designs of swirls, stars and spots. Symbols from ancient cultures have been found: there are webs, knots; even a complete diagram of a DNA structure! Many designs are based on complex mathematical and geometrical patterns. All of them are perfect and precise.

How Are They Made?

No one knows. But we do know that the crops – usually wheat, barley or rye – are pressed down flat against the ground to make the patterns.

- It's done with care – the crops are not cut down or damaged during the process
- Each circle or pattern is usually made in one direction, lying in either a clockwise or an anti-clockwise 'swirl'
- In some places the stalks are even beautifully woven together
- The circles usually appear from April to September – the growing seasons for crops and the best time to produce a distinctive pattern

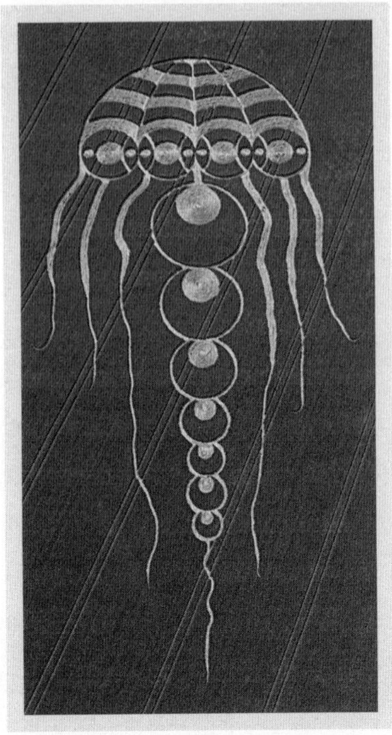

This pattern 'cropped' up in an Oxfordshire field in 2009. Something fishy about it?

A Message from Outer Space?

In 2001 two remarkable crop designs appeared close to a place called the Chilbolton Observatory in Hampshire. One showed a human face; the other was a pattern that looked like some kind of code.

Computer experts quickly realized that the message was in binary code – which is used as a way of encoding data for computers. Binary code is also one of the ways in which SETI – the Search for Extra-Terrestrial Intelligence (see page 305) – tries to communicate with possible aliens in the universe.

Back in 1974 SETI transmitted a message from a radio telescope – you can see it below. The message contained, among other things, information about the Earth's population, our solar system and the chemical elements that exist on Earth (as detailed on the middle diagram). It was directed at a star cluster called M13, which is about 25,000 light years away from us.

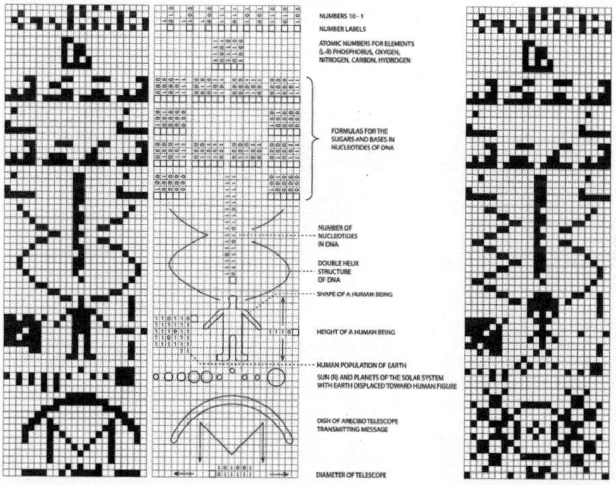

Take a look at the image on page 268 – taken from the crop circle. It looks very similar to the original message, doesn't it? In fact, it is an exact copy of the message sent by SETI, but with a few minor adjustments – for instance, 'silicon' has been added to the list of chemical elements.

Many people believe that this crop marking is a 'reply' message made by aliens! As aliens probably don't speak English very well, they have used the same binary code to reply to our original message, which was sent from Earth 27 years before. If this were true, it would be absolutely incredible – a letter from aliens! Made of wheat! An ET Wheat Meet!

However, before you get too excited, you should know that SETI – who take this sort of thing very seriously – were not impressed by the alien 'message'. They think that if an intelligent alien were trying to contact Earth, it would be way too advanced to be just making marks in fields.

But there's more. Things got even stranger the following year (2002), when this 120-metre-long image was found near Winchester, Hampshire:

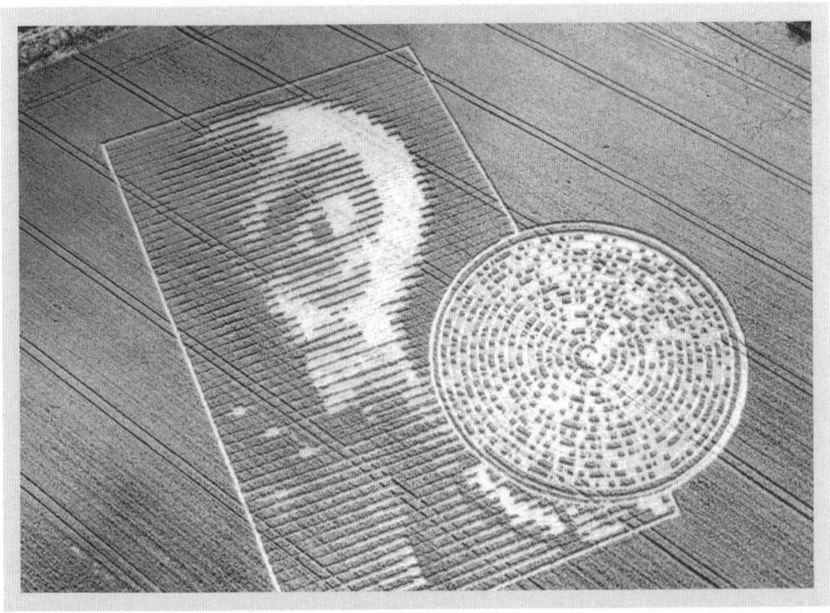

This amazing picture clearly shows the head of an alien, with three small shapes to the left which might be UFOs. A large circle containing symbols was decoded by researchers. The message appears to read:

Beware the bearers of FALSE gifts & their BROKEN PROMISES. Much PAIN but still time. [Damaged word.] There is GOOD out there. We OPpose DECEPTION. Conduit CLOSING (BELL SOUND).

Any idea what this means? Nope, me neither. The jury is split on this one. Many are convinced that this crop circle is some kind of weird letter from aliens (who sound really confused – maybe they're just learning English?), while others think it is all a hoax. Particularly as the alien 'face' looks like something from a bad TV show . . . So – what do you think?

MY MISSION

I could spend many, many nights camping out in fields to see if any crop-circle makers eventually turn up. Or I could try and see how difficult it really is to make a crop circle of my own. Because, let's face it, if I can do it, then anyone can!

Let me show you my crop-circle kit. I'm rather proud of it.

KIT LIST

A PLANK OF WOOD – just over a metre long, with holes drilled in each end

A LENGTH OF ROPE – about three metres long; each end of the rope needs to be put through the hole in the plank and securely knotted

EXTRA-LONG MEASURING TAPES

MARKERS – I'm using small bits of wood to stick in the ground

NIGHT-VISION GOGGLES

A FRIEND TO HELP – you can't do this on your own

As this is my first attempt, I've kept it relatively simple – no jellyfish or alien faces for me. Just a large but perfect circle, with some smaller circles around the outside. I've done a sketch of my circles and have worked out how big they are going to be.

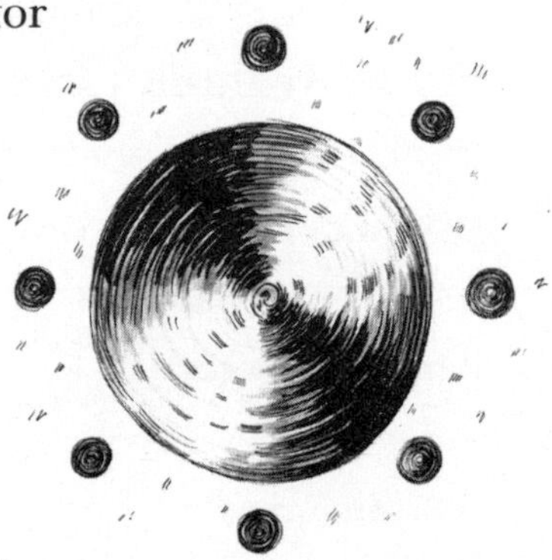

Now all I have to do is find a field and wait for a moonlit night . . .

MISSION COMPLETED

My crop circle turned out surprisingly well! I used a method called planking (which has nothing to do with the internet phenomenon of lying down like a plank in a public place; I'm simply using a plank in a public place).

Not this:

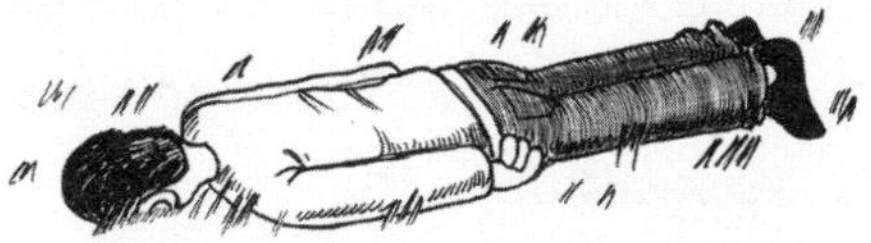

But this:

How to Make a Crop Circle

1. Find a public field with very long, straw-like grass. Farmers get a bit cross when you trample all over their livelihood, no matter how cool your pattern is!
2. Decide on the centre point of your circle and place a stake in the ground.
3. Get your helper/friend to stand on one end of the plank, to keep it still. This is the centre point of your circle.

4. The rope should be knotted through the plank holes. Loop the rope over your shoulders, with the plank on the ground in front of you. Put one foot on the plank, pressing down hard onto the ground. This flattens down the crops quite well.
5. Walk around your centre point in a complete circle while pressing down hard on the plank – and there you have it! A perfect, if small, crop circle. The plank has pressed down all the crops underneath it.
6. To make it bigger, all you need to do is to reposition your plank on the outside of the circle you have already made and walk around again. Each time you go around the circumference you will get a bigger circle – until it's massive!

So how did I manage to enter and leave the field without leaving any trace of my footsteps? No, not by levitating (now that would be impressive) but by walking on tractor tracks already made in the field so that no one could see where I had trodden. Clever!

Despite my success with a basic circle, I'm still struggling to see how the really complicated designs could be made, especially in the dead of night. Could a bunch of people with some planks of wood and pieces of rope really produce something as precise and fantastic as this?

© DIGITAL VISION/ GETTY IMAGES

Could this be achieved with an all-night planking marathon?

WHAT DO YOU THINK?

People have come up with all kinds of bizarre ideas to explain what causes crop circles, from hovering helicopters to rolling hedgehogs! Here are the four most likely explanations (no hedgehogs included):

1. Crop Circles are Made by Wind

Could the patterns be caused by a natural force that is moving the crops around? Some people think so. They point to whirling winds called 'dust devils', which spin around madly, picking up lots of dust and dirt along the way. As all the tiny particles of dust whirl about, they bump into each other and produce an electric charge. Apparently some dust devils even give off a glowing light because of this electricity. Which would explain why unusual balls of lights have been seen moving in and around crop-circle fields.

But could a mini wind really carve out the incredibly complex designs that are sometimes found? And wouldn't these whirlwinds have been noticed by crop-circle investigators before now?

2. They are Created by Natural Energy

A scientist called Dr Hans Jenny thinks the circles are caused by a different kind of 'natural' force – the force of sound. The idea is that vibrating sound frequencies could cause something solid – our crops – to be shaped into a geometric pattern.

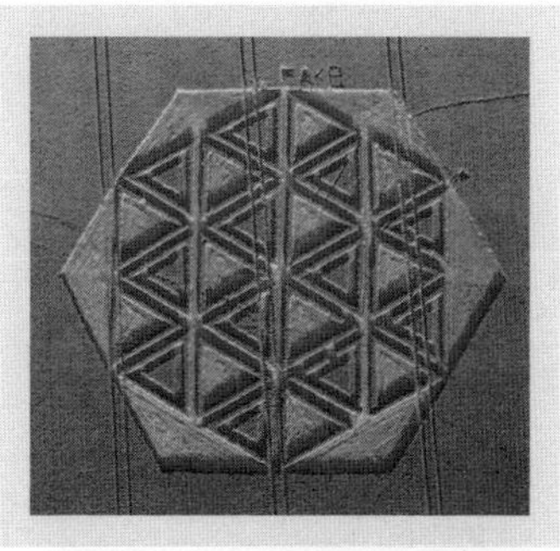

Crop circles really get your head in a spin!

It's not as crazy as it sounds. Quite a few witnesses to crop circles claim to have heard a strange noise in the fields, usually before the circle appears. It's been described as a bit like a cicada (a kind of grasshopper) – a trilling sound. In the 1980s the noise was even recorded during the night by a group of researchers in England.

The recording was sent to the important-sounding NASA Jet Propulsion Laboratory in California. The experts there didn't think that it came from an insect or any other kind of creature – they said it was a mechanical noise and probably of 'intelligent' origin. You can draw your own conclusions from that – aliens or humans?

A fascinating experiment, performed in the 1960s, measured the effect of different kinds of music on the growth of plants. It found that:

- Thrashing heavy metal music made the plants bend away from the speakers – and sometimes die!
- Gentle classical music encouraged the plants to bend towards the music source

But there are other explanations for an unknown force of energy that could be behind the circles.

Mystical Lines

In the 1920s a man called Alfred Watkins discovered that certain ancient sites – such as standing stones, churches, forts and castles – could be connected by drawing invisible lines.

He named these 'ley lines'. He said that a ley line was a straight line connecting five sacred sites that were within five kilometres of each other.

Some people believe that ley lines are actually channels of energy that flow under the Earth's surface. They think that ancient civilizations knew all about them, which is why they built their special places on these pathways – to make the most of the Earth's energy at powerful points.

Could crop circles have some kind of connection with these invisible lines? Could energy from ley lines have something to do with the energy making the circles?

People have noticed that there are strange things going on in some of the circles, all connected to energy. Some say that mobile phones, compasses and other electrical devices don't work properly if they are inside the circles. One idea is that the energy in crop circles alters the electromagnetic field, affecting the working of the equipment.

Perhaps it's no coincidence that England has a large number of ancient sacred sites (therefore ley lines) – and also has the most crop circles?

Note: My top gardening tip – play relaxing music to your plants and flowers!

3. Crop Circles are Hoaxes!
Could there be groups of crop-circle artists, creeping out at night to mystify and amaze the world with their designs? If this is true, then one thing's for sure: the circle hoaxers are not only brilliant at making circles – they're brilliant at keeping secrets. And so far, no one has ever 'grassed' on them!

So if the circles are secretly being made by humans, how are they doing it? Lots of people have tried to work this out. They've tried the same methods that I used to make my experimental circle – a simple kit involving wood and rope. Some have suggested that the hoaxers might use stools to move from one piece of the pattern to the other, which stops them from making too many giveaway marks in the crops.

A more recent idea has been suggested by a Professor Taylor from the University of Oregon. He thinks that the hoaxers are using gadgets called 'magnetrons' to make the patterns with. Ever heard of a magnetron? You could probably find one in your kitchen right now. It's a powerful tube found inside a microwave oven. It's the part that generates the microwaves, creating heat. The idea is that a creative person with a hand-held magnetron could flatten the crops much more easily than with a plank, and make really ambitious and complex circles – like some of the ones we've seen. Some researchers have even noted that a few crops show evidence of being blasted with microwave radiation.

One thing's for certain, though – some of the crop circles are definitely being made by humans. How do we know? They've admitted it . . .

Field of Fakers

In 1991 two men, Doug Bower and Dave Chorley – known as Doug and Dave – confessed that since 1978 they had made hundreds of crop circles. They even made a film for the BBC demonstrating how they used planks, rope and wire to make their circles. Doug and Dave are said to have made more than 200 crop circles during their time as hoaxers.

© JOZE POJBIC/ GETTY IMAGES

One of Doug and Dave's efforts. Not bad!

Other experiments have shown that humans can definitely make some impressive crop circles using simple equipment.

But even though this pair owned up to making their crop circles, does it mean that all the many hundreds of crop circles found around the world are hoaxes too? Perhaps it's a bit like UFOs – just because some of them are fakes doesn't mean all of them are . . .

4. Crop Circles are Made by Aliens

Some people believe that the circles are the work of intelligent aliens. They think that the patterns may have been formed by alien landings, perhaps made by their spaceships hovering over the ground.

There are even witnesses who say they have seen strange glowing balls of light and heard inexplicable noises – high-pitched sounds and strange crackling – around the fields when the crop circles are found (possibly ball lightning? – see page 228). One person thought they saw a tube of light coming down from the skies and making the pattern.

In Wiltshire in the summer of 2009, a policeman approached three tall mysterious blond-haired figures standing close to a crop circle that had appeared a few days earlier. There was a weird crackling sound and he said that the plants appeared to be moving. As the policeman got closer, the three figures ran away 'faster than any man he had ever seen'. Could they have been humans – or something from out of this world?

There is also the question of the mysterious patterns, which some think are coded messages left by aliens. The best examples of these are the 2001/2002 crop faces and signs found in Hampshire (page 270).

If this is the case, what exactly are the aliens trying to communicate to us? Look back at the 'message' on page 270. Perhaps making a circle is their way of saying 'hello'? Or maybe they just really enjoy making artistic patterns in our fields – using planet Earth as a canvas for their creative ideas?

YOU DECIDE

Crop circles are definitely one of the most perplexing mysteries around. And no one has managed to come up with a satisfactory answer. Is it all a conspiracy, or are creatures from another planet responsible? It's up to you!

MYSTERY 5

The Existence of Aliens

THE MISSION . . .

. . . to find out if there are aliens anywhere in our universe . . .

BURNING QUESTIONS

- Is there life on other planets or moons?
- What would a real alien look like?
- How can we find an alien?

MISSION DETAILS

As mysteries go, this is a biggie. Perhaps the biggest of all time? Is there life 'out there'?

Humans have always gazed up at the stars and planets, wondering if there are other worlds up there – and what kinds of creatures might be living on them. Would they be anything like us – or completely 'out of this world'?

But even though we are getting to know much more about our solar system, and what lies beyond it, we're really none the wiser. And if aliens *do* exist, are they responsible for all the weird stuff we've investigated in this book, like UFOs and crop circles?

My mission is to search out aliens – but there's one big problem. The size of the search area . . .

THE LOCATION

Ever heard the expression 'looking for a needle in a haystack'? It pretty much sums up our problem. The universe is the biggest thing you can possibly imagine. Actually it's so big, you *can't* imagine it. Words like 'massive', 'immense', even 'humongous' (is that a real word?) just don't do the job.

To make things even more mindboggling, scientists believe that the universe is getting even bigger. It's expanding as you're reading this book! (Though I'm not quite sure *how* scientists know this – they must have such long tape measures . . .)

To get an idea of the scale of things:

- Our planet, Earth, is one of eight planets currently orbiting the Sun, our star. This is our solar system. Huge
- But it's only one of many, many solar systems. All these solar systems together make up a galaxy. Our galaxy is called the Milky Way
- And it doesn't stop there. Astronomers think there may be billions of other galaxies out there, each with its own group of solar systems! It's all too much for my little brain to cope with . . .

All these galaxies, along with all the other stuff in space – like meteorites, comets, dust and gas – make up the universe. So we have our location. But where in the universe do we start?

THE EVIDENCE

Aliens are everywhere! In books, stories, movies and TV programmes, there's no shortage of little green men, man-eating monsters and cuddly extra-terrestrials.

Humans are fascinated – and terrified – by the idea of aliens (I'm not too proud to admit that I still hide behind the sofa when *Doctor Who* is on). And it's no surprise, with so many scary movies and TV shows around. Who wouldn't be nervous about the idea of unfriendly aliens arriving in flying saucers, desperate to get their claws on Earth? More 'extra-terror-estrials' than cuddly ETs?!

But, scary or not, how far have we got in our real-life search for aliens?

Note: By the way, 'extra-terrestrial' is a Latin phrase meaning anything that comes from outside Earth. But it is often used to mean 'alien' – especially when shortened to ET. *ET* is also the name of a famous movie about a cute and cuddly alien who gets stranded on planet Earth and needs to phone home. You've probably seen it. . .

The Age of Space Travel

Up until the 1950s and '60s we'd been able to observe space – but never to reach it ourselves. Everything changed with technology. In 1957 the very first human-made satellite, *Sputnik 1*, was sent into space by the Russians. From then on, space was big news. The Americans and Russians got really competitive with each other to see who could complete each space 'first' – things like:

- The first living creature in space (a dog called Laika in 1957 – that was the Russians)
- The first person to orbit the Earth (Yuri Gagarin in 1961 – the Russians again)
- And the biggie – the first human to set foot on the Moon (this time the Americans won)

The 1969 trip to the Moon was probably the most incredible event that has ever happened in our history. Think about it – for the first time ever, a human set foot on another world! Millions of people watched as astronaut Neil Armstrong stepped onto the Moon's surface, uttering the famous words, '*That's one small step for man, one giant leap for mankind . . .*'

Proud Neil flies the flag for the good old USA.

So, did Neil and his space companion, Buzz Aldrin, find any ETs on the moon? Nope: going to the Moon proved once and for all that there was a disappointing lack of aliens living on our closest 'heavenly body'.

Meanwhile, back on 1960s Earth, Neil's moonwalk had made space the coolest thing ever. Kids were pretending to be astronauts, just like him. Space toys were the number one Christmas present. People were reading science fiction comics and watching great new TV shows like *Star Trek* and *Doctor Who*. All featured thrilling space adventures and a bizarre collection of aliens (which looked like they'd been made out of toilet rolls and cling film, but no one seemed to care).

People started going out to watch sci-fi movies at their local cinema. These films seemed to have one thing in common – scaring the living daylights out of the public. Movies like:

- *Invasion of the Body Snatchers* – aliens invade Earth by taking over the bodies of humans, one by one. Spooky . . .
- *The Day of the Triffids* – weird alien plants (called Triffids) try to take over our planet. Doesn't sound possible, but these are plants are killers – and they can 'walk'. Eeek!
- *The Blob* – when a meteorite lands on Earth, a jelly-like blob emerges. Sounds harmless, but it soon grows, then starts eating humans . . .

© ALLIED PICTURES/ THE KOBAL COLLECTION

But the thing is, despite all these fantastic – and horrible – aliens we've invented, we actually have *no idea* what a real alien would look like.

Here on Earth, creatures have evolved to suit all the many different environments in our world, and we have thousands of different species on our planet.

Think about it: if other planets had a similar number of different species, suited to their very different environments, the possibilities are endless! Aliens might look nothing like what we've imagined.

Whatever we find, we'll just have to hope that real aliens aren't as scary as the ones we've made up in movies!

Alien Abduction

Plenty of people think they've seen a UFO or an alien, or even both. Some even believe that they have been kidnapped by aliens and taken on board their spaceship.

Take, for example, Travis Walton, a logger from Arizona, USA. At the end of a long day in November 1975, he and six colleagues were driving home at dusk when a bright light in the distance caught their attention. It seemed to be coming from a strange silver disc, about six metres in diameter and hovering in the air, wobbling from side to side. The men had never seen anything like it before, and Travis (who was either very brave or very foolish – you decide) thought he would investigate. As he got closer to the UFO, his friends saw a beam of bluish-green light whoosh out of it and strike his body. Poor old Travis was jolted upwards into the air, and he landed, outstretched and unconscious, on the ground. His (less brave) friends quickly drove off, convinced he was dead, and terrified that the same thing would happen to them. When they'd calmed down, they drove back to the same spot – but there was no sign of Travis or the weird disc.

The police were called and an extensive search took place for the missing man, but nothing was found. It was a mystery. What on earth had happened to Travis Walton?

Five days later, Travis appeared at a local petrol station in a nervous, panic-stricken state. His story?

Travis said he had been abducted by aliens and held in their spaceship. The aliens he described were short and bald, with big heads and large staring eyes. Travis was so terrified to find the aliens looking at him that he passed out – then found himself at the petrol station when he woke up. He had been missing for five 'Earth' days, yet he was convinced that he had only been gone for a few hours. This kind of 'time-slip' crops up quite often in reports of alien encounters.

Travis Walton's experience remains one of the most talked-about alien mysteries, and his story was later made into a book and film. Some think that, because there were seven witnesses to the UFO, the story must be true; others think that the whole thing was a big hoax, made up by Travis and his friends.

Travis Walton – innocent victim of aliens or hoaxer?

Whether you believe him or not, his description of the aliens does fit that of others who say they have seen ETs. People like Betty and Barney Hill, who say that in September 1961 they were followed in their car by an alien spacecraft. They then 'lost' two hours of time. The couple later remembered being taken up into the craft and meeting aliens.

Betty says that she even asked one of the aliens where it had come from and that he showed her a map of the stars. Good to know that you can always rely on an ET to help you with directions . . .

The aliens that the Hills and Travis Walton encountered are now officially known as Grey Aliens – the most common description given by those who say they've seen one.

Grey features:

- The size of a small human – 1.5 metres
- Large black eyes
- Small nose and mouth
- Large head
- Pale grey skin
- Smooth and hairless

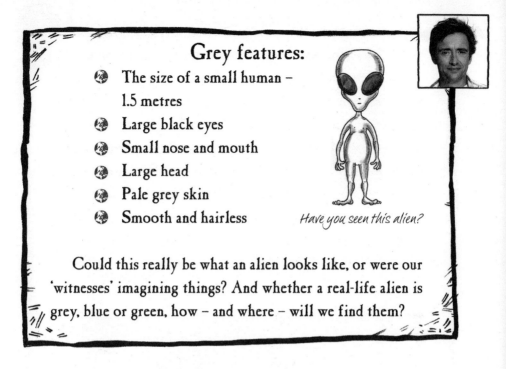

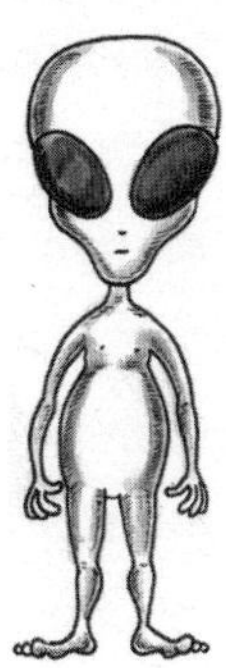

Have you seen this alien?

Could this really be what an alien looks like, or were our 'witnesses' imagining things? And whether a real-life alien is grey, blue or green, how – and where – will we find them?

The Search for Life

Finding an alien isn't as simple as getting into a rocket and jetting off into the stratosphere. Manned missions – that's missions with humans on board – are incredibly difficult to organize and cost billions of pounds. They can also be very risky for the astronauts who take part in them. I mean, would you fancy being blasted through Earth's atmosphere in a rocket to the unknown? Added to the 'challenging' journey are other risks, including:

- High levels of dangerous radiation in deep space
- Violent solar storms
- And, if anything goes wrong on your mission, no one is going to be able to rescue you . . .

If you think about it, astronauts are *really*, *really* brave!

A less risky – and cheaper – way of finding out about other planets is to send unmanned probes. These are specially designed robotic craft which can travel to and land on distant planets, making fantastically long journeys that humans could not survive. These robotic probes can take photographs, pick up soil and rock samples – even whip up a quick spag Bol (I'm joking). In this way we've been able to find out lots more about other places where ETs might be discovered.

A sky crane lands the rover Curiosity on the planet Mars in 2012.

So far, we've landed probes on planets like Venus and Mars, and explored several different moons looking for evidence of life. Missions such as *Voyager*, *Galileo* and *Magellan* have brought us information about places we can only dream of visiting ourselves.

What are we looking for?

It's quite simple, really. To find life, we really need to find a planet that's like ours – good old planet Earth.

Why? Because our planet has been mega-successful when it comes to creating life. Earth has the most amazing variety and number of different life forms, so it makes sense for scientists to look for other planets that have similar conditions to ours.

What life needs

- **Wonderful water**: Life here on Earth probably began in water. And nothing can survive on our planet without it. Luckily, research has revealed that liquid water is pretty common in our solar system. Probes have found evidence of the existence of water on Mars and Europa (one of Jupiter's moons); on the planet Venus; and also on Titan and Enceladus (both moons of Saturn), and Ganymede and Callisto (both moons of Europa)

- **Creative carbon**: Did you know that you are a carbon-based life form? You do now! Every cell of every living thing on our planet contains carbon

Carbon is a crucial part of what makes life happen. It is an element that combines with other elements – hydrogen, nitrogen and oxygen – to make the complex chemicals that life needs. And there's a lot of carbon out there in space – because it is made by stars!

All living things that we know of need carbon, but some scientists think it might be possible for an alien life form to be based on another element. Some think that silicon could be that element. If that happened, no one knows what the results would be like. Sci-fi writers have imagined all kinds of weird silicon-based life forms: in his story *A Martian Odyssey*, Stanley Weisbaum described a slow-moving creature, over half a million years old, which poos silicon bricks. Ouch!

An artist imagines a silicon life form created from crystals. Or is it a giant prawn?

- **The right light**: Living creatures need sunlight for energy and warmth. Earth lies in what's been nicknamed the 'Goldilocks Zone' – in just the right position. It isn't too close to our sun – if it was, it would be so hot, all our water would evaporate (and we'd be finished). But it isn't too far away from the Sun either – if it was, it would be too cold, dark and frozen for anything to survive

Like Baby Bear's porridge, Earth is 'just right' when it comes to being the perfect distance from our sun, and the perfect temperature for life to thrive.

Here are a few places in our solar system that we are currently exploring to see if the conditions are right for life:

Is there life on Mars?

We call Mars the Red Planet because it is covered in iron oxide – aka rust. Mars is smaller, colder and drier than Earth, but even so, there are hopes for finding life here one day. NASA have so far made seven landings on Mars with robotic probes – the latest was *Curiosity* (great name) in August 2012.

Most importantly, there is water on Mars – though most of it is frozen in Mars's ice caps, because it's so cold there. Scientists think that Mars was once much warmer, so if the water was liquid in the past, life of some kind could have existed. The surface of the Red Planet shows that it may once have had seas and rivers.

Nowadays it is probably too cold and dry for anything to be living on the surface, though scientists think there might still be something underground – perhaps bacteria or simple life forms. Even that would be a major breakthrough, because bacteria are the basic beginnings of all life, even here on Earth. The earliest evidence for life on our planet has been found in Australia – in 3.4-billion-year-old mats of bacteria called stromatolites. So if scientists can find bacteria on other planets, it tells us that the potential for many more life forms to evolve is there.

The search continues – and even though the journey to Mars would be extraordinarily difficult for humans to manage, scientists are trying to find a way to make it possible.

The Martian Mix-Up

People have long thought that there were aliens living on Mars – not because of science but because of a language mistake.

Back in 1877, an Italian astronomer called Schiaparelli announced that he'd spotted some interesting things on the surface of the planet Mars – long vertical lines that he called 'canali'.

I can speak a little Italian, you know: *pizza, pasta, panini*... I'm practically bi-lingual. Sadly, many people aren't as gifted as 'moi' (French – just testing) when it comes to languages. So there was a slight problem over the word 'canali': the English thought it meant 'canal', though it actually means 'channel' in Italian. What's the difference? Channels can occur naturally, while canals are most definitely made – by someone – or something...

An astronomer called Percival Lowell heard about the 'canali' and got very excited. He reasoned that if there were canals on Mars, there must be intelligent beings living there who had built the canals. The idea soon got around and a name was coined for the Mars-dwelling creatures – Martians!

There was no evidence for this – but the idea of Martians caught people's imaginations. Ever heard of *War of the Worlds* by H. G. Wells? In this famous book, Wells created a frightening vision of the future where alien machines from Mars landed on Earth and started to destroy everything in sight.

Help! The Aliens Are Coming!

© MARY EVANS PICTURE LIBRARY

Chaotic crowds learn never to compete with a Martian in a three-legged race!

Amazingly, the hysterical crowd scenes described by H. G. Wells in his fictional story actually happened in real life in the USA. In 1938 famous director Orson Welles made a radio play of *War of the Worlds* – with disastrous results. The actors in the play were so convincing that many listeners thought that it was a real-time news broadcast. Believing that Martians were invading Earth, panicking crowds fled their homes! Maybe they thought the Martians were looking for food – perhaps Mars bars, mars-malade or mars-mallows??

In real life, Martians may not turn out to be anything like the tripods of H. G. Wells's famous book – but wouldn't it be just a-mars-ing to find life on the Red Planet?

More Homes for Aliens?

Lying beyond the Earth and Mars are the two giant gas planets, Jupiter and Saturn. There's not much chance of anything living in these freezing places as their atmospheres are full of poisonous gases. But both have a number of moons orbiting them – and these moons have totally surprised scientists with their possibilities.

Incredible Europa

One place that scientists are really excited about is Europa, one of the moons of the planet Jupiter. You might not have heard of it, but Europa was discovered a long time ago, in 1610, by Italian astronomer Galileo Galilei.

Too clever for their times?

Imagine living hundreds of years ago, long before the telescope was invented. You can see the Sun and the Moon but you don't know anything scientific about the universe. Would you have believed that the Earth was at the centre of everything – and that all the planets and everything else revolved around our world? Most people did. Wrongly, of course!

It wasn't until 1514 that a Polish astronomer called Copernicus came up with a big, big idea. He published a book saying that he believed that the Earth moved around the Sun.

This shocking revelation was just too much for people in the sixteenth century – especially those in charge, who really didn't like their ideas being challenged. Poor old Copernicus's book was trashed. He probably would have gone to jail (these were harsh times) but he died soon afterwards.

In the 1600s, however, an Italian physicist, mathematician and all-round brainiac called Galileo used a proper telescope for the first time. Galileo discovered all sorts of amazing things about the planets and moons, and declared that

Copernicus had been right all along (and he had!). For this Galileo was sentenced to life imprisonment, in 1633.

If either of them had been born in different times, they might have been as respected and admired as, say, Professor Stephen Hawking is today. Life can be very unfair. . .

Images from probes have shown large areas of water on Europa's surface, which are probably huge oceans or lakes. It's unbelievably cold on Europa – a freezing -160° C on the surface – so it is covered in a thick crust of ice, between three and seven kilometres thick (that's thick – if there is life on Europa, they could ice skate without worrying. . . !). But experts believe that warmer waters lie underneath the crust.

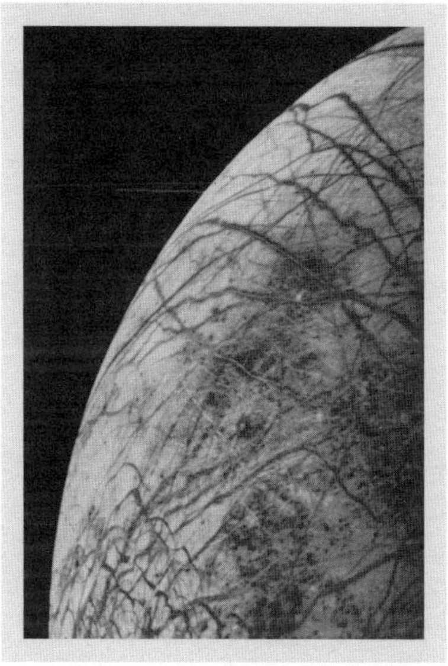

This is how icy Europa might look when lit by the Sun.

This is because the massive gravitational pull of Jupiter creates enough heat to warm up Europa's interior, but not quite enough to melt the icy crust on top. This fact, along with the discovery of some fascinating new creatures on Earth, has made scientists think that Europa's waters may hold some very interesting finds.

'Black Smokers'

Deep down in some of Earth's oceans are smoking black plumes called hydrothermal vents. They happen when cold sea water on the sea floor meets hot magma bubbling up from below the Earth's surface. When the hot fluid bursts through a crack into the sea water, you've got yourself a hydrothermal vent. Also known as a 'black smoker'.

I said earlier that all life needs sunlight to survive. But it turns out the experts weren't quite accurate (yes, even boffins are sometimes wrong). No one thought that life could possibly exist at the very bottom of the sea, where no sunlight can penetrate. But we recently discovered that not only are there bacteria, shrimp and crabs in the darkest depths, there is a weird new creature on the black-smoker block – the tube worm.

Scientists have found lots of red and white tube-shaped creatures, about a metre long, which are completely blind and have no mouth (very attractive!). More incredibly, this new species has found a way to survive without any light at all – something we just didn't believe was possible. Clearly scientists don't have all the answers!

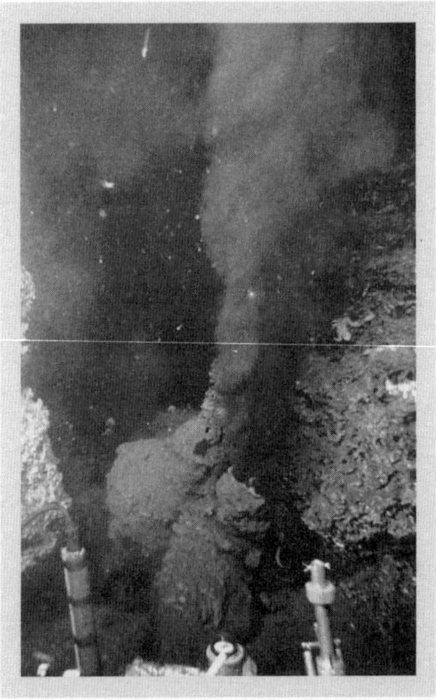

These vents are smokin'!

Experts think that Europa could possibly have hydrothermal vents, like Earth. If so, could alien creatures be living deep in its waters, around the vents? Something even weirder than a blind, mouthless tube worm maybe . . .

To find out for sure, a mission to Europa would need to land, penetrate the massively thick icy crust, explore the deep waters, and somehow bring any life forms back to Earth – but where there's a will . . .

Life Is Tough

Everywhere we look on our planet, life is flourishing – even in places where we once thought it was impossible. In recent years, scientists have found life forms alive and well in some very unusual places, not just the oceans. Like the driest desert in the world (the Atacama in Chile) and the freezing ice of Antarctica.

These tough species are called 'extremophiles' – things that can survive in extreme environments in which no normal life form would have a chance.

The existence of extremophiles has made the chances of finding life on other planets even better. Because now scientists know that life might be able to begin and survive on other worlds that have hostile environments.

More missions are being planned for the 2020s – to Europa, and to Jupiter's other moons – which will hopefully tell us more.

Terrific Titan

Titan is the largest moon of the planet Saturn. Scientists are excited about Titan because it is a bit like Earth was many years ago. It has nitrogen, like Earth, and is covered in mountains, lakes and river beds. It is much, much colder, though, and there is no liquid water, which is a big problem. Or is it?

In 2005 the *Cassini-Huygens* space probe finally reached Titan after a seven-year journey. It sent back pictures of oceans, made not of water but of liquid methane. Scientists have been thinking about an exciting possibility for Titan: could alien creatures have evolved that use liquid methane to live rather than water? They might look and behave in a completely different way to us Earthlings, because they would have developed using a different chemical structure. Mind-blowing . . .

The probe also told us that hydrogen gas detected in Titan's atmosphere seems to be flowing down and disappearing at its surface. One reason for this could be that the hydrogen is being used up – breathed – by alien life forms.

Moons, Planets and Stars . . .

OK – with all this talk of moons, I have to admit, before I started on this mission I wasn't really sure what the difference was between a planet, a moon and a star. Here's some help in case you don't know either (go on, admit it):

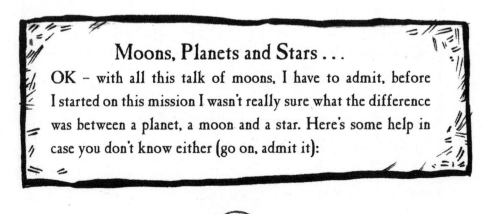

- A **star** is a huge, hot burning ball of gas, which makes energy and light. Our sun, for example
- A **planet** orbits a star. It can be rocky, like Earth, or a gas giant like Jupiter. It doesn't burn but is illuminated by light from its star
- A **moon** orbits a planet. Some planets have many moons – so far, 63 moons have been counted orbiting Jupiter. That makes our single Earth moon seem a little bit sad, doesn't it . . .

In our solar system we have a total of eight planets. Here they are in order of distance from the **Sun** (starting with the closest): **Mercury**, **Venus**, **Earth**, **Mars**, **Jupiter**, **Saturn**, **Uranus** and **Neptune**.

If you look at older books or websites, you may read that our solar system has nine planets – that's because Pluto got 'downgraded' in 2006. In other words, it was kicked out of the solar system by scientists. Poor old Pluto!

Far, Far Away . . .

So we've looked at aliens that might be found within our solar system – but what about even further afield?

In 1995 the very first planet outside our solar system was discovered. It is orbiting a star called 51 Peg. Since then we've gone on to discover many more distant planets with an incredible piece of technology . . .

The Kepler Telescope

In 2009 a gigantic space telescope was launched into space by NASA, the US space agency. Its mission? To find Earth-like planets outside our solar system. The Kepler Telescope is currently observing about 100,000 stars.

How does it find new planets? This amazing telescope looks at changes in the brightness of stars. A dip in a star's light could mean that an orbiting planet has just moved across its face.

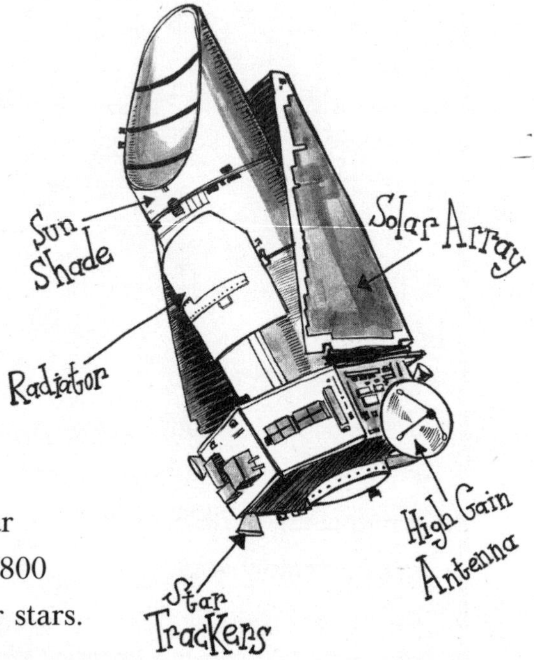

Using this equipment, astronomers have so far discovered more than 800 new planets orbiting other stars.

These strange new worlds are called exoplanets. So far we've discovered that:

- About 54 of these exoplanets are of a similar size to Earth
- They also happen to be in their 'Goldilocks Zone' – just the right distance from their sun

But this is just the tip of the exoplanet iceberg. There might be many, many more of them. But because these planets are in other solar systems, the distances involved are incredible. Even sending unmanned probes to an exoplanet would be a marathon task.

How can we find life if it is so far away?

The Alien Hunters

Some people really do have dream jobs – chocolate taster, waterslide tester, computer-game designer all spring to mind. But one of the coolest jobs of all has got to be that of 'alien hunter'. Which is exactly what the people at SETI do.

© DR SETH SHOSTAK/ SCIENCE PHOTO LIBRARY

A houseful of alien hunters . . .

So what is SETI exactly? The word stands for the Search for Extra-Terrestrial Intelligence – an organization set up in 1984. The people who work for SETI have one aim –

to find signs of intelligent alien life. They are looking for thinking, feeling beings who can properly communicate with us.

They do this, not by zipping up a space suit and blasting off into the stratospherespace, but by using advanced technology to try and detect signals made by intelligent life forms.

SETI are currently scanning the stars, looking for radio and laser transmissions from distant civilizations in far-off solar systems. To do this, they need top-notch technology: roll out some more great gadgets . . .

The All-Sky SETI Optical Telescope – (OSETI)

This impressive telescope was launched in 2006 and scans the night sky with a huge 72-inch mirror, looking for laser signals that might be transmitted by distant extra-terrestrials. This tasty bit of kit can apparently process one terabit (a trillion bits!) of data – that's as much data as in all the books in the world – every second! So it should be able to cope with whatever our intelligent aliens might throw at it.

Listening to the skies

Perched in the Californian desert are a row of radio telescopes that look like giant dishes. Their job is to detect 'noise'; specifically noise that might be coming from other civilizations.

Not an easy job, given that there is so much other noise around us, like man-made signals from our TV stations, radar and satellites.

The Allen Telescope Array (for that is what they are called) listens out for narrow-bandwidth radio signals coming from outside the solar system. Because these signals don't occur naturally, finding one would mean that something intelligent must have made it.

The Allen Telescope Array on its noise-busting mission.

What they want to find is called a 'beacon' – a clear and definite signal that has been sent by intelligent aliens who are trying to communicate with us.

WOW!!

Has a beacon signal ever been found? Maybe!

In the summer of 1977 a radio telescope in Ohio, USA, picked up an incredibly exciting signal. So exciting that the astronomer on duty wrote *WOW!* on the printout when he spotted it.

Incredibly, it's been known as the WOW signal ever since.

The signal was coming from somewhere near the constellation Sagittarius, and appeared as a series of numbers and letters on the printout (so not an actual sound).

SETI thinks that it was not made by anything human and that it could have come from intelligent aliens with a very powerful transmitter. The signal has never been repeated – but the alien hunters at SETI are ready and waiting for the next one to come along.

Some even think that aliens might have been listening in to accidental signals from Earth for a long time. Our planet began transmitting radio and television signals about 100 years ago, and some of these transmissions will have leaked into space. A faraway alien might be picking up those signals right now. Let's just hope they haven't tuned in to more reruns of *Come Dine with Me* . . .

Message in a Space Bottle

So if aliens are trying to communicate with us, are we doing them the same favour? Well, kind of. Back in the 1970s, messages to aliens were placed on board the *Voyager* and *Pioneer* probes. They've now been travelling for more than 30 years and no one knows exactly where they are, or if an alien has picked them up. So what exactly have we put in our space-age 'message in a bottle'?

- The two *Pioneer* probes have gold-coloured plaques on their sides, showing the date the mission left and the location of Earth in the universe. They also have illustrations of a man and woman on them, who are supposed to be everyday Earthlings. The man is waving in a friendly way – hopefully, showing the aliens that we humans come in peace, even though some of us have forgotten to put any clothes on

What?
Maybe an alien is scratching its head over this picture at this very moment!

- On board *Voyager* are some vinyl records (which we once used to play music – just ask a grown-up). Fortunately, full instructions for playing the records are also included, just in case aliens aren't familiar with ancient Earth rituals

The records contain different sounds from the Earth: laughter, heartbeats, footsteps, a volcano, thunder, the wind, rain and sea – even the sound of a chimpanzee! (This could be very confusing for an alien – it might think that all we Earth dwellers do is monkey around . . .)

There are greetings in 55 different languages, and pictures of humans, animals, plants and buildings. There's music too. We're not sure who made the selection, but it includes Beethoven and a blues singer called Blind Willie Johnson.

Voyager is now known to be at the outer limits of our solar system and it holds the record for being the most distant human-made object in the universe. Bet Blind Willie never thought he would get so far with his music!

MY MISSION

Going on a space mission would quite literally be 'a blast'. But, much as I would love to zoom off into the galaxy in search of aliens, it's just not possible – yet. One of the biggest problems is time.

Take a trip to Mars, for example. There's a very good reason why we haven't sent any human astronauts there. The total journey time from Earth to Mars would be up to a whopping 300 days, depending on the position of Earth and Mars at that time (remember, both planets are constantly in orbit).

So nearly a year to get there – then you'll need to spend some time on the Red Planet – and then get back to Earth again. That's a very long time to be in a spacecraft. Long enough to drive you a bit crazy – you might come back an 'astro*nut*' rather than an astronaut!

Despite the time issue, space experts are working hard on a

way of getting humans safely to the Red Planet – which will, hopefully, be in your lifetime. Maybe one day you'll be the first person to set foot on Mars!

If you are that person, this is what you'll need to take along:

KIT LIST

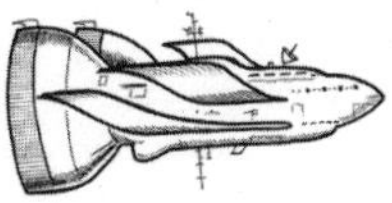

A MEGA MARS SPACECRAFT – it doesn't exist yet, but when it does, it will need to carry a huge amount of stuff (the technical term is 'payload'). Enough oxygen, food, water and fuel for a two-year trip – it will be the heaviest spacecraft ever . . .

ENTERTAINMENT – to make the two years a bit more bearable, you'll want a selection of movies, games and music to while away the hours

PRESSURIZED SPACE SUIT AND HELMET – when you leave the craft to explore, you'll need this specially designed suit to withstand the freezing Martian temperatures and the incredible amount of dust on the Red Planet

MECHANICAL GRABBER – this special tool retrieves and collects objects – because your gloved fingers will be about as useful as a packet of sausages

ROBOTIC ROVER ASSISTANT – to carry your air supply, communications system, tools and generator

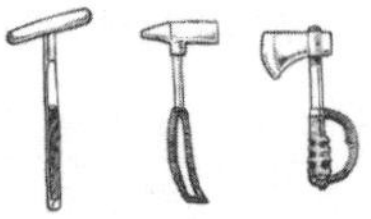

SPACE TOOLS – to probe the surface, you will need a specialist axe, hammer and a corer (for taking soil samples)

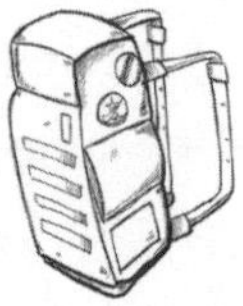

BACKPACK – contains enough power to keep you alive for eight hours once off the craft

Here, boy! A robotic rover in action – every astronaut's best friend.

MISSION COMPLETED

For the moment, the nearest I'm going to get to outer space is a visit to my local science museum. But I could make up for it by planning a very different type of holiday . . .

The First Ever 'Space Vacation'

Sometime in the next few years, a Virgin Galactic spacecraft will blast off from Earth at speeds of up to 4,000 kph. Passengers will experience what it is really like to travel into outer space and will get an incredible view of Earth from above. Awesome!

They'll be travelling in a rocket-powered space plane, which will be launched from an aircraft at around 50,000 feet, just above the Earth's atmosphere. The journey will be short but fun – passengers will float and spin around as they experience micro-gravity!

But I'd better start saving up. It won't be cheap – but many would say it was worth it for the ultimate trip of a lifetime. For now, I'll just put my name on the waiting list . . .

WHAT DO YOU THINK?

1. Aliens Do Exist

Do you believe that we are not alone in the universe? Many astronomers would agree with you. This is why:

Sheer Numbers

It's all a numbers game. There's a well-known saying:

'Give enough monkeys enough typewriters, and one of them will write Shakespeare.' The planetary argument is similar. There are just *so many* planets out there. Scientists think that there are billions of them in just our galaxy, the Milky Way. And there are billions more galaxies, each with billions of stars!

Some experts think that at least half of these stars will have planets orbiting them. And the chances are that some of the planets will be similar to Earth and will have developed life forms.

Unfortunately, it would take so long for a human to travel to another solar system that we'd be dead years before we arrived at our destination. So we'll keep relying on even more advanced space probes and telescopes to do the faraway investigating for us.

Perhaps one day SETI will pick up a clear and direct message from an alien in a distant solar system. Maybe aliens are watching us right now – and laughing at our primitive inventions!

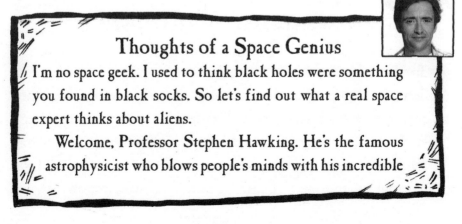

Thoughts of a Space Genius

I'm no space geek. I used to think black holes were something you found in black socks. So let's find out what a real space expert thinks about aliens.

Welcome, Professor Stephen Hawking. He's the famous astrophysicist who blows people's minds with his incredible

ideas – such as the real possibility of time travel. He knows pretty much everything a human can possibly know about the universe and has written lots of amazing books about the subject.

So, what does Prof Hawking think about aliens? To put it simply, he doesn't believe that we are the only life form in the universe. He once said:

'To my mathematical brain, the numbers alone make thinking about aliens perfectly rational... The real challenge is to work out what aliens might actually be like.'

This view is backed up by the super-brainy scientists at SETI. Who, of course, wouldn't be spending all their valuable time searching for alien signals if they didn't truly believe that intelligent life could exist in the universe. As SETI say: *'Given a suitable environment and sufficient time, life will develop on other planets.'* Evidence enough?

2. Aliens Don't Exist

Perhaps you're one of these people who don't believe anything unless you see it with your own eyes? And the chances are you've not come across an alien yet. (Though if you ever do encounter a real-life ET, please do let me know.)

To date, not a single person, not even an astronaut – or Stephen Hawking, for that matter – has come up with a proper recording of an alien, or a photograph, or any other hard evidence. There are thousands of stories, reports and cases, but all of them could be put down to hoaxes or genuine mistakes.

And if aliens and UFOs were visiting us on a regular basis, as so many seem to believe, why would they be so shy about making themselves known to us humans? Why send garbled messages in code or make weird lines and circles on Earth's surface? And why would we still not have any proper evidence, like a captured UFO?

There's certainly a lot of nonsense talked about aliens. And many scientists don't believe that any of the weird monsters that appear in movies like *Men in Black* will bear any resemblance to real aliens.

The kind of ET normally seen in films – but would they be anything like real-life aliens?

It's true that many space experts believe that alien life forms of some kind do exist. But maybe – like the scientists who thought that life couldn't exist without sunlight – they're just wrong? Really, the only way to prove aliens exist is to find one!

YOU DECIDE

Do aliens exist or not? It's 'make your mind up' time. So head to the back of the book to make your notes! The answer is out there – somewhere. In the meantime, we'll keep on looking . . .

WANT TO KNOW MORE?

George's Secret Key to the Universe, George's Cosmic Treasure Hunt, George and the Big Bang – Lucy and Stephen Hawking (Corgi)

The Alien Hunter's Handbook – Mark Brake (Kingfisher)

Monster Tracker: The Alien Hunter's Guide – Gomer Bolstrood (Watts)

Can Science Solve? The Mystery of UFOs – Chris Oxlade (Heinemann)

The Twilight Realm: Aliens – Jim Pipe (Wayland)

Ask Uncle Albert: 100½ Tricky Science Questions Answered – Russell Stannard (Faber & Faber)

www.nasa.gov

NASA for kids – **www.nasa.gov/audience/forkids/kidsclub**

www.nationalgeographic.com

www.planetary.org/explore/for-kids/

ANCIENT TREASURES

MYSTERY 1

Pirate Treasure

THE MISSION . . .

. . . to find out if there are hoards of pirate treasure out there, just waiting to be found . . .

BURNING QUESTIONS

- Did pirates really bury their treasure?
- Did they make maps to find it again?
- Where did the treasure come from?

Hoards of glittering treasure – 'chest' what a pirate needs!

MISSION DETAILS

Ahhaaar, me hearties! Yo ho ho and a bottle of rum! Heave ho! Land ahoy! Shiver me timbers!

Talking like a pirate – brilliant! *Ahhaarrr!!* I could do it all day. Actually, I tried to once, but Mrs Hamster got a bit tired of it and made me stop.

Pirates are just the best though, aren't they? I mean, they had the best outfits for a start – it's the only thing I'll wear to a fancy-dress party, whatever the theme. And they did all the best stuff.

- They went on thrilling voyages across the seven seas
- They flew skull-and-crossbone flags and fought with swashbuckling swords . . .
- Some had talking parrots, hooks for hands and peg legs all at the same time! I should imagine a one-legged talking parrot that perched on a hook would have been worth a fortune.

Long John Silver, Captain Hook and Captain Jack Sparrow are just a few of the splendid sea dogs who have appeared in movies, TV shows and books. But what about *real* pirates? Was it all 'ha ha' and 'ho ho' on the high seas? Well, no, not quite.

Eye-patch, parrot, earrings, hat – he's got all the pirate paraphernalia!

In the past, being a pirate was a serious – and often deadly – business. All that sword-fighting and ship-burning and sailing to far-off places with unknown diseases was pretty risky stuff. Plus, if you got caught by the authorities, you'd be hanged and your body left to rot in public. Not much of a welcome home after a long voyage . . .

Because it was so dangerous, some historians think that pirates of the past could have expected to live just two years. Two years? Perhaps a pirate's life wouldn't have been for me, after all . . .

So why did pirates risk their lives? For treasure, of course! (With a few bottles of rum thrown in.)

So jump on board to find out the truth about real pirates, and whether any of those famed pirate treasure chests are still out there . . .

THE LOCATION

Wherever there was a shipping route, there was probably a pirate. Ever since the first boats and ships set sail, pirates have been around to prey on them.

- The ancient Greeks and the Romans were attacked by pirates in the Mediterranean Sea – the Roman emperor, Julius Caesar, was even kidnapped by them
- Scandinavian Vikings were the bearded pirates of the north, raiding and invading in their longships
- Chinese pirates in ships called junks ruled the seas around China up until the eighteenth century.
- And in the sixteenth century, pirates called corsairs sailed the Barbary Coast of North Africa

One of the most famous periods of pirate history was during the seventeenth and eighteenth centuries, when terrifying pirates like Blackbeard became legendary. They even called it the Golden Age of Piracy. I mean, probably not at the time, but we've certainly called it that since.

The Spanish had colonized the New World in the sixteenth century, taking huge territories in Central and South America. (See pages 382 for more on the Spanish explorers.) Spanish ships called galleons carried fabulous wealth from these lands through the Caribbean and across the Atlantic back to Spain. And where there's a ship full of valuables, well yes, you guessed it, there's a pirate. The galleons, inevitably, were attacked by pirates, some of whom were called buccaneers – the real Pirates of the Caribbean . . .

The Spanish Main – where pirates roamed the waters.

THE EVIDENCE

Pirates have been romanticized throughout history, but in reality, attacking and robbing ships at sea was nothing to be proud of. Pirates used threats and violence to steal pretty much anything they could. Silver, gold and other treasures were obviously at the top of a pirate's wish list, but food, drink and clothes were all taken on board, so to speak.

Pirate ships were usually smaller and speedier than the ones they preyed on. The pirates could sneak up alongside their chosen ship and leap aboard quickly, before the crew had a chance to defend themselves.

But, like everyone else, pirates had to stop and rest sometimes. And after months at sea (all that deck-swabbing, mainbrace-splicing and sea-shanty singing can be very tiring, you know) a pirate crew would need to find somewhere to land, stock up on food and drink, and perhaps do a spot of trading. Maybe even have a bit of entertainment?

Pirates were always on the lookout for 'pirate-friendly' places – and what better spot than a nice quiet island?

A desert island – every pirate's dream . . .

Let's find out more about a few pirates who used islands as hiding places . . .

The Life – and Death – of William Kidd

© THE ART ARCHIVE/ PRIVATE COLLECTION/ EILEEN TUESDAY

Here's looking at you, Kidd

Legendary pirate William Kidd had a fearsome reputation. He once killed a member of his own crew by throwing a heavy iron bucket at him. That's one way to kick the bucket . . .

Kidd started off his pirating career as a privateer (I'll explain what one of those is in a minute), sailing to places like the West Indies and the Caribbean. He had plenty of piratical adventures, but his biggest haul was when he got his hands on a massive Armenian ship called the *Quedagh Merchant* in 1698. It was stuffed full of valuable silks, gold, silver and other riches. What a steal!

But this treasure trove was to be Kidd's downfall . . .

Two years before, Kidd had set sail on the *Adventure Galley*, with a crew of 80. His mission: to capture all French ships, plus any pirates in and around Madagascar. During the voyage the *Quedagh Merchant* was spotted in the distance, and Kidd did what any self-respecting pirate/privateer would do. He abandoned his own ship and took command of the much nicer new vessel.

But Kidd didn't know that some of the riches aboard the ship were owned by a powerful minister in India. The minister complained about Kidd, and the British government declared him a wanted criminal and known pirate. By this time Kidd was on his way to New York. When he arrived there, he was none too pleased to find himself arrested, then shipped back to England.

William Kidd was put on trial in 1701 and found – 'Guilty, m'lord.'

He was hanged at Execution Dock in London. Unfortunately, the first rope snapped and Kidd fell into the dirt below. No wonder his name was mud . . .

Another rope was found, and the second attempt was successful. Kidd's body was then covered in tar and suspended in chains as a warning to others. That's one way of 'hanging' around!

What happened to the treasure?

Before he reached New York with his loot, Kidd had heard the bad news of his forthcoming arrest. So he stopped at an island close to the coast – Gardiner's Island – to bury his treasure for safekeeping. He was hoping he'd be let off the charges and would soon be back.

Keep digging, men! Captain Kidd's in a 'hole' lot of trouble.

Kidd gave Mrs Gardiner (who owned Gardiner's Island) a length of gold cloth and a sack of sugar in return for letting him use her land. When he left, he warned the Gardiner family that if the treasure wasn't there when he got back, they'd be in big trouble . . . but of course, he never did make it back.

When Kidd was on trial, the Gardiners were ordered to produce his treasure as evidence. It was a stunning stash, containing:

Bars of gold and silver

Gold dust

Glittering rubies, diamonds and other jewels

Rolls of luxurious silk

57 bags of sugar (sugar was very valuable in those days: if you had a sweet tooth, you'd have needed a very big wallet, as well as a good dentist)

In November 1704 the treasure was sold off for a total of £6,437 (a lot of money in those days) and the cash was used to build a hospital. A plaque on Gardiner's Island marks the spot where the treasure was buried.

So – the treasure was found. But was it? Many believe that there is even more treasure that Kidd buried or hid during his adventures. Several locations have been suggested, mainly islands in Nova Scotia (a province of Canada) and Connecticut, USA. Others think that he might have buried his loot on a Caribbean island. Stories and rumours about the treasure are rife. Here's just one of them:

Dead Man's Creek . . .

The story goes that Captain Kidd and his men went upriver searching for a place to bury their treasure. They found a good spot close to Clarke's Island, in the Connecticut river, Northfield, Massachusetts. Kidd then decided that something was needed to warn others away from the loot. Something really scary. What about a dead body? But whose . . . ?

The men drew lots to see which of them would be the unlucky victim. The unfortunate pirate was 'despatched' and his body left to rot at the burial place.

Over the years a legend of a curse grew up around the treasure. It said that, if the gold was found, it could only be dug up if three people did the digging at the same time (we have no idea why). They had to do it at midnight, and the full moon had to be directly overhead. The three diggers must form a triangle around the spot and work in silence. If anyone spoke, the mission would fail.

Unsurprisingly, the remainder of Kidd's treasure has never been found!

Pirate or Privateer?

What's the difference? They all did the same thing – attacking ships at sea.

A privateer, however, was a kind of 'official pirate' who had permission from his country to loot and plunder other ships. Privateers like William Kidd were sent by their governments to go on voyages and commandeer (which is just a nicer way of saying 'steal') enemy ships, also 'commandeering' their riches whilst they were at it. Of course, there was an official motive here: by taking over their enemy's ships, they weakened enemy naval forces, which came in very handy during a war. Any booty that the privateer found would be split between him, his crew and his government. Share and share alike!

Pirates, however, had no such permission and were working for themselves, as sort of self-employed villains. Unlike privateers, if they were caught, they could be hanged. Much riskier . . . but at least they were their own bosses.

Captain Henry Morgan was a very famous privateer who worked for the English and fought the Spanish during the seventeenth century. He attacked cities as well as ships, and became extremely rich. He was eventually knighted by King Charles II and made governor of Jamaica. He even has a brand of rum named after him! Yo ho ho and a bottle of Captain Morgan!

William Kidd became a legendary figure in the years following his death – but are the stories of his missing buried treasure really true?

Here are some other famous pirates who were also said to have buried treasure . . .

Benito 'Bloody Sword' Bonito

BBSB, as we shall call him (though I shouldn't to his face, if you were to meet him) was a Portuguese pirate whose favourite activity was attacking and looting Spanish ships in the seas off Central America, then setting them on fire. He wasn't also nicknamed the 'Terror of the Atlantic' for nothing.

You can see where Benito got his nickname from. Check out the sword . . .

In 1819 Benito pulled off a famously cheeky stunt. He discovered that a huge amount of Spanish gold was being carried by mule overland to Acapulco, Mexico. So he and his men captured all the guards and dressed up in their uniforms. They coolly loaded the treasure straight onto Benito's own ship, the *Mary Deare,* then sailed to Cocos Island in the Pacific Ocean.

Benito was later killed, but his treasure was never found. Some think that his gold may be worth millions. And people are still looking for it . . .

What happened to the treasure?

The beautiful Cocos Island lies about 600 kilometres off the coast of Costa Rica. It has lush rainforests, roaring waterfalls, underground caves, even an ancient volcano. A fantastic place for a game of pirate hide-and-seek – and, of course, perfect for burying treasure . . .

A 1622 Spanish map showing the location of Cocos Island.

Cocos Island was once said to be a popular pirate hangout. The pirates would land there, find a good spot to bury their treasure – and hopefully remember where it was when they came back.

But, as you know, pirates didn't usually live very long (remember the two-year lifespan?). Many think that the island is still home to hoards of treasure, left by those unlucky pirates who perished elsewhere.

BBSB was one of them. He was said to have buried his treasure here under the cliffs – some say in a secret tunnel. It may still be there . . .

Captain Thompson and the Treasure of Lima

Cocos Island is thought to be the hiding place for another famous hoard of treasure, said to be worth hundreds of millions of pounds. It was brought here by an English captain, who disappeared, never to be seen again . . .

Hopeful treasure hunters should be on the lookout for:

Two solid gold life-size statues of the Virgin Mary

273 jewelled swords

Candlesticks of gold and silver

Bars of solid gold

 Hundreds of coins, diamonds and rubies

 Golden crowns . . . and more

Obviously if you're looking at that lot, then you've already found it and I suggest you nip to the bank. But where did it all come from?

The Treasure of Lima came from – no prizes for guessing – Lima, the capital city of Peru. In 1820 the Spanish ruled the region and were worried about a possible uprising against them. The governor of Lima asked a British trader called Captain Thompson to safeguard the valuable hoard (much of which came from local cathedrals and churches) on his vessel. The plan was eventually to ship it over to Mexico, where the Spanish also ruled.

But Captain Thompson betrayed the governor. He sailed straight for Cocos Island, where he and his crew buried the loot.

His plan was foiled when he and the crew were later captured by a Spanish warship. Most of the men were executed. Captain Thompson and his second-in command escaped death by promising to take the Spaniards to the treasure. They kept their word, but once they had all landed at Cocos Island, the pair quickly ran off into the forest.

Neither the men nor the treasure were ever found.

What happened to the treasure?

Over the years, many treasure hunters have landed on Cocos Island in the hope of getting rich. Even one of the presidents of the USA, Franklin Roosevelt, visited three times, hoping to strike gold.

One man was so sure that there was treasure on the island that he spent nearly 20 years searching for it. August Gissler, a German, arrived in 1889 – and didn't leave until 1908. In fact, he stayed for so long that the Costa Rican government made him the island's governor! But Gissler only ever found a few coins.

Why is the treasure so difficult to find? One of the problems is that the island has many networks of unexplored caves and tunnels – brilliant for hiding stuff, but not so great for finding it again. Over the years various earthquakes may have destroyed landmarks and features that would have helped identify its location.

In case you're wondering whether it's worth buying a plane ticket to Cocos Island for your summer holiday (and packing a metal detector), bear in mind that whoever finds the treasure probably won't be getting rich overnight. It would now automatically become the property of the Costa Rican government.

But fear not, my salty sea dogs! Cocos Island isn't the only island that is still rumoured to have treasure buried on it.

The Real Robinson Crusoe

Crusoe – the most famous castaway in the world.

Have you ever heard of *Robinson Crusoe*? It's a famous book written by Daniel Defoe, about an Englishman called Robinson Crusoe who is shipwrecked in 1659.

In the book, Crusoe is stranded on an island off the coast of Trinidad for a mammoth 28 years, two months and nineteen days. Crusoe knows this because he makes a notch with his knife in a piece of wood for every day that passes by (it must have been a very long piece of wood . . .).

The desert island isn't the paradise of most castaways' dreams. Crusoe describes it as *'a dismal unfortunate island, which I call'd the Island of Despair.'*

Though, after 28 years, I'm not surprised he was a bit fed up with his surroundings!

Crusoe relieves the boredom by investigating a cave.

During his very long stay, Robinson Crusoe survives a serious illness, an earthquake and violent hurricanes. And he later discovers that he is not alone –

there are cannibals living on the island! When he rescues a man from the hungry cannibals' clutches, the man becomes Crusoe's friend. Crusoe calls him Friday, because he rescued him on a Friday. Simple, but easy to remember and better than calling him, say, 'Beans' because that's what he happened to have had for lunch that day. Or 'Headache' because he had one when he found him . . . you get my drift. Anyway, I digress . . .

Years later, when a shipload of mutineers turns up one day, Crusoe engineers an adventurous escape plan and returns by ship back to his life in England.

Now, Robinson Crusoe was a completely fictional character – but Daniel Defoe based his story on a real-life person: a privateer called Alexander Selkirk, who survived alone for four years after being left on an uninhabited island in the Pacific Ocean.

In 1704 Selkirk was on a privateering voyage as a member of the crew of the *Cinque Ports*. Following several violent clashes with the Spanish Armada, they stopped off at Más a Tierra (it wasn't called Robinson Crusoe Island then – because the book *Robinson Crusoe* hadn't yet been written, silly!). The crew were tired, hungry and sick, and the ship was badly damaged. Selkirk didn't think it would make the rest of the voyage and he argued with the captain about its seaworthiness. Whether Selkirk was deliberately marooned, or whether he thought it was safer to stay on the island rather than board the leaky old boat, we'll never know. But Selkirk never got back on the ship. Which was just as well, as it later sank, and most of the crew were drowned. A lucky escape . . .

For the next four years, Selkirk survived on fish, berries and wild goat (there were herds of them living on the island – in fact, they were his only company, apart from some rats and cats). Then, one day in 1709, he caught sight of a British ship passing by. Selkirk was picked up by a couple of privateers, and sailed back to London, where he became a mini-celebrity. Daniel Defoe heard his incredible story and *Robinson Crusoe* was published in 1719.

Now, Alexander Selkirk didn't have any treasure with him in 1704. So why is Robinson Crusoe Island – now famous for its castaway connection – also a top spot for treasure hunters?

Alexander Selkirk has fun playing with the local 'kids'.

The Real 'Treasure Island'?

Like Cocos Island, Robinson Crusoe Island was a handy stop-off point for pirates. It is part of the archipelago of Juan Fernández in the Pacific Ocean, about 600 kilometres from the coast of Chile – but, more importantly, it was on one of the Spanish navigation routes. *Aharrr!*

Legend says that a Spanish galleon carrying treasures from South and Central America landed on the island in 1715. Its master, Captain-General Don Juan Esteban de Ubilla was said to have buried its cargo here, in a cave. Ubilla left the island, but before he could return to get the treasure, he was killed in a violent hurricane.

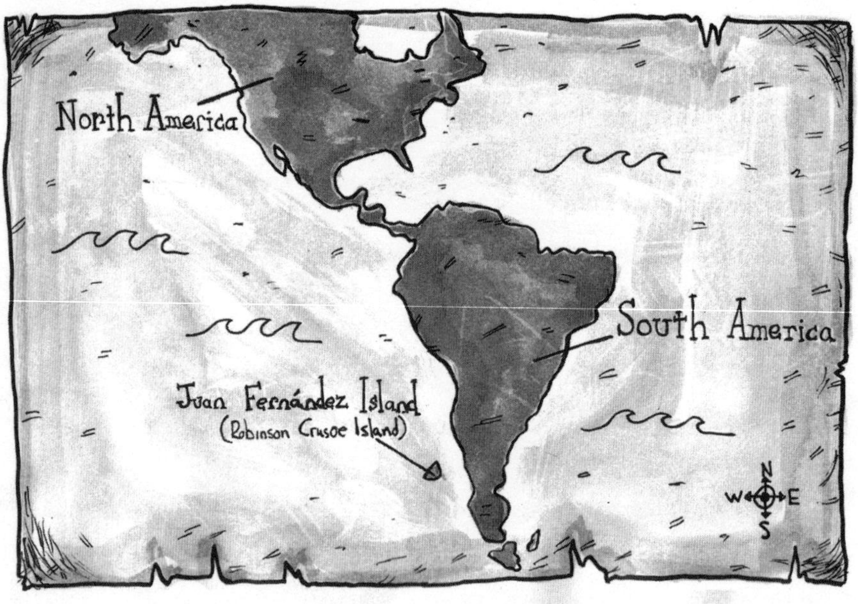

Ubilla was said to have carved an S-shaped map of South America onto the cave wall where the treasure was buried.

Then, in 1761, an English pirate called Cornelius Webb turned up. He'd been sent by British Admiral Lord George Anson on a secret mission to find Ubilla's treasure. Webb found the gold, and before he left he was said to have carved the name of his boss – ANSON – into the wall of the cave. He also carved a rose because of a lovely jewelled rose that was part of the treasure.

Webb sailed off, but a terrible storm set in and broke the ship's mast, so he was forced to return to Robinson Crusoe Island. The ship now needed repairing, so he and his men set off to the nearest Chilean port for help. Before they left, they re-buried the treasure, at a location near the original cave.

A shocked Webb then discovered that his crew planned to mutiny and take the treasure for themselves! So he blew up his ship, killing everyone but himself, and escaped by rowing away in a small boat.

The Pirate Code

Blowing up the ship was certainly an explosive way for Webb to punish his crew. But betraying your captain was always a serious matter for any sailor, pirate or not.

Pirates knew that they weren't above the law. Before a voyage the pirate crew would elect a captain, and everyone would have to agree to a set of rules before they set sail.

For example:

- **No stealing** – this may sound strange, given that pirates stole for a living, but it meant that pirates couldn't steal *from* each other. Trust was vital, especially when you had valuable treasure and needed to share it out fairly
- **No fighting** – again this meant no fighting *with fellow pirates*. Best to save your energy for fighting crews of treasure-laden ships!
- **No acts of tyranny** – things like keeping a secret from the others or deserting the ship

If you broke the rules, one of the worst punishments was to be marooned on a desert island with no food or water (a bit like Selkirk). If your crime was really bad, you might even get tied up and shot. But, strangely, walking the plank was not the usual pirate punishment – that's all a bit of a myth (and a bit of a myth-tery too . . .).

Back to Webb, the only survivor of the ship – and the only person left who knew where the treasure was buried. He sent two letters back to the admiral in England, telling him the location, but Anson suddenly died and the documents were lost, never to be seen again. Webb himself died soon afterwards.

The treasure is said to contain:

More than 800 bags of gold

200 gold bars

21 barrels of precious stones and jewellery

A two-foot-high gold and emerald rose

160 chests of gold and silver coins

Treasure hunters over the years have searched high and low for it.

Pieces of Eight!

The silver coins in Webb's treasure chests were probably 'pieces of eight' – something you might have heard being shouted by a pirate, or squawked by a parrot, in a seafaring movie.

'Pieces of eight' were Spanish coins made of silver, so-called because they were worth eight Spanish reales at the time. Even more valuable were gold coins called doubloons. Any pirate would have been happy to get his hooks on either!

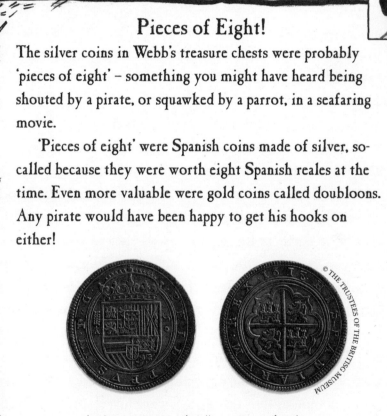

Also known as Spanish dollars, 'pieces of eight' were used by many different countries.

Modern Day Treasure Hunters

In 2005 a group of Chilean investigators announced that they had literally struck gold on Robinson Crusoe Island. They claimed to have found several buried barrels using a mini robot called 'Arturito'. Arturito – who had already helped solve crimes in Chile by locating buried weapons – used GPR (ground-penetrating radar) to scan the ground.

The robot was said to have found an 800-tonne hoard buried about fifteen metres down on the west side of the island. But the treasure – if it does exist – has still not been dug up! The company that owns the robot says that it is too difficult to reach and that the job is too big for them. Strange – it makes you wonder how sure they are about their find . . .

Another keen treasure hunter is an American called Bernard Keiser. He's been looking for the treasure since 1998, and is convinced that a place called Selkirk's Cave holds the key to the location. But because Robinson Crusoe Island is a protected area, he can only use basic tools such as shovels and spades. No mining or explosives are allowed (which would obviously be a lot quicker).

In 2004 Keiser and his team were excited to discover a small amount of Chinese porcelain, thought to be nearly 900 years old. Keiser believes that these pieces are just a tiny part of the treasure hoard and proof that it really exists. Other fragments, such as buttons and bits of old bottle, date from the 1600s.

Keiser is still looking, and now hopes to use new mining methods to locate the loot. Perhaps he'll strike it lucky one of these days?

The Myth of Maps

There is one thing that I'm sure Keiser, and all treasure hunters, would love to find: a treasure map! I can see it now: a furled, brown-edged roll of parchment with a skull and crossbones at the top and a drawing of a desert island. In looped, inky handwriting would be directions for finding 'X' – the spot where the treasure is buried.

Sadly, the idea that pirates made treasure maps is probably another pirate myth, a bit like walking the plank. No one has yet found an authentic map that was used by a real pirate. (Let's face it: anyone who did would have been off like a shot to find the spot.)

If you think about it, it was probably safer for a pirate to keep the secret location in his head, rather than risk drawing it on a piece of paper that could easily fall into someone else's hands. This 1883 map, drawn by a Spanish cartographer, is about the closest thing to a real treasure map you are likely to see.

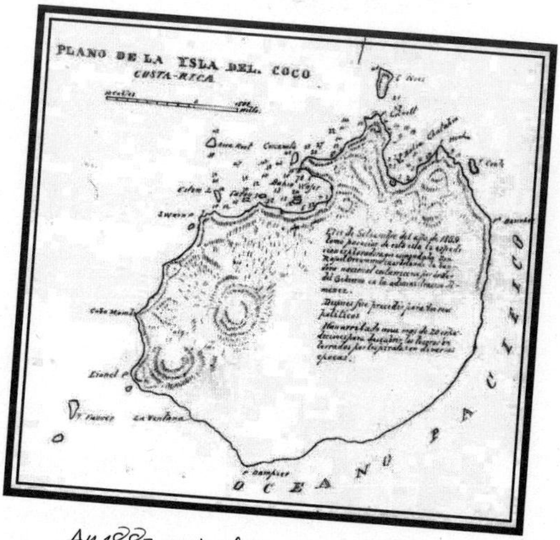

An 1883 map of Cocos Island, which says that 20 expeditions have landed there to find treasure.

MY MISSION

'X' marks the spot, so they say. But how can I find pirate treasure when so many others have failed? And when there aren't any maps?

Undaunted, I'm heading for Robinson Crusoe Island to see exactly what's in Selkirk's Cave.

In 1761 Cornelius Webb found Spanish Captain Ubilla's gold hidden at this spot, inside a rocky tunnel. He used explosives to blow out the rock, creating a larger cave, before loading the treasure onto his ship. It is also where both Ubilla and Webb are said to have made their famous marks on the wall. But, most importantly, the treasure is said to have been re-buried by Webb somewhere close by . . .

Just to make the experience really authentic, I'm going to be a proper castaway for a few days. Once I've been dropped off by a fishing boat, I'll be alone on this part of the island, with only my thoughts – and, of course, a bit of kit – for company.

KIT LIST

- WATER – an essential for a desert-island castaway. If I run out, I'll collect rainwater – hope it rains . . .
- FOOD – best to avoid unknown, possibly poisonous berries and fruits. So I'll watch the local wildlife, see what they eat and follow their example

- KNIFE – I'll use it to make a spear by sharpening a pointy end of a long stick. Ideal for catching fish in shallow waters, but I'll need to move fast
- MATCHES – a fire is essential, to keep warm, for cooking, and for scaring off wild animals. If my matches get damp, I'll have to rub two sticks together instead – but that could take a very long time. A smoking fire also makes a good signal to alert passing ships and planes if I need rescue
- TORCH – to explore the dark cave (no electricity here)
- SPADE AND BAG – in case I find any treasure!
- ALEXANDER SELKIRK'S BOOK – did I mention he'd written a book? Well, he did, and it will come in very useful while exploring the island

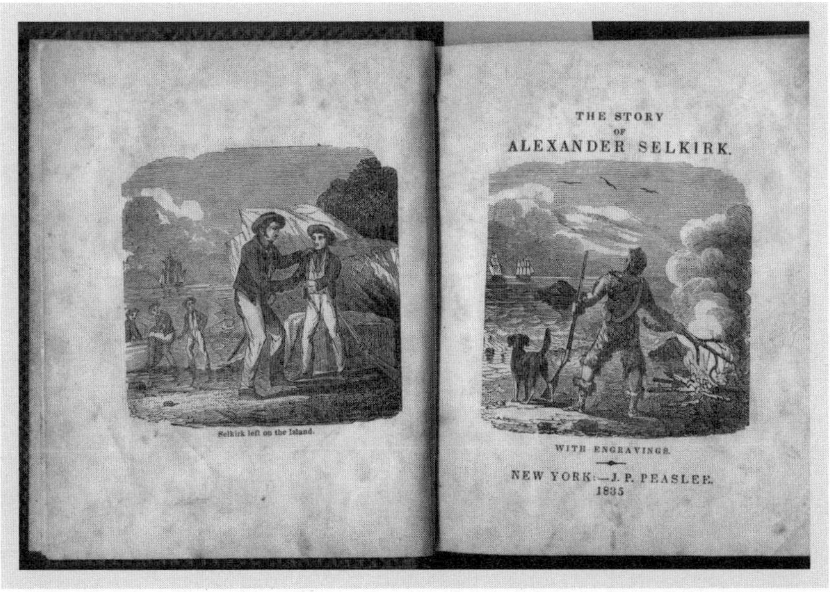

In 1713 Alexander Selkirk wrote all about his four-year island adventure.

I'm feeling pretty confident about my stay. I mean, if Alexander Selkirk managed to survive here all those years ago, I'm sure I can manage it. Selkirk only had a Bible, some clothes, a musket (an old-fashioned gun) and a few tools, including a small axe for chopping wood. When his clothes wore out, he had to wear goat-skins. In 1709 the captain of the ship that picked him up said that Selkirk looked even wilder than the island's goats! He must have looked 'furry' strange . . .

MISSION COMPLETED

My journey began with a long flight to Valparaiso, a large bustling port in Chile. From here I went by fisherman's boat to the island – a 72-hour trip on some very choppy waters. After a lot of 'ups and downs', and a few sick-bags, I was very relieved to arrive at a bay on the north of Robinson Crusoe Island – the closest place to Selkirk's Cave. The island itself looked just like a huge piece of volcanic rock jutting out from the sea, surrounded by high cliffs, and with a large mountainous peak at its centre.

At least I didn't have to build my own shelter. I made my bed for the night in the cave – a large jagged hole, about three metres high, in the side of the rock face. I spent most of the night imagining what it must have been like for Selkirk – alone here over the years, and not knowing when, if ever, he would get home again.

Using my torch, I started reading Selkirk's book. But when I got to the part where rats gnawed his feet while he was asleep at night, I decided it was best to stop . . .

In the morning (I checked – my toes were still there!) I had a good look at the cave walls. There were lots of names and dates scratched into them, presumably made by the many visitors who've been on the island since Selkirk's day. But among them I found the carvings I was looking for: the S-shaped map, the name ANSON and a carving of a rose. Proof that Ubilla and Cornelius Webb were most definitely here. But was it proof of the treasure?

Bernard Keiser thinks so – he believes the treasure was once hidden right here, in the cave. But where? I dug hard with my spade and succeeded in making lots of very small holes. None of which had any treasure in them. The trouble is, the treasure could be anywhere – and it could be buried really deep. After two days of fruitless digging, it was time to give up and get some fresh air.

So I climbed up a steep path through thick forest to reach 'Selkirk's Lookout'. This is a high point where Alexander Selkirk used to sit and watch for passing ships, and where he eventually spotted the one that would save him.

The fishing boat returned to pick me up three days later. I was tired, hungry (spearing fish didn't work – I almost speared my foot instead) and, sadly, treasure-less.

WHAT DO YOU THINK?

1. There is Pirate Treasure Out There Still

Legend has it that pirates always buried their treasure. But is this actually true?

People (and dogs) have always buried things that are precious to them – nothing surprising about that. In the days before banks existed, hiding your valuables was probably the best way of keeping them safe. Pirates were no different. Burying treasure on a desert island could have been just like putting money in a bank for them.

But, realistically, how many pirates would have become so rich that they were forced to bury their stash, rather than spend it all at once?

We know that some did. There's William Kidd and Gardiner's Island, and even our own Sir Francis Drake. He was the first Englishman to circumnavigate the globe, and led the English naval fleet to victory over the Spanish Armada in 1588. But you may not know that Drake was also a privateer. He and his men raided a Spanish mule train at a place called Nombre de Dios in 1572, and stole more gold and silver than they could possibly manage. So they buried it, returning a few days later to retrieve what they could, and sailed for England with their haul. Proof that burying treasure – and finding it again – can actually work . . .

History tells us that in many parts of the world piracy was, for hundreds of years, very big business – no one really knows exactly how many pirates there were. It also tells us that pirates didn't live long lives. So why shouldn't there still be undiscovered treasure left to find? Surely treasure hunters, past and present, wouldn't have spent so much time and money looking for it if they weren't convinced that it existed.

We've looked at just a few places where pirates could have buried their treasure. But there are many, many more islands and secluded spots around the world where pirate treasure could potentially be hidden. We just need to find it!

2. Pirate Treasure is a Myth

Would pirates really have bothered saving their treasure 'for a rainy day'? Think about it – if you were a pirate, would you have risked leaving your fortune in a hole on an island in the middle of nowhere? What were the chances of ever getting it back again? (Pretty poor, judging by the pirates we've been finding out about.)

Let's face it – pirates, by their nature, were more likely to be spenders than savers. Any stolen loot would have been divided up among the pirate crew, who would have had plenty of things to spend it on: parrots, eye-patches, peg legs . . . well, a pirate's got to look the business, hasn't he? And if you're only going to live two years, what's the point in saving?

Bear in mind too that ships of the past carried a lot of valuable cargo that couldn't actually be buried, like spices, fabrics, tobacco and food. Pirates could easily sell or trade these items

– so that's what they did.

But where did all the stories about buried treasure come from, if many weren't true?

Robert Louis Stevenson's *Treasure Island* was published in 1883; it is probably the most famous pirate adventure story ever written. It tells the story of young Jim Hawkins, who finds a treasure map and embarks on an incredible adventure involving a one-legged pirate called Long John Silver, a treasure chest, a desert island and a map. This book was so popular (and still is – find yourself a copy!) that it changed the way people think about pirates. After 1883, legends and myths about pirate treasure, islands and maps were everywhere – and have been ever since.

And perhaps that's all they are. Stories. Because if hoards of pirate treasure did exist, surely they would have been found by now?

YOU DECIDE

A-harr!! Everyone loves a swashbuckling pirate adventure. But now it's up to you to decide if real buried treasure is still there for the finding – or not. Head to the back of the book and mark your 'x' on a spot!

MYSTERY 2

The Curse of the Pharaohs

THE MISSION . . .

To find out if Tutankhamen's tomb had a terrible curse on it . . .

BURNING QUESTIONS

- Are curses for real?
- Who was Tutankhamen?
- What happened to those who opened up his tomb?

MISSION DETAILS

One of the most famous curses in history is thought to have happened after an Englishman made a stunning discovery of treasure. And it's sooo scary, it'll make you want your mummy!

In April 1922 Howard Carter made an amazing find. After years of searching, he and his team finally discovered the tomb of the ancient Egyptian pharaoh Tutankhamen.

When the underground chamber was opened up, piles of priceless treasures were revealed. And inside a beautifully decorated sarcophagus (a stone coffin) lay the mummified body of the young pharaoh, only eighteen years old when he died.

© LEEMAGE/THE BRIDGEMAN ART LIBRARY

Howard Carter opens the sarcophagus – what's 'under wraps'?

Howard Carter must have thought he was the luckiest person in the world . . . but was he?

Soon afterwards, strange and sinister things began happening to some of those involved.

Could the ancient Egyptians have placed a curse upon anyone who dared to open up this precious tomb? Let's find out more . . .

THE LOCATION

Tutankhamen's tomb wasn't easy to find. It took Howard Carter five hard years of research – and a serious amount of digging – before he made his sensational discovery in a place called the Valley of the Kings, near the city of Luxor (once called Thebes) in Egypt.

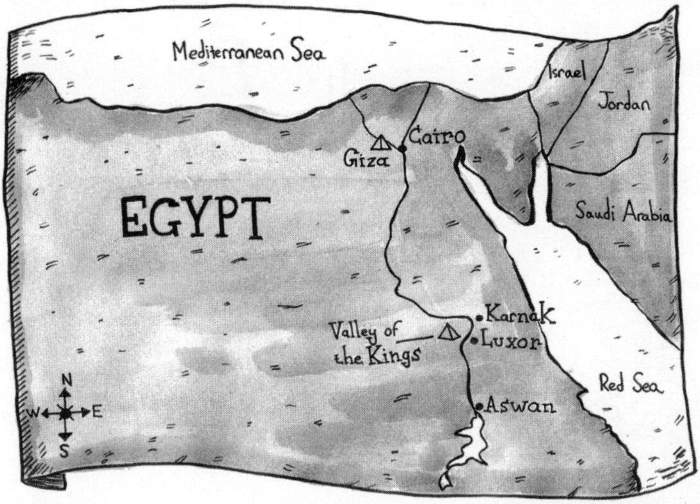

The Valley of the Kings is a large rocky valley surrounded by mountains. It was once an important burial place for the ancient Egyptians – there are more than 60 underground tombs here. Most of them have several rooms inside, connected by corridors and steps. They were made for the great pharaohs (and their families), who ruled from around 1500 to 1100 BC. Tutankhamen's tomb is one of these.

The Valley of the Kings – one of the most visited places in Egypt.

Thousands of people come here every year to see the tombs – and many nearby temples and ruins – at what's been called 'the world's greatest open-air museum'.

But what about Tut? Tutankhamen's body can still be seen in his original tomb, but all his lavish treasures are on display (under very high security!) at the Egyptian Museum in Cairo. No chance of any grave robbers digging their way in there . . .

THE EVIDENCE

The tomb of Tutankhamen was one of the most exciting finds of the 20th century. It is the only ancient Egyptian tomb that has ever been found intact, complete with treasures.

And no one was more excited than the man who worked so hard to find it . . .

Howard Carter was a talented and keen archaeologist who had got his very first job in Egypt in 1891, when he was just seventeen.

But it wasn't until 1917 that he got properly started on the project that was to make him famous all over the world.

At the time, most experts thought that all the tombs in the Valley of the Kings had been discovered. Not Howard Carter. He believed that there was still one more tomb to be unearthed. That of a little-known king called Tutankhamen.

But the dig would be expensive and Carter needed money to pay for it. Luckily, he found the perfect sponsor in Lord Carnarvon, who was not only wealthy, but a massive fan of Egyptology, which is, well yes, you've guessed it. . .

Carter and his team dug for five long years, looking for the missing pharaoh. By 1922 Carnarvon (and his wallet) was ready to give up, but Carter persuaded him to be patient for just a little longer.

The Big Find

The final season's excavation began. On 4 November 1922 a member of the team was digging in the sand with a stick, when he hit a stone step. Carter was immediately alerted. A day's excavation revealed the top of a flight of steps and what seemed to be a blocked entrance covered in mysterious oval stamps. Carter recognized one of them – the royal necropolis seal, showing a jackal and nine captives. Could he have finally found what he'd been searching for?

The Burial Chamber. The intact necropolis seal upon the doorway of the third funerary shrine of Tutankhamun.

Carter – though incredibly excited – calmly ordered the secret stairway to be temporarily filled in again, and quickly got in touch with Lord Carnarvon in England. Carter later wrote:

Anything, literally anything, might lie beyond that passage, and it needed all my self-control to keep from breaking down the doorway, and investigating then and there . . .
(*The Tomb of Tut-ankh-Amen* by Howard Carter, 1923)

Lord Carnarvon arrived in Egypt a few days later, and on 23 November the pair broke through the blocked doorway, revealing a passageway beyond. It was filled with rubble, all of which had to be cleared. By 26 November they had reached a second sealed door. Carter peered in, holding a flickering candle. Lord Carnarvon asked, 'Can you see anything?' – to which Carter replied: 'Yes, wonderful things!'

The incredible sight that greeted Howard Carter.

Inside the 3,300-year-old antechamber of Tutankhamen's tomb lay piles of glittering golden objects – things like:

Solid gold chariots

Gilded animal couches – a cow, a hippo and a lion

A golden throne, a bed, chests and chairs

Clothes, including a leopardskin cloak with a golden head and silver claws

 Two life-size statues of King Tut 'guarding' the tomb

Tut really was the King of Bling!

The objects were crammed into the room quite untidily. Historians think that Tutankhamen probably died unexpectedly, so everything was done in a bit of a rush.

In February 1923 Carter and his team finally entered the last room – the burial chamber. Inside was a massive golden shrine (like a big box). Inside that were three more shrines, then a stone sarcophagus, which in turn contained three coffins. *Phew!* It was a bit like opening a giant Egyptian pass-the-parcel!

Inside the final solid gold coffin was the mummified body of the boy-king Tutankhamen, wearing the famous gold and blue death mask.

Tutankhamen – a golden boy with a taste for blue eyeliner.

The body had lain undisturbed for more than 3,000 years. Maybe it was best kept under wraps . . .

Tutankhamen – the Boy-King

Can you imagine becoming king at the age of just nine? Would you be ready to act as supreme ruler and be treated as a god on Earth? If the answer's 'yes', then you and Tutankhamen would have had a lot in common.

Tut became pharaoh (that's what they called kings in ancient Egypt) in about 1337 BC, when he was just a lad. He reigned over Egypt for nine or ten years.

Tut wasn't a particularly famous pharaoh and not that much is known about him – apart from the fact that he died at about the age of eighteen. Ah, yes – the downside to being a royal in those days (and during much of history) is that you might get murdered by a power-hungry relative who wanted your throne. Is this what happened to Tut?

Some experts think so. An X-ray of his body showed damage to his skull – was he killed by a blow to the head? One theory is that his adviser, a powerful man called Ay, arranged for Tut to be killed so that he could become the next pharaoh. 'Skullduggery' in the royal court? Ay!

But a more recent scan in 2006 showed another injury. Tut's leg had been broken just below the knee not long before he died. Some think he may have had a hunting accident and then died of an infection.

Tut may have lived a short life, but hopefully it was a good one. Given the amount of stuff he was sent off with, Tut was certainly well-prepared for whatever the afterlife had in store for him. Pharaoh-nuff, as they say!

© P.PLAILLY/ E.DAYNES/ SCIENCE PHOTO LIBRARY

Is this what Tut could have looked like? A modern reconstruction of his face.

Grave-robbing, Egyptian Style . . .

It took months to carefully explore and excavate Tut's entire tomb. No wonder – there were a whopping 5,398 objects inside it! But why?

The ancient Egyptians believed in an afterlife, and preparing a dead person for this momentous journey to 'the other side' was very important to them.

They had to have everything they could possibly need in the next world. Things that would help them carry on living in luxury – from the best quality food and clothes to beautifully crafted furniture, chariots to get around in and beds to sleep on. All these items were placed in the tomb alongside the body. Trouble was, these things were not only useful but incredibly valuable. So, naturally, robbers tried to break in. The Egyptians did everything they could to foil the burglars:

- They used the best architects to design the tombs
- They created cunning false doorways to fool intruders
- Hidden chambers were concealed behind other rooms
- Thick slabs of stone blocked passageways
- Some think that they even placed a curse on whoever disturbed the pharaoh . . .

Unfortunately, most of these safeguards failed. From ancient times, grave robbers found ingenious ways to get into all the hidden places. Which is why all the tombs in the Valley of the Kings (apart from King Tut's) had been completely stripped of their treasures years before Howard Carter appeared on the scene.

Note: Only Very Important Dead People – pharaohs, queens, nobles, etc. – got the VIP treatment. Commoners like you and me would have been buried in the sand, with a couple of household objects, if we were lucky. Great: itchy sand and a kettle for company for all of eternity. Just as well we weren't born in ancient Egypt . . .

Even King Tut's tomb had been broken into. Evidence showed that there had been at least two attempted robberies of the tomb, probably very soon after Tutankhamen's burial. Luckily they didn't get as far as any of the really valuable stuff in the antechamber and beyond.

Did any of those grave robbers suffer the wrath of a curse? We will never know . . .

The Curse Begins . . .

Have you ever heard of the 'Curse of the Mummy'? If you think it's what your mum yells at you when you've forgotten to tidy your room – it's actually much worse (if that's possible) . . .

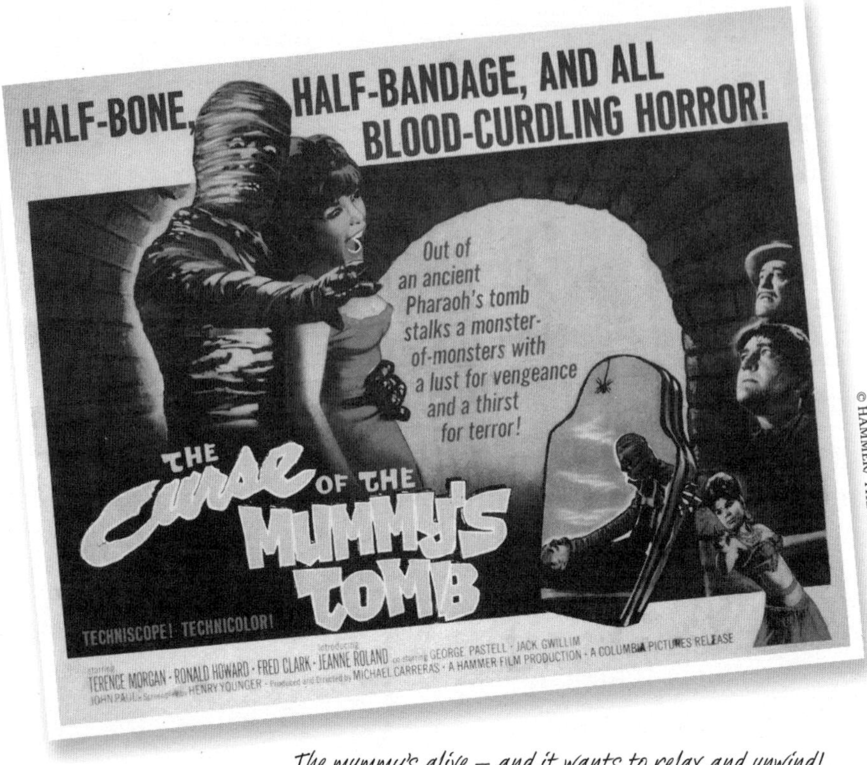

The mummy's alive – and it wants to relax and unwind!

The story of the Curse of the Mummy has been seen in lots of horror movies, old and modern. It goes like this:

When its ancient tomb is disturbed, a huge, hideous mummy comes to life and starts lumbering about dangerously, attacking everyone around it. With its flapping bandages (or is it toilet roll?) and beady eyes, it's really not the kind of mummy you'd want to come and tuck you up in bed at night.

However, you'll be relieved to hear that in real life there is no evidence that an Egyptian mummy has ever risen from its

tomb and started threatening people. Phew . . .
But did the Egyptians have other kinds of curses, just as bad as a living mummy?

Leave my mummy alone!

The ancient Egyptians believed that if a person's body was stolen or interfered with, their spirit would not be able to return to their mummified body at night and there would be no afterlife for them.

That's why threats have been found inscribed on some tomb entrances. The punishments sounded horrible – enough to terrify anyone who dared tamper with a tomb. Take a look at this one, written in hieroglyphics on the entrance to the Third Dynasty tomb of Petety at Giza.

The gods will not allow anything to happen to me. If anyone does anything bad to my tomb, then the crocodile, hippopotamus and lion will eat him.

Imagine being eaten by a croc, a hippo and a lion – a pretty 'wild' way to go . . .

Other threats found on different tombs and statues include:

I shall seize his neck like that of a goose.
He shall die from hunger and thirst.
His relatives shall detest him.
He shall be miserable and persecuted.

I'm sure there were others. You might make up your own:

He shall stub his toe really badly on the coffee table and spill his drink.
His alarm clock shall go off at random times for the rest of his life and he shall never get a good night's sleep.
He shall forever be losing his pen just when he needs it.

I could go on . . . but I shan't because we need to get back to King Tut and his own, special curse.

The Curse of Tutankhamen

So, Tut. Was there any sign of a curse on his tomb?

Some say that the following words were inscribed in hieroglyphics by the entrance to the tomb when it was found:

They who enter this sacred tomb shall swift be visited by wings of death.

Wings of death! Sounds really scary. But strangely no trace of this 'curse' remains – it seems to have mysteriously vanished over time. Did this message ever really exist or was it just made up?

Whether it did or not, weird stuff soon started happening . . .

- Just two months after the tomb was opened, tragedy struck. In February 1923 Lord Carnarvon was bitten on the face by a mosquito and the bite became infected. He died in April

- At the moment of Lord Carnarvon's death, all the lights in Cairo – the capital city of Egypt – suddenly went out
- At the same time, in England, Carnarvon's faithful dog, Susie, let out a mournful howl – and dropped dead!
- Spookily, when Tutankhamen's mummy was finally unwrapped in 1925, it was found to have a wound on the left cheek – in exactly the same place as Lord Carnarvon's fatal insect bite! Oo-er!

Rumours began to spread of a mysterious curse, and the newspapers reported stories of a vengeful King Tut who had placed a curse upon anyone who opened the tomb. The British Museum in London was inundated with gifts of Egyptian relics from owners who were scared that they might be punished by the curse too . . .

The deaths continued. In the years following the discovery, eleven people connected with the discovery of the tomb died in strange circumstances. Among them were:

- Aubrey Herbert, Lord Carnarvon's half-brother. He died in hospital after having his teeth removed in September 1923. He had just returned from a visit to Luxor
- Lord Carnarvon's other half-brother, Captain Richard Bethell (who was also Howard Carter's personal secretary), was mysteriously found dead in his bed in November 1929

- Bethell's father, Lord Westbury, jumped to his death from the top of his apartment in February 1930
- Just four days later, Edgar Steele, the man in charge of handling the tomb artefacts at the British Museum, died in hospital following a minor operation
- Jay Gould, a businessman, visited the tomb and in 1923 died of pneumonia
- Sir Archibald Douglas-Reid, the man who X-rayed Tutankhamen's mummy, died mysteriously in 1924

But what happened to Howard Carter, the main man behind the excavation? Incredibly, he lived to the age of 65 – and never believed in curses! He stayed in Egypt, working on the excavation until 1932, then returned to London, where he spent his time touring and giving lectures about Egypt.

Other Famous Curses

What is a curse exactly? It's a kind of bad wish or spell that someone believes has been placed on an object or a person. Superstitious people might believe in curses – but how superstitious are you? Take a look at these two famous curses and see what you think:

The Hope Diamond

Beautiful, sparkling and incredibly valuable – most people would think themselves lucky to own a real diamond. But maybe not this one. The Hope Diamond is said to bring bad luck and disaster to its owner. It's a huge, deep blue diamond,

about the size of a walnut. But it's worth a bit more than your average nut – about 250 million dollars more!

The Hope Diamond has had a long history of different owners – and some have certainly had more than their fair share of bad luck:

Can a jewel really be unlucky?

- The man who was said to have first stolen the diamond – Jean-Baptiste Tavernier – was later killed by wild dogs in Russia. Unlucky . . .
- Another owner, King Louis XVI of France (along with his queen, Marie Antoinette) lost his head in 1793 during the French Revolution. Very unlucky . . .
- A wealthy American, Evalyn McLean, bought the diamond in 1911. Her son was killed in a car crash and her daughter died at the age of 25. The family newspaper went bankrupt and Evalyn's husband later became insane. Incredibly unlucky . . .

The Hope Diamond sounds a lot more hope-less than hope-ful. But why is it supposed to be cursed?

It's said that the stone was originally stolen from India, taken from the forehead or the eye of a statue of the Hindu goddess, Sita. Perhaps this is Sita's revenge for having her precious diamond taken away from her? A kind of evil eye?

The diamond was given to the Smithsonian National Museum of Natural History in Washington, DC, USA, where it is currently on display – but no one has ever offered to buy it from them . . .

Tecumseh's curse

This curse was supposed to have been placed upon all American presidents by an angry native-American chieftain called Tecumseh. It was in revenge for being defeated by William Henry Harrison – a future US president – in the Battle of Tippecanoe, in 1811. Tecumseh was said to have sent Harrison a message saying that every 20 years an American president would die . . .

Spookily, following his prediction, seven presidents *did* die – and all of them were elected in a year ending in a zero. Each of those election years was exactly 20 years apart. Weird . . .

The seven dead presidents:

1840: **William Henry Harrison** – died from pneumonia, 1841
1860: **Abraham Lincoln** – assassinated April 1865
1880: **James Abram Garfield** – assassinated July 1881
1900: **William McKinley** – assassinated September 1901
1920: **Warren Gamaliel Harding** – died from food poisoning, 1923
1940: **Franklin Delano Roosevelt** – died from a stroke in 1945
1960: **John Fitzgerald Kennedy** – assassinated November 1963

In March 1981 President Ronald Reagan survived an assassination attempt. Some say this marked the end of the curse, as none of the presidents since then have followed the pattern.

What do you think?

MY MISSION

Probably the best way of finding out if a tomb is cursed is to:

1. Open up an Egyptian tomb; then . . .
2. See if a terrible fate befalls me.

BUT this idea falls down in two very important places. Firstly, I don't think there are many, if any, Egyptian tombs left for me to find. Secondly, even if there were, I'd be more than a bit nervous about breaking open that sealed doorway. I mean, what if ancient Egyptian curses do exist? Being eaten by a croc, a hippo and a lion isn't likely to happen in my neck of the woods (unless the local zoo has a break-out), but you never know . . .

So, instead, I'm going to the place where there are more ancient Egyptian tombs than you can shake a stick at. The Valley of the Kings, of course. I'll get to see the real Tutankhamen's tomb for myself. And see if the atmosphere feels, well, cursed in any way . . .

KIT LIST

- LARGE BOTTLE OF WATER – essential in a hot, dry climate
- HIGH-FACTOR SUN-BLOCK AND SUN HAT – there are no shady trees here to shelter under
- STURDY TRAINERS – many of the tombs have crumbly, uneven surfaces and steps – it would be easy to take a tumble. And I don't want to end up with a broken leg – that would be spookily like King Tut!

- A HEAD TORCH – it can be pretty dark in some of the tombs and I'll need to see where I'm going – and have my hands free in case I stumble
- A PEN AND NOTEBOOK – for taking notes of any interesting hieroglyphics I might come across
- A TUTANKHAMEN HISTORY BOOK – would be useful
- CAMERA WITH A FLASH – for taking shots in those dark chambers

MISSION COMPLETED

Wow. Egypt was hot. Really hot! Temperatures here can reach 120° Fahrenheit (49° Celsius). So I had to get going very early in the morning, before the heat got too much. My visit to Tutankhamen's tomb started with an alarm call at 5 a.m.

The entrance to the tomb would have been easy to miss – it's just a plain rectangular doorway cut into the rock. Once inside, you walk through a narrow passageway and turn right into the antechamber. It looked very different from when Howard Carter first found it – there are no heaps of glittering treasure here any more, just a bare room. All the tomb's riches have long since gone to the Egyptian Museum in Cairo.

Then it was straight on to the burial chamber. Inside, it was hot, humid and packed with people desperate to get a glimpse of the famous pharaoh. The room was small, with beautiful golden walls covered in paintings of Egyptian figures and animals. In the middle, protected by glass, lay King Tut himself.

© D E A PICTURE LIBRARY/ GETTY IMAGES

Here lies King Tut.

It was all super-spooky. The small, dark chamber. The mummified corpse of Tutankhamen, who had been lying here for more than 3,000 years. I nervously wondered if he might rise up out of his sarcophagus for a quick 'coffin break'. Yes, I've definitely been watching too many 'Curse of the Mummy' horror movies . . . but now that I've seen a real Egyptian mummy, I can see why they make such good subjects!

Despite my nerves, I survived my visit – no signs of any strange infections or lights going out, or anything else weird. And I feel very lucky to have seen the real King Tut because he won't be here for much longer. Tut is a really popular guy – he gets up to a thousand visitors a day! And that's the problem. If all those people carry on tramping through the most popular tomb in town, there won't be much left of it in a few years' time. To stop the damage, Tut's tomb will soon be closed to the public, but an exact replica is being made for visitors to see at the Valley of the Kings.

WHAT DO YOU THINK?

1. The Curse of Tutankhamen Doesn't Exist

Yes, people *did* die after the tomb was discovered – but maybe those people would have died anyway? If the tomb really had been cursed, surely everyone present would have died or had something awful happen to them?

Let's look at the facts. There were 22 people present when the tomb was first opened in 1922 – and by 1934 only six of them had died. There were just ten people there when Tut's mummy was finally unwrapped – and none of them died very soon afterwards.

There's no doubt that Lord Carnarvon's death was very strange. But was it all just a coincidence? The story of all the lights going out in Cairo at the moment of his death is true, but if you've ever visited Cairo, you'll know that blackouts do happen – and in the 1920s the electricity supply was even more unreliable than it is now.

And what about Howard Carter? As the main leader of the expedition and the first to enter the tomb, he should have been a prime target for Tut's revenge. But he lived to the age of 65.

Howard Carter himself never believed in a curse (if he had, he probably wouldn't have chosen a career as an Egyptian archaeologist!). And there has never been any writing found on Tut's tomb that resembles a curse, despite the story of the spooky 'wings of death' inscription found on the entrance, which could easily have been made up by the press.

Some experts say that Egyptian curses simply don't exist. They think that tomb inscriptions were just messages meant to frighten off enemies. They believe that all the stories of cursed mummies were made up by newspapers and films in the West to frighten audiences. If that's true, it worked!

2. The Tombs are Toxic

There could be another reason to explain why some people who visited Egyptian tombs got sick, or even died. Some experts think that there could be dangerous bacteria inside them. But how did it get there?

As well as treasures, the Egyptians put food, plants and other living things into the tombs. These items would have decayed, creating a perfect breeding ground for bacteria. And once the tombs were opened up, the bacteria could have escaped, making people close by really ill.

It's also possible that the Egyptians deliberately poisoned their tombs to defend them from intruders.

The ancient Egyptians certainly knew their poisons. They extracted toxic substances from all kinds of plants, minerals, animals and insects. It's possible that they placed these lethal poisons inside the tombs, waiting to wreak havoc on anyone who disturbed the sleeping pharaoh. Experts say that some poisons can live for hundreds of years if they are sealed up in a space with no light or air.

BUT if the poisonous air was to blame, wouldn't all the people present at the opening of a tomb have got sick in some way? And that didn't happen with Tut's tomb.

3. The Curse is Real!

If you think that Tutankhamen's curse is real, firstly you have to believe that curses exist. Secondly, you have to believe that Egyptians cursed their tombs.

We know that the Egyptians believed in magic. They called it 'heka' and thought it was the magical force responsible for creating their world. Heka was used by most Egyptians, from the lowly to the noble.

Imagine a world where priests perform magical rituals to protect the pharaoh, scorpion-charmers use magic to get rid of poisonous creatures, and nurses use magic to heal the sick. People called 'protection-makers' offer you amulets – small, magical objects to wear or carry for protection.

Some of this magic was used to try and harm others. Historians know that Egyptian ceremonies were performed to curse enemies. Drawings of enemy gods were stamped on, burned, then dissolved in buckets of urine!

A baboon to protect you – one of many different kinds of Egyptian amulets.

The names of human enemies were written on clay pots or figures and then burned, broken or buried.

The ancient Egyptians did everything they could to protect their precious tombs. If they went to all the trouble of building hidden rooms and blocking up doorways, mightn't they have used their magic to put a curse on the intruders too?

You might also think that the deaths following Tut's discovery prove that the curse was real. Some of the ways in which the people died were indeed strange and mysterious. Even stranger is the tale of Susie the terrier who, thousands of miles away at the Carnarvon family home, dropped down dead at the very moment when Lord Carnarvon died in Egypt. How can anyone explain that?

Many people around the world seem to believe in curses – but are you one of them? Turn to the end of the end of the book and cast your vote!

YOU DECIDE

Do you think that an ancient curse caused the deaths of those associated with Tut? Or do you think that all curses are just made-up nonsense, invented to scare superstitious people. It's your call!

MYSTERY 3

The Legend of El Dorado

THE MISSION . . .

. . . to find out if the legendary kingdom of El Dorado really exists . . .

BURNING QUESTIONS

- Where is El Dorado?
- Why is everyone so desperate to find it?
- Is it real – or imaginary?

MISSION DETAILS

A city of glittering gold. Sparkling jewels, and riches beyond your wildest dreams . . .

This is El Dorado. Hopeful treasure hunters have spent years looking for it – and some have even lost their lives during their quest. How hard would you try to find a place like this?

Treasure hunters dream of such a golden opportunity . . .

The mystery of El Dorado began in the sixteenth century, when explorers from Spain began arriving on the coasts of Central and South America. There was a lot to conquer – a massive continent, which they called the 'New World'.

The explorers soon realized that the New World, with its vast resources of gold and silver, could make them very rich and powerful. So when they heard about a legendary ceremony that involved throwing away piles of precious gold and jewels, their ears pricked up. Treasure for the taking? *'Si, señor!'*

The ceremony was supposed to take place near a mountain lake, where a local tribe called the Muisca welcomed a new chief by covering him in a sticky substance, then showering him in pure golden dust. Like a precious golden statue, the chief would drift out onto the water on a raft. They named him El Dorado – 'the gilded one'.

El Dorado would then jump into the lake, washing off the golden dust, accompanied by cheers and shouts. 'Water' way to celebrate!

Then – and this was the really interesting part for the Spaniards – piles of jewels and treasures were thrown into the water as a gift to their lake-dwelling god.

From this ritual, rumours grew of an entire kingdom awash with gold and other precious treasures.

The legend of El Dorado has survived for hundreds of years – but the real El Dorado has never been found . . .

THE LOCATION

Lake Guatavita can be found high up in the Andes mountains, about 50 kilometres from bustling Bogotá, the capital city of modern-day Colombia.

The circular lake lies inside a crater, which was created by a massive meteorite strike about 2,000 years ago. The Muisca knew nothing of meteorites. They believed the almighty bang was caused by the arrival of the sun god, who then made his home at the bottom of the lake. Must have been a really 'deep' guy . . .

THE EVIDENCE

The Spanish first heard the story of El Dorado from native South Americans they had captured. These tales were backed up by others, like Colombian writer Juan Rodríguez Freyle, who in 1636 wrote:

By that lake of Guatavita they made a great raft of reeds, decorating it as beautifully as they could . . . They undressed the heir, anointed him with a sticky earth and dusted him with ground and powdered gold, so that he went in the raft completely covered with this metal. The golden Indian made his offering, casting all the gold and emeralds he had brought into the middle of the lake . . .

The guy on the right is blowing golden dust over the new chief. Bet there were lots of volunteers

It didn't take the Spanish long to find the lavish lake of legend. But getting the treasure out of the lake was another matter (this was way before scuba-diving had been thought of). The only way was to drain the lake of water – but how?

Draining Disasters

- In 1545 two conquistadors and a large group of workers used 'buckets' made from hollowed-out gourds (a sort of large fruit) to scoop water from the lake. They must have done some serious scooping because, amazingly, they managed to lower the water level by three metres! It took them three months – but their super-scooping was in vain. A little gold was found, but nothing like the riches they had imagined

- In 1578 treasure hunter Antonio de Sepúlveda had a better idea. Why not cut a huge chunk of earth out of the rim of the lake and lower the water level that way? Great idea, Antonio! He went ahead, but the earthworks collapsed and many workers were killed. Again, only a small amount of gold was found

- In 1898 a group of 'experts' from London dug a tunnel which opened up in the centre of the lake. Success! Most of the water drained away. But it left behind a deep, sticky mud that was too sludgy to investigate – by the next day, the mud had been baked solid by the hot sun. Finding a mere £500 worth of gold, the Londoners gave up. And the lake soon filled again

- Several other attempts were made over the years using mechanical earth movers, but nothing much was found. It almost seemed as if the God Who Lived in the Lake didn't want anyone to find his treasure; treasure which could have looked like this:

© THE ART ARCHIVE / ALAMY

The beautiful raft of legend . . . definitely worth its weight in gold.

This raft was found inside a Muisca clay jar, hidden in a cave south of Bogotá, in 1969. It shows the El Dorado ceremony in action. Are there more treasures like this to be found?

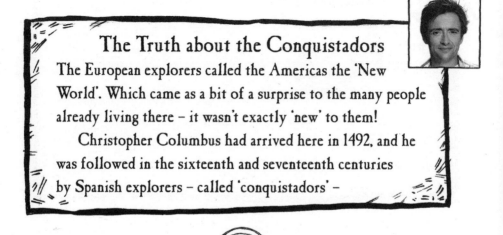

The Truth about the Conquistadors

The European explorers called the Americas the 'New World'. Which came as a bit of a surprise to the many people already living there – it wasn't exactly 'new' to them!

Christopher Columbus had arrived here in 1492, and he was followed in the sixteenth and seventeenth centuries by Spanish explorers – called 'conquistadors' –

eager to conquer these lands. But native South Americans had been living on the continent for many hundreds of years before the Europeans arrived – and changed everything.

- Many conquistadors saw the locals as savages, and exploited them, robbing their towns and villages and taking their treasures. Battles sometimes broke out between the Europeans and the American Indians, but local bows and arrows were no match for smoking Spanish guns
- The Spanish wanted to change the locals' religion. They brought priests with them, so that they could persuade the natives to become Catholics, just like them
- The arrival of the explorers brought other deadly consequences – diseases like measles and flu. The locals had never had these illnesses before, and thousands died. Some experts think that 90 per cent of the population were killed by European diseases

Between them, the Spanish, closely followed by the Portuguese, colonized much of South and Central America. They became rulers and were incredibly powerful in the region for more than 400 years. (The English, meanwhile, were busy colonizing many other parts of the world, including North America.)

Stories like that of El Dorado encouraged Europeans to journey further into the continent to find as much gold as possible. Were they adventurous explorers – or greedy invaders?

A Change of Location

So – if the treasure of El Dorado wasn't at the bottom of Lake Guatavita – where was it?

The search eventually moved from Colombia to Venezuela and Guyana in the east.

Rumours began spreading that El Dorado could be found much further east. After the lake fiasco, the Spanish turned their attention to the eastern foothills of the Andes, and several explorers set out to see what they could find. Including a particularly famous conquistador called Gonzalo Pizarro.

Pizarro – finding El Dorado would certainly have been a feather in his cap . . .

Pizarro's quest

Pizarro was living in Ecuador when he heard a story told by the locals about a wonderful place full of gold and spices that could be found in the mountains of the east. Here lived a tribe so rich that they covered their chief in gold. Believing it was the fabled El Dorado, Pizarro went east in 1541. He didn't exactly travel light, taking with him:

- Hundreds of Spanish soldiers
- About 4,000 native South Americans
- 4,000 pigs (for food)
- Horses, dogs and llamas (for carrying supplies)
- A large river ship called a brigantine
- His friend and lieutenant, Francisco de Orellana
- . . . And the kitchen sink (just joking)

Despite all this preparation, the expedition didn't go well. The going was really tough and many of the men died along the way from disease and attacks by unfriendly locals.

Orellana and a few men sailed down the river in search of food but never returned (apparently Orellana's men wouldn't let him turn back because they didn't want to share the food they had found with the others!).

Incredibly, Orellana eventually ended up discovering the mighty Amazon river and becoming the first known person to travel down its entire length! Despite this great achievement, he never found El Dorado – and neither did Pizarro.

Martínez and Manoa

But more rumours were emerging about El Dorado's location. In 1542 a Spaniard called Juan Martínez told his strange story. He had been part of an expedition that went off with a bang when their supply of gunpowder accidentally exploded. Martínez got the blame, and his punishment was to be tied up and set adrift in a boat on a river. Presumably to a watery end . . .

Martínez would probably have died, had he not been captured by a group of locals. He said he was then blindfolded and marched for four days to an unknown location. When his blindfold was taken off, he found himself in an incredible city, full of houses made of shining gold and precious stones. He was taken to a palace and met the king, who was called El Dorado. Just like the story, El Dorado was bathed with gold dust every day.

Martínez begged for his freedom; El Dorado refused at first, but later changed his mind and set him free. The Spaniard eventually managed to get to the city of Margarita, where he told everyone his incredible tale. It was indeed incredible – and to this day no one knows whether he made the whole thing up or not.

Martínez was convinced that the city he had been taken to was called Manoa, on the shores of a great lake named Parima. Parima was then part of Guyana, in north-east South America.

An ancient map shows the location of Manoa – but did it ever exist?

Manoa became the next hot spot for El Dorado hunters, and the Spanish mounted five major expeditions to find it.

Going for Gold

The quest for gold was tough – with soaring mountains, steamy rainforests and huge plains to cross – but Pizarro, and others like him, didn't mind risking their lives on dangerous expeditions. They had a taste for treasure – and they wanted more.

They were inspired by another Spanish explorer, Hernán Cortés, who had already defeated the mighty Aztecs in what is now Mexico. Pizarro, who'd set out from Spain in 1530, went on to do a similar thing in South America, battling the Inca of Peru.

The Inca Empire was huge, dominating the mountains of the Andes for about 4,000 kilometres, all the way from the coast to the Amazonian rainforest. The Incas ruled over more than 12 million people. But it took just two years for Pizarro and his men to defeat them and take their gold and silver, using some underhand tactics along the way.

The sneaky Spanish arranged a meeting with a powerful Inca emperor called Atahualpa. But they kidnapped him and demanded a huge ransom of gold, equivalent to millions of pounds today. Once they got the gold, instead of setting Atahualpa free, as they had promised, they killed him. The Spanish then invaded Cuzco, the most important city of the Inca Empire.

One of the first Spaniards to enter Cuzco couldn't believe his eyes at the sight of so much gold. He described seeing decorations, figurines, animals, vases, pots, jewellery – everything seemed to be made of gold!

'They had also a garden, the clods of which were made of pieces of fine gold; and it was artificially sown with golden maize, the stalks, as well as the leaves and cobs, being of that metal.'

No wonder the Spanish got a taste for treasure. And a real determination to find El Dorado . . . whatever it took.

Raleigh – Truth or Myth?

It wasn't only the Spanish who wanted gold. You're sure to have heard of Sir Walter Raleigh. (No, he didn't invent the bicycle . . .)

Raleigh was actually a famous English courtier and explorer. He was also a great favourite of the powerful Queen Elizabeth I.

There are a few good stories about him. But which ones are true? See what you think:

Sir Walter – so 'frilled' to meet you!

STORY – Sir Walter Raleigh once laid his fine cloak over a muddy puddle so that Queen Elizabeth wouldn't have to get her royal toes dirty. What a gentleman!

TRUTH – Though this kind of thing probably happened to her all the time, sadly it never happened with Sir Walter. The cloak-and-puddle story is a myth, one that was probably made up by a historian called Thomas Fuller, who was known for 'exaggerating'.

STORY – Following one of his expeditions, Sir Walter brought the first potato back to England. It's been one of the nation's favourite vegetables ever since.

TRUTH – He didn't. Potatoes were introduced to Europe by the Spanish, and they gradually became popular throughout the continent, and in Britain. But they are still one of the nation's favourite veggies.

But one thing people don't generally know about Sir Walter – and this one is actually true – is that he believed in the legend of El Dorado. So much so that he organized, at huge expense, two expeditions to South America in search of the fabled treasure.

Sir Walter really wanted to impress good Queen Bess (well, who wouldn't?). So in 1595 he left England, taking five ships with him. He had a plan. He would sail to the island of Trinidad, leave the ships there, then travel to the mainland of Guyana in smaller boats and sail along the Orinoco river to find the legendary city of Manoa.

Raleigh and his men got as far as the Orinoco river but then gave up. They had some good excuses. The conditions were terrible, the rainy season was starting (and we're not just talking drizzle – this is the rainforest, remember!). Also, the Spanish were dangerously close behind them.

But Sir Walter's dream didn't end there. In 1617 he set sail again, this time with fourteen ships and about 1,000 men, including his son, Walt. Most of the men got as far as the Orinoco river. But the Spanish (who weren't very happy about the Brits being on their territory) caught up with them and during the fighting Raleigh's son was killed.

The English searched in vain for about two months, all the while fending off Spanish attacks. They found nothing, and Sir Walter returned home a sad and dejected man, with only one ship left and deserted by many of his men. Because he had breached the conditions of his Royal Charter, once home, Sir Walter was imprisoned and sent for trial.

In 1618 he was executed at the Tower of London under the order of King James (Queen Elizabeth had died in 1603). Raleigh apparently asked to see the axe that would cut off his head and said:

'This is sharp medicine . . . that will cure all my diseases.'

A bit of an understatement – but he seemed to take his punishment well . . .

To the very end, Sir Walter still thought that El Dorado existed. Like the cast of *Glee*, he just never stopped believin'.

Four hundred years later, and we have to ask: *Did the gold of El Dorado even exist in the first place?*

In his 1849 poem 'El Dorado', writer Edgar Allan Poe summed up the problem:

Gaily bedight,
A gallant knight,
In sunshine and in shadow,
Had journeyed long,
Singing a song,
In search of Eldorado.

But he grew old –
This knight so bold –
And o'er his heart a shadow
Fell as he found
No spot of ground
That looked like Eldorado.

MY MISSION

Those looking for an 'El Dorado' don't have to go too far these days:

- There are towns called El Dorado in Venezuela, Mexico, Argentina, Canada and Peru
- El Dorado International Airport is located in Colombia
- But the place with the most El Dorados is the USA – at least thirteen states have a town named after the legendary city!

Finding the real El Dorado is going to be much, much harder. I'm going to follow in Sir Walt's steps (hopefully, without losing my head) and see if I can locate the lost city of Manoa. Martínez said it was on a salt lake called Lake Parime, close to the Orinoco river in what is now Venezuela.

It's a long, long journey, starting with a flight to the massively big and busy Venezuelan city of Caracas. From there, a twelve-hour bus trip takes me to the banks of the Orinoco, where I will board a small canoe to make my way downriver. 'Orinoco' (apart from being the name of a Womble – ask your parents!) actually means 'a place to paddle' – and I'll certainly be doing a lot of that. But as it is one of the longest rivers in South America (2,140 km), I won't be attempting its entire length . . .

I won't be having a refreshing swim either, despite the heat. Apparently there are electric eels (shocking!) and piranha, who might just fancy a bite . . .

I'd prefer to come back intact, ready to take on more mysteries!

KIT LIST

A large part of the Orinoco river flows through steamy, humid rainforest and mangrove swamp. I'll need to be fully prepared:

LIGHTWEIGHT FIBREGLASS CANOE AND PADDLES – with space to store all my supplies

TENT AND HAMMOCK – I'll need to sleep raised above the rainforest floor because of all the insects, scorpions and snakes . . .

A GOOD MOSQUITO NET – there'll be hundreds of mosquitoes around at dusk and dawn

EXTRA-STRONG INSECT REPELLENT – those pesky mozzies again, plus a whole variety of other biting insects. Repellent spray should make them buzz off!

CAMERA AND BINOCULARS

COMPASS – the rainforest is huge and you can easily get lost if you wander off route. And there's not much chance of being found if you do . . .

HEAD TORCH – it's pitch dark in the jungle at night

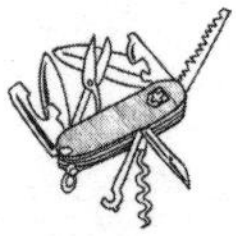

SWISS ARMY KNIFE WITH ATTACHMENTS – will come in handy for lots of jobs

SUN HAT/SUN-SCREEN/SUN-BLOCK

WATER-PURIFICATION TABLETS/WATER BOTTLE FOOD

JUNGLE SURVIVAL GUIDE – full of useful tips for rainforest survival

MISSION COMPLETED

I'm sweaty, hot and tired – after paddling thousands of metres in a canoe, I'm now wondering why I didn't use the motorized version . . .

But the long journey was brightened up by the most amazing wildlife, bringing a smile to my sweaty face. Creatures like giant river otters, howler monkeys, brightly coloured parrots and toucans. Not all the wildlife was welcoming, though. Large caymans (a sort of croc) and river pythons got me paddling as fast as I could in the other direction!

But the best sight of all had to be the pink river dolphins. Yes, pink dolphins! These friendly freshwater dolphins have long snouts and are found in very few places in the world – but luckily the Orinoco river is one of them. A friendly pod (that's the name for a group of dolphins) popped their heads out of the water to investigate my canoe.

But what about El Dorado? There are now lots of towns and villages close to the Orinoco river that didn't exist in Walter Raleigh's day. (The journey would have been much, much harder then.) Which meant that there were quite a few people around to talk to. I spoke to lots of friendly locals on the river banks, but no one I met along the way had heard of the town of Manoa. There was no sign of it. Some ancient maps show the lake – but were these made up by explorers? I just don't know.

WHAT DO YOU THINK?

1. El Dorado is a Myth

Could El Dorado be just a story? But if so, why have so many people risked their lives to find it? It's a myth-tery!

Perhaps the rumours got out of control. The Muisca tribe's ancient tradition of throwing treasure into a lake is well-known. But did the Europeans' greed for gold make them imagine more? Perhaps they were so dazzled by the riches of the Aztecs and the Incas that they persuaded themselves that there must be more wealth out there. The kingdom of El Dorado fitted the bill perfectly.

There is another possibility. Maybe the native Americans made up a lot of the stories about El Dorado. But why?

As you know by now, the Spanish conquistadors weren't exactly popular with the locals. Think about it: what would you do if you were faced with a bunch of strange people with guns arriving at your village and demanding information about a 'golden kingdom'? You could tell them that El Dorado didn't exist – and risk their anger. Or you could tell them what they wanted to hear. Inventing a fictional city and telling the Spanish it was hundreds of kilometres away from your own village would have been a sure-fire way of getting rid of the annoying intruders. Hopefully for a very, very long time . . .

We know that old-fashioned adventurers weren't able to find El Dorado. And modern-day explorers – with all the GPS technology that they didn't have hundreds of years ago – haven't been able to find it either. Does that tell us that it never actually existed?

2. El Dorado Exists

Some people think it's likely that there was indeed a golden city full of treasures. The Inca were fabulously wealthy – the richest civilization anywhere in South America. (At least, they were until the Spanish arrived . . .)

The Incas mined gold and silver and used it for decorating buildings, making statues and crafting many beautiful treasures. The city of Cuzco, in Peru, boasted a golden palace, temples with roofs of gold, even a golden fountain. But their love of gold wasn't just about money; gold was the sign of their sun god and symbolized his power. Golden objects were used for offerings to the gods.

Sadly, many of these precious treasures were taken by the Europeans and melted down to be made into gold bars. But was all of it?

Some people believe that groups of Incas may have run away and set up their own hidden empire in a secret location, filled with riches that they had taken with them. Deep in the rainforest or high up in the mountains would have been an ideal place to hide. Perhaps Manoa was the Incas' hidden city? Or maybe there is another secret kingdom somewhere?

The area of South America we are talking about is vast, with thousands of kilometres of unexplored rainforest. Even now, archaeologists are still finding new evidence of ancient hidden civilizations deep in the jungle. The golden kingdom hasn't yet been found – but this doesn't mean its remains aren't out there somewhere . . .

We also know that European explorers on the Orinoco river did see Indian traders carrying gold, jewellery and other precious items. They said the goods came from Manoa – but the actual location of this place was never revealed.

The Spanish were convinced that there was a hidden city that the locals were keeping from them. Were they right?

YOU DECIDE

'Looking for El Dorado' describes someone who is searching for their life's great wish or ambition, but who has never found it. Will we ever find the real El Dorado? You must decide . . .

MYSTERY 4

The Crystal Skull Conundrum

THE MISSION . . .

. . . to find out if an ancient civilization made mysterious crystal skulls . . .

BURNING QUESTIONS

- How were the skulls made?
- Are they all fakes?
- Do crystal skulls have supernatural powers?

MISSION DETAILS

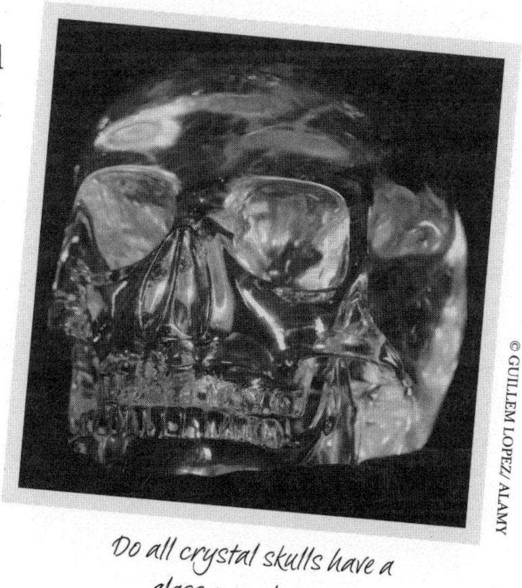

© GUILLEM LOPEZ/ ALAMY

Do all crystal skulls have a glassy-eyed stare?

Have you ever seen a crystal skull? It's a beautiful but spooky-looking thing – a realistic human skull carved from sparkling quartz crystal.

People have always been fascinated by these skulls. Some believe they possess strange supernatural forces: even the power to heal – or to curse . . .

A few think that the skulls might even have come from the legendary island of Atlantis (if it ever existed) or that they were brought to Earth by alien visitors!

But what do the experts think? At one time most of them thought that the skulls were made by the Aztecs or the Mayans, hundreds of years ago. But now there is a big debate over the skulls' origins and exactly how they were made. Are they bony phoneys – or the real deal?

It's time to delve deeper into the strange, sparkling world of crystal skulls . . .

THE LOCATION

To see a crystal skull for yourself, you'd have to visit one of the world's great cities. There are three famous skulls currently on display in museums in London, Washington DC, and Paris. The rest are in the hands of private owners around the world.

You may even spot a crystal skull in a shop window when you're out and about, but don't get too excited if you do. There are plenty of souvenirs around that are just copies of the original skulls, mostly made from glass.

THE EVIDENCE

A skull might not be the first thing you'd think of putting on display in your bedroom (except maybe at Halloween), but some civilizations thought differently.

Skulls were really important to several of the ancient peoples of Central America (often called Mesoamerica by historians). The Aztec god of death Mictlantecuhtli (try saying that really quickly) was shown as a skeleton or a person wearing a skull. The Mayans and the Aztecs liked to build structures called skull racks – a gruesome 'wall' of skulls! Some racks were made of real skulls belonging to battle victims and unfortunate locals sacrificed to the gods. Others were carved of stone.

I bet the ancients 'racked' their brains to think of this idea . . .

Skull patterns were used to decorate shrines and temples, and colourful masks were made from real human skulls inlaid with turquoise and jade.

Human skulls were sometimes used for religious rituals. In 2012 a hoard of 50 skulls was found buried near Mexico City, thought to have come from human sacrifices more than 1,000 years ago – it's enough to chill you to the bone . . .

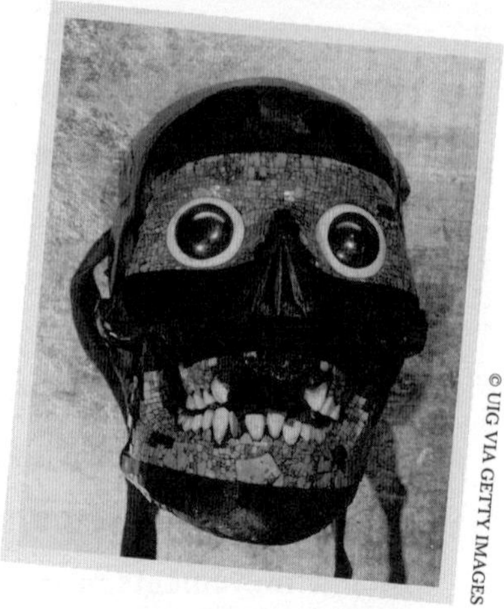

© UIG VIA GETTY IMAGES

An Aztec skull mask – note the real teeth. You could wear it to a party but there'd be no body to go with . . .

And if you visit Mexico today, you'll see that skulls are still really popular – in art, festivals and architecture. (Though, you'll be relieved to hear, no longer for human sacrifices.) Mexican kids can even eat tiny sugar skulls from the sweet shop – mmm, crunchy!

© DAVID PEDRE / GETTY IMAGES

Mexicans celebrate the Day of the Dead to remember their loved ones. Check out this bunch of boneheads!

The crystal skulls we're talking about are supposed to be very special. Many believe that they were made by either the Aztecs or the Mayans. But who were these people, exactly?

Pyramids, Sacrifices and Deadly Ball Games

Civilizations such as the Aztecs, the Mayans, and others, once lived in a region called Mesoamerica, which includes parts of Mexico, Guatemala, Belize, Honduras and El Salvador.

The Mayans lived mainly in the rainforests of the Yucatán peninsula of Mexico from around 900 BC. Their civilization peaked around 300 AD – the height of their achievements in art, learning and culture. But then, mysteriously, they began to abandon their cities. Some think the forests couldn't support so many people. Others blame war or drought. Whatever happened, by 800 AD the Mayans had all but disappeared . . .

The Aztecs lived in central Mexico from the fourteenth to the sixteenth century, eventually ruling over a huge empire under their leader, Montezuma. They built an impressive capital city called Tenochtitlán (now Mexico City). In 1519 the Spanish conquistadors, led by Hernán Cortés, attacked the Aztec Empire. The Aztecs were on their way out . . .

A mighty Aztec warrior 'wings' it!

Each group had different languages and ways of life – but they also had quite a lot in common.

- Both Aztecs and Mayans ruled large, powerful empires
- They worshipped many different gods and made sacrifices to keep them happy. Animals, birds and insects were often used as offerings at religious ceremonies. And sometimes human beings too . . .
- They built amazing cities, temples and stone pyramids, used for religious ceremonies. You can still see their ruins today – many tourists visit these ancient sites to marvel at them

Marvelling at the Chichén Itzá stepped pyramid in Mexico.

© JAN COBB PHOTOGRAPHY LTD / GETTY IMAGES

- They played a notorious ball game, in which you had to try and get a rubber ball through a ring without using your hands or feet. Players used hips, thighs and upper arms in an attempt at 'keepy-uppy'. Sound like fun? You wouldn't have been laughing if you'd been the leader of the losing side. He would probably have his head cut off (remember that skull rack from earlier?). Losing doesn't get any tougher than this . . .

An ancient ball court today. Could you get a ball through that ring without using your hands?

Yes, we know quite a lot about the Aztecs and the Mayans. But nowhere have historians found evidence that they made crystal skulls. Or what they would have been used for. Maybe they were just beautiful works of art – or perhaps they had more significance?

The Legend of the Thirteen Skulls

Some people believe that there are just thirteen real crystal skulls in existence. They think that the skulls have incredible powers – but only if they are all brought together in a certain way.

Twelve of the skulls must be arranged in a circle and the largest, thirteenth, skull placed in the middle. When this happens, it is said that the skulls will have the combined power and wisdom that humankind needs to survive the future. Impressive!

But, confusingly, some people believe the complete opposite – that if all thirteen crystal skulls are gathered together, it will bring about the end of the world! No wonder no one's ever tried it . . .

Thirteen – a lucky or unlucky number when it comes to the skulls?

It's All Over – or Is It?

Talking of the end of the world, chances are you'll remember a certain date – Friday 21 December 2012. It was memorable because this was the day some people believed our world would come to an end. And it was all because of the ancient Mayans.

The Mayans were good at maths and astronomy and they devised advanced calendar systems. And it just so happened that their calendar ended on 21 December 2012.

Some took this as a 'sign' that everything was over for the human race! When the fateful day arrived, they were probably hiding under their tables waiting for a meteorite to strike the Earth – but nothing happened. I guess the believers are all feeling a bit silly now . . .

A Mayan calendar on a large stone tablet found in Mexico.

Is it too far-fetched to believe that a few pieces of crystal could contain enough power to save – or end – our world?

One crystal skull was thought to be so powerful, it was said to bring nothing but unhappiness to those around it . . .

The Skull of Doom

Actually called the Mitchell-Hedges skull (but let's face it, the 'Skull of Doom' sounds much more exciting), this skull has had a spooky reputation for years. It was owned by a man called Frederick Mitchell-Hedges, who claimed it had evil powers that were once unleashed by Mayan priests to strike people dead. Other stories have said that it emits blue lights from its eyes and crashes computer hard drives!

But where did the doom-laden skull come from? And how did its owner know all this?

Mr Mitchell-Hedges was a proper old-fashioned explorer who travelled the world in the early 1900s, seeking adventure and challenge (sounds right up my street). On this particular trip he was accompanied by his teenage daughter, Anna. Their story – which sounds like something out of an Indiana Jones movie – starts when the pair began investigating the ruins of an ancient Mayan temple in Belize.

© 2006 TOPFOTO/FORTEAN

F. A. Mitchell-Hedges with a group of Chucunaque Indians. And a pipe.

According to Anna, she noticed something shining through a crack in a pyramid and alerted her father.

Unable to reach the object, the pair returned to the spot the following day, but it took a long while to move enough stones to make a decent-sized opening at the top of the pyramid. An apprehensive Anna was then lowered inside. She later said:

With two ropes tied around my body and a light strapped to my head, I was lowered into the darkness, terrified of the snakes and scorpions that might be down there.

This definitely sounds like a movie – perhaps Indi-Anna Jones!

Anna said she saw a shining object, which she grabbed and wrapped in her shirt. Once in the light, she could see that it was a transparent skull, made of crystal, heavy, and about two-thirds the size of a real skull. It had a moveable, detachable jaw, unlike other crystal skulls that have been found.

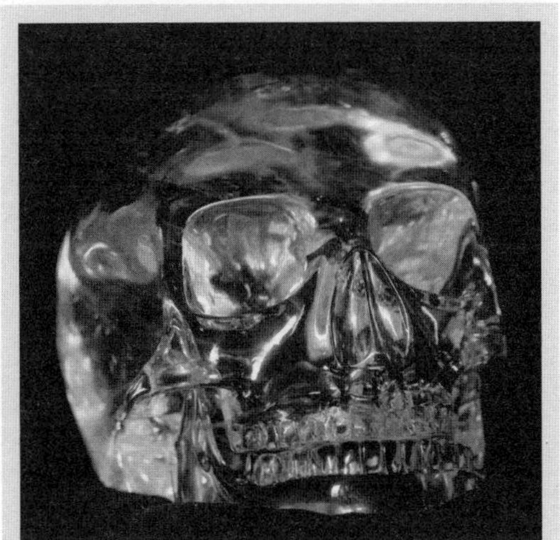

The Skull of Doom – as evil as it looks?

© GUILLEM LOPEZ/ ALAMY

The crystal skull made the pair famous. Mr M-H even wrote a book about it. He claimed that it was made by at least five generations of Mayans, who had slowly shaped it out of a piece of rock crystal by painstakingly rubbing it down with sand. (We have no idea how he knew this, as he couldn't possibly have been there at the time . . .)

But some think that our intrepid explorer had an over-active imagination. Around that time there happened to be a popular adventure story called *The Crystal Skull.* It featured a spooky skull stolen by a character called Lyndon Cromer, an academic who robbed ancient sites to get his hands on precious artefacts.

A suspicious-looking Lyndon Cromer turns headhunter . . .

Was Frederick Mitchell-Hedges 'inspired' by this novel to come up with an equally exciting story about his own crystal skull?

We'll never know – but there are certainly those who disagree with the Mitchell-Hedgeses' version of events. Some say that their story just doesn't stand up. There were no photographs and no witnesses, so we only have their word for it.

Moreover, Anna Mitchell-Hedges has always been very unclear about the actual date of the find. It was sometime in the mid-1920s, but she can't remember exactly when . . . Also her story of being lowered down into a pyramid on a rope does sound a bit like a movie, rather than real life. Does it all sound rather suspicious to you?

Many people would say so. They think that the skull might have been bought from a London art dealer in October 1943 – years later than it was said to have been found.

Anna later toured the world giving private viewings of the 'Skull of Doom'. It made her and her father famous – but only they knew the real truth about where it came from . . .

Skulls – Fakes or Finds?

So, what's the latest verdict on the other crystal skulls?

- London, England: For years the British Museum believed the skull in their collection was an ancient treasure. But now they think it's a modern fake.

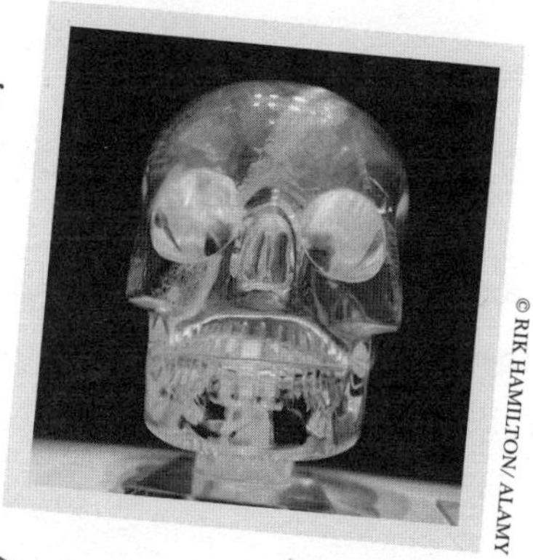

© RIK HAMILTON/ ALAMY

- Washington, DC, USA: The skull on display at the Smithsonian National Museum of Natural History arrived mysteriously by post in 1992. It had an anonymous note claiming it came from Aztec times. It is the largest of the skulls, about 38 cm high and weighing in at fourteen kilos. The museum thinks it is a fake – so much so that they even included it in an exhibition called 'Modern Fakes'

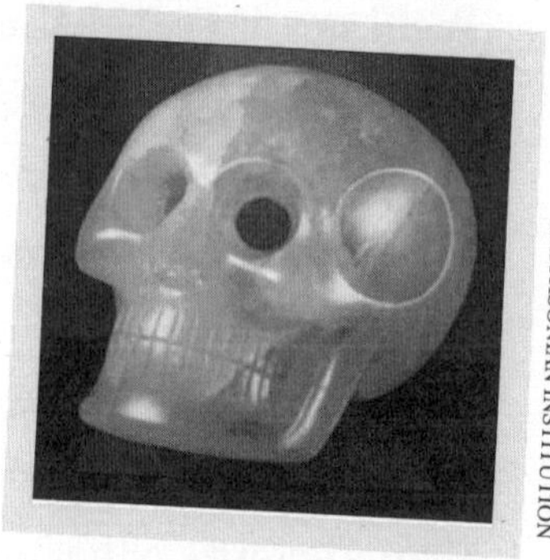

© JAMES DI LORETO/ SMITHSONIAN INSTITUTION

- Musée du Quai Branly, Paris: The Paris skull is small – just ten cm high. But, unlike the others, it has a hole drilled through its centre, so it may have been mounted on something in the past. The museum describes it as 'Pre Columbian with Mexican origin' – so they have not declared it a fake

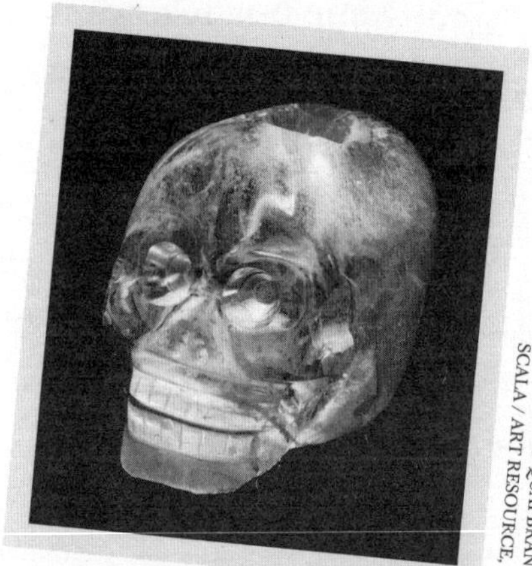

© MUSEE DU QUAI BRANLY/ SCALA / ART RESOURCE, NY

Skull Power

Some people believe that crystal skulls have incredible abilities. Take a look . . .

Computer Crystals

Ancient computer? No, I don't mean your very old laptop, but the skulls themselves. Some think that because the skulls are made out of the same type of quartz crystal that is inside modern-day computers, they might have a similar function. They think that their existence could even be proof of an ancient civilization even more advanced than our own.

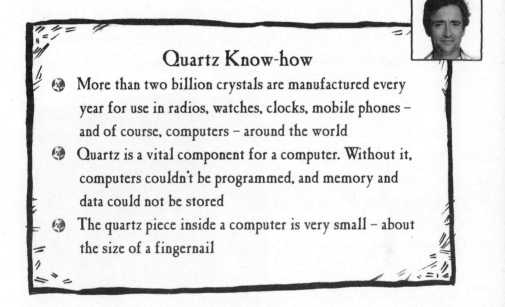

Quartz Know-how

- More than two billion crystals are manufactured every year for use in radios, watches, clocks, mobile phones – and of course, computers – around the world
- Quartz is a vital component for a computer. Without it, computers couldn't be programmed, and memory and data could not be stored
- The quartz piece inside a computer is very small – about the size of a fingernail

So, what do you think – if a crystal chip inside a computer can store data, could a crystal skull also be a device for storing information? But how? You can't exactly plug it in . . . Some people think that we just have to discover the right way to 'read' the skulls. But at the moment, nobody knows how.

Crystal Doctor

Some believe that crystal skulls have special energies which can be used to help people, healing sickness and disease. They point to the fact that crystals were thought by ancient civilizations such as the Egyptians and the Mayans to have healing powers. Others believe that crystals have special psychic abilities and can foretell the future. But no one has ever proved any of this.

Could these ideas just be a lot of skull silliness, perhaps influenced by books – and movies like *Indiana Jones and the Kingdom of the Crystal Skull*, in which the skull of the title contains incredible knowledge and wisdom? (It also belongs to a bunch of intelligent alien archaeologists, who claim the skull back, then take off in a flying saucer – but not until they've activated a portal into another dimension and caused chaos on Earth!)

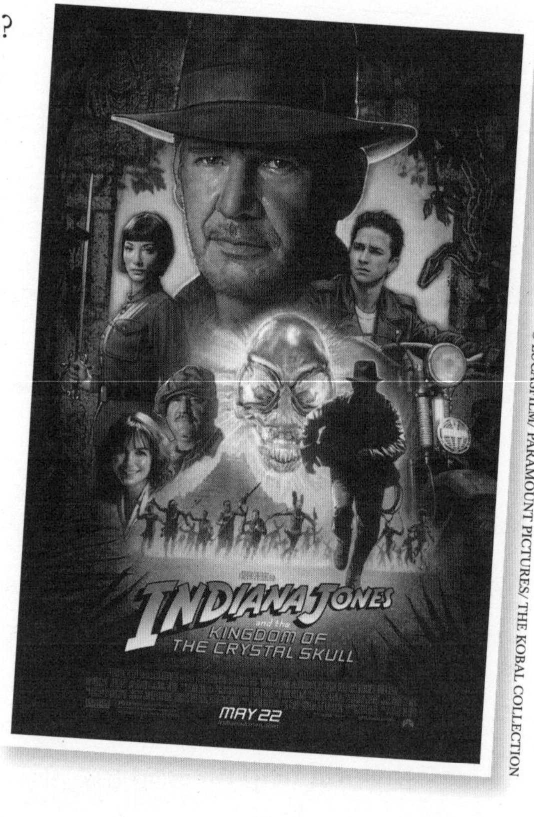

© LUCASFILM/ PARAMOUNT PICTURES/ THE KOBAL COLLECTION

It's total fiction – but are all these claims about the skulls fictional too?

MY MISSION

Let's make no bones about it (sorry) – I could do an Indiana Jones, grab myself a battered leather hat and a whip, and travel all the way to Central America to find out more about the ancient Mayans and Aztecs.

OR I could visit the British Museum in London (a handier distance from my home) to see for myself one of the legendary crystal skulls we've discussed in this book.

I think you've guessed my choice.

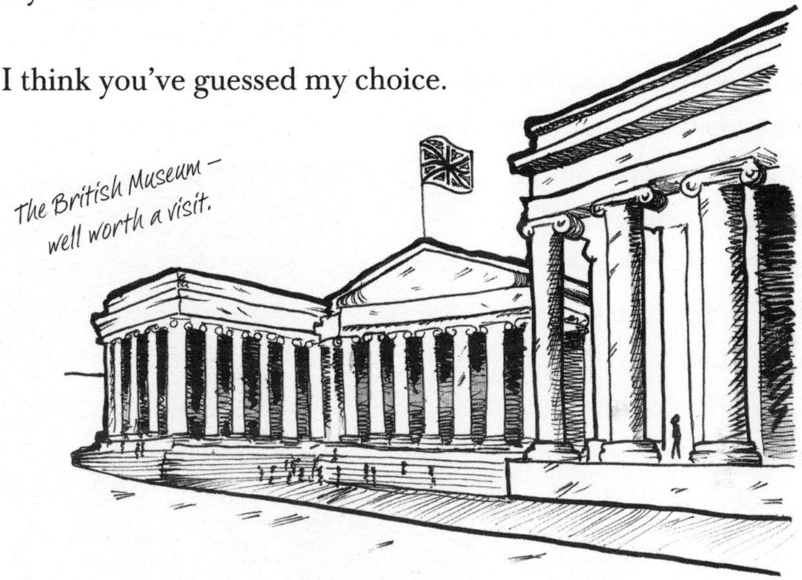
The British Museum – well worth a visit.

KIT LIST

A day trip to a museum is one of my simpler missions (phew!) so I shouldn't need too much. Just:

- A BRITISH MUSEUM GUIDE BOOK – it's a big place so this will help me find my way around

- COMFY SHOES – lots of walking and standing involved
- BOTTLE OF WATER/SNACKS IN A BACKPACK – need to keep those energy levels up
- TRAVELCARD – to get me there and back on the London Underground
- NOTEBOOK AND PEN
- MAGNIFYING GLASS – to get an even better close-up view of the crystal skull

MISSION COMPLETED

Using my trusty guide book, I made my way to where the famous skull is on display, in a room called 'Living and Dying'. I knew I was in the right place because so many people were clustered around a single glass case. I eventually managed to squeeze in through the crowds and see the skull for myself, close up.

It was a beautiful sight, about 25 cm high, and sparkling in the light.

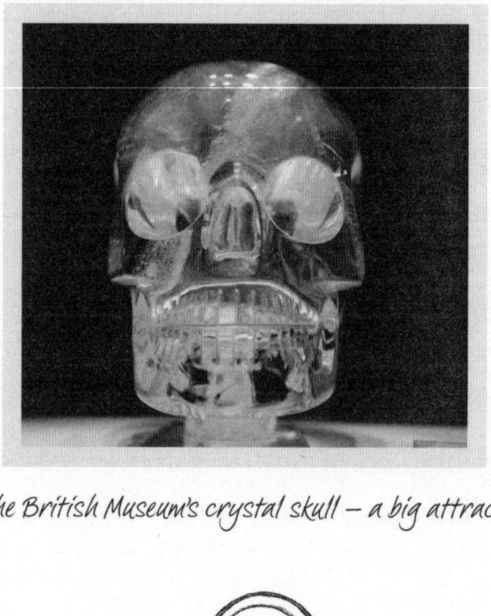

The British Museum's crystal skull – a big attraction.

Note: By the way, if you ever get the chance to visit the British Museum, you're in for a treat. Among the eight million objects in its collection are spooky ancient Egyptian mummies, the famous Rosetta Stone and a mysterious statue from Easter Island – as well as many other fabulous treasures from all over the world. And if you know where to look, you'll soon find their spectacular crystal skull.

I found out more about the history of the skull. The British Museum bought it from Tiffany of New York in 1897, believing that it was a genuine Aztec relic, purchased from a Spanish officer in Mexico. The description on the skull says that it was originally thought to have been Aztec but is now believed to have made in the nineteenth century.

But the museum website is slightly different. It says of the skull's origin: *'The question remains open . . .'*

WHAT DO YOU THINK?

1. Crystal Skulls are Fakes

In the 1990s the Smithsonian National Museum of Natural History and the British Museum decided to find out the truth about the crystal skulls in their collections. The skulls were closely examined by experts under light and scanning electron microscopes. They all thought the same thing: marks on both skulls showed that they had most likely been carved and polished using high-speed cutting and polishing tools called rotary wheels. These are modern tools, which weren't around in Aztec or Mayan times. The museums decided that the skulls must have been made much later, probably in the nineteenth century.

The Mitchell-Hedges skull was examined by an expert from the Smithsonian, who also found similar 'modern' markings.

The British Museum now believes that all the crystal skulls in existence are probably fakes.

But why would someone bother to 'fake' a crystal skull?

In the nineteenth century, people became very interested in ancient cultures and their histories. Museums, collectors and shops around the world were looking to buy all kinds of interesting objects, from ancient Egyptian relics to Aztec pottery. A crystal skull would have been worth a lot of money – particularly if it was thought to come from one of the Mesoamerican civilizations.

In the late 1900s a French dealer called Eugène Boban sold some of these skulls to museums, claiming they were ancient relics, but no one knows where he got them from.

Some think they could have been made in Germany – in a town called Idar-Oberstein, to be exact, once known as the capital of the gemstone industry. In the 1870s craftsmen working here bought large numbers of quartz crystals from Brazil. Could these have been the beginnings of our crystal skulls?

But what about the skulls' mystical powers? We've heard lots of stories from people who believe in their strange abilities, but no one has put the skulls through a proper scientific test to prove it. In real life, crystal skulls do look very mysterious and it's easy to see why many believe that they are magical, supernatural objects. But I certainly didn't see any evidence of powerful energy beaming out from the British Museum skull . . . maybe it's just me?

A lot of people would really like to think that the crystal skulls are supernatural objects used centuries ago by Mayan or Aztec priests. It's just much more exciting than finding out the skulls were made about 50 years ago in a German factory! But perhaps that's all the skulls really are?

2. Crystal Skulls are Genuine

How can anyone prove that the skulls were made by the ancient Aztecs or Mayans?

One of the big problems is how to date the skulls. For carbon-based things like bone, cloth, wood, animals and humans (yes, we're made of carbon too), archaeologists can use a method called carbon dating to work out how old something is. But there's no such test for quartz crystal. Because it doesn't decay or change over time, there's no scientific way to find out when it was made.

The main argument for the skulls being fakes is that the markings shown on the surface of the skulls look as if they have been made by modern instruments. But is this really the case?

We know that Mesoamerican civilizations did carve stone and minerals – archaeologists have discovered body decorations, like lip plugs, ear spools and beads. These were often carved from obsidian, a hard dark volcanic stone (not crystal). But while most experts don't believe that any such civilization would have used a rotary wheel cutter, a few say it's possible that they could have used some kind of wheel for carving.

Were the Mesoamericans more advanced than we think? Could they have used tools that weren't even supposed to exist more than a thousand years ago?

We know that skulls were important in both Aztec and Mayan cultures but, so far, no skull made from crystal has ever been found by archaeologists at one of their ruins. If one day a sparkling crystal skull is dug up at such a site, we'll finally have our evidence.

YOU DECIDE

Mystical objects – or modern fakes? Your decision . . .

But whatever you decide and note down at the back of the book, most people will agree that crystal skulls are beautiful objects which deserve to be on display in museums, however and whenever they were made.

WANT TO KNOW MORE?

Tutankhamun – The Life and Death of a Pharaoh – David Murdoch (Dorling Kindersley)

King Tut's Curse! – Jacqueline Morley (Book House)

The Life and World of Tutankhamen – Brian Williams (Heinemann)

Eyewitness Guide: Pirate – Richard Platt (Dorling Kindersley)

Fact or Fiction: Pirates – Stewart Ross (Aladdin/Watts)

Terror on the Amazon – The Quest for El Dorado – Phil Gates (DK Readers)

Sir Walter Raleigh and the Quest for El Dorado – Marc Aronson (Houghton Mifflin)

Unexplained: An Encyclopedia of Curious Phenomena, Strange Superstitions and Ancient Mysteries – Judy Allen (Kingfisher)

www.britishmuseum.org

www.nationalgeographic.com – Great for all kinds of information about the world. You can search the site for their views on the mysteries in this book.

DECISION TIME

So, we've looked at the evidence (which sometimes got a bit too close for comfort, if you ask me). Now it's time for you to sort the facts from the fiction and solve some of the world's greatest mysteries once and for all . . .

WEIRD WATERS

Mystery 1: The Lost City of Atlantis

Notes

____

____

____

____

____

____

Possible explanations:

☐ *1. The Minoans and the Atlanteans Were One and the Same*

☐ *2. Atlantis Is Buried under Mud Flats in Spain*

☐ *3. Atlantis Was Once Part of Cyprus*

☐ *4. It's Just a Story*

☐ *5. Aliens on Atlantis*

☐ *6. Other* ____________________________

Mystery 2: The Mary Celeste

Notes:

Possible explanations:

☐ *1. Sea Monster Attack*

☐ *2. Plundering Pirates*

☐ *3. Foul Play*

☐ *4. Mutiny*

☐ *5. A Curse*

☐ *6. A Sea Quake or Spout?*

☐ *7. A Potential Explosion?*

☐ *8. Alien Abduction!*

☐ *9. Other* ____________________

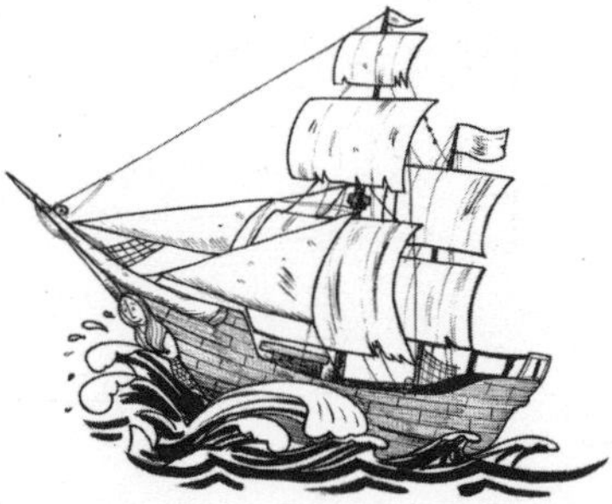

Mystery 3: Mythical Mermaids

Notes:

Possible explanations:

- ☐ *1. Mermaids Are Sea Cows*
- ☐ *2. Mermaids Are Real*
- ☐ *3. Mermaids Are Made Up*
- ☐ *4. It's Just a Story*
- ☐ *Other* ______

Mystery 4: The Bermuda Triangle

Notes:

Possible explanations:

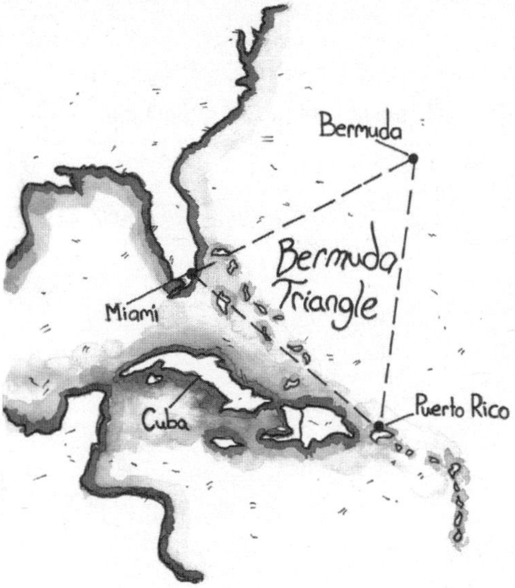

☐ *1. Electronic Fog*

☐ *2. Aliens!*

☐ *3. A Time Portal*

☐ *4. Wild Weather*

☐ *5. A Flatulent Ocean?*

☐ *6. Death by Atlantis?*

☐ *7. Accidents Will Happen*

☐ *8. The Environment*

☐ *9. Other* ______________________________

Mystery 5: The Philadelphia Experiment

Notes

____

____

____

____

____

____

____

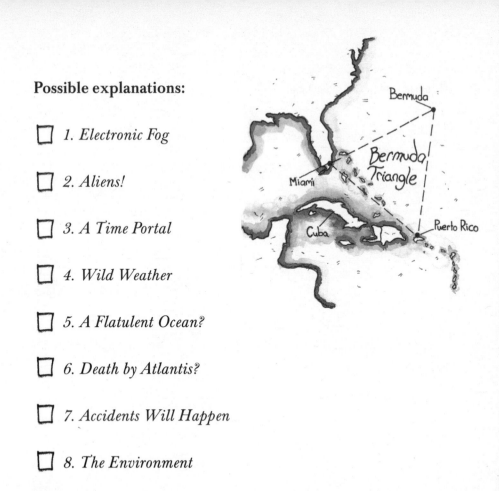

Possible explanations:

☐ *1. It Happened – But How?*

☐ *2. It Never Happened*

☐ *3. Other*

CREEPY CREATURES

Mystery 1: The Loch Ness Monster

Notes:

____

____

____

____

____

Possible explanations:

☐ *1. Nessie Is a Plesiosaur*

☐ *2. Nessie Is a Giant Eel*

☐ *3. Nessie the Elephant?*

☐ *4. Nessie Is Tree Gas!*

☐ *5. Weird Waves*

☐ *6. Other* __________________________________

Mystery 2: Yeti

Notes:

____

____

____

____

____

____

Possible explanations:

☐ *1. The Yeti Doesn't Exist*

☐ *2. A Trick of the Sun?*

☐ *3. The Yeti Exists: It's a Giant Ape*

☐ *4. The Yeti Exists: It's a Man (Sort of . . .)*

☐ *5. Other* ______________________________

Mystery 3: Vampires

Notes:

____

____

____

____

____

____

____

Possible explanations:

☐ *1. Vampires Don't Exist: Fear of Disease*

☐ *2. Vampires Don't Exist: Fear of Death*

☐ *3. Vampires Do Exist*

☐ *4. Other* ____________________

Mystery 4: Werewolves

Notes:

____

____

____

____

____

____

Possible explanations:

☐ *1. Werewolves Don't Exist: Fear of Animals*

☐ *2. Werewolves Don't Exist: Sickness and Disease*

☐ *3. Werewolves Don't Exist: Wolf Poison*

☐ *4. Werewolves Do Exist*

☐ *5. Other* ____________________

ALIEN ENCOUNTERS

Mystery 1: The UFO Enigma

Notes:

Possible explanations:

☐ *1. UFOs Are Sent by Aliens*

☐ *2. UFOs Are All Explainable*

☐ *3. Other*

Mystery 2: The Roswell Incident

Notes:

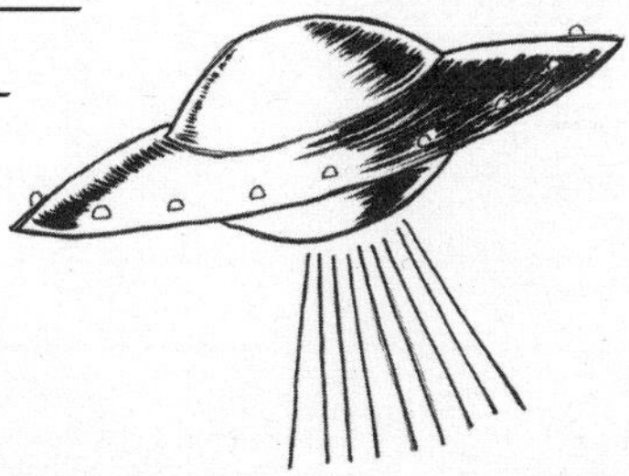

Possible explanations:

☐ *1. The Object Was an Alien Spaceship*

☐ *2. The Object Was a Spy Balloon*

☐ *3. Other* ____

Mystery 3: The Nazca Lines

Notes:

____

____

____

____

____

____

☐ *1. The Nazca Lines Were Made by Humans*

☐ *2. The Lines Were Made by Aliens*

☐ *3. Other* ____

Mystery 4: Crop Circles

Notes:

____

____

____

Possible explanations:

☐ *1. Crop Circles Are Made by Wind*

☐ *2. They Are Created by Natural Energy*

☐ *3. Crop Circles Are Hoaxes!*

☐ *4. Crop Circles Are Made by Aliens*

☐ *5. Other* ______________________

Mystery 5: The Existence of Aliens

Notes:

Possible explanations:

☐ *1. Aliens Do Exist*

☐ *2 Aliens Don't Exist*

☐ *3. Other* ______________________

MYSTERIOUS TREASURES

Mystery 1: Pirate Treasure

Notes:

Possible explanations:

☐ *1. There Is Pirate Treasure Out There Still*

☐ *2. Pirate Treasure Is a Myth*

☐ *3. Other* ____________________

Mystery 2: The Curse of the Pharaohs

Notes:

Possible explanations:

☐ *1. The Curse of Tutankhamen Doesn't Exist*

☐ *2. The Tombs Are Toxic*

☐ *3. The Curse Is Real!*

☐ *4. Other* ______________________________

Mystery 3: The Legend of El Dorado

Notes:

____

____

____

____

____

____

Possible explanations:

☐ *1. El Dorado Is a Myth*

☐ *2. El Dorado Exists*

☐ *3. Other* ____________________

____

Mystery 4: The Crystal Skull Conundrum

Notes:

____

____

____

____

____

____

____

____

Possible explanations:

☐ *1. Crystal Skulls Are Fakes*

☐ *2. Crystal Skulls Are Geniune*

☐ *3. Other* ______________________________